W9-CZY-622

EDO CULTURE

EDO CULTURE

Daily Life and Diversions in Urban

Japan, 1600–1868

Nishiyama Matsunosuke

Translated and edited by Gerald Groemer

University of Hawai'i Press

Honolulu

© 1997 University of Hawai'i Press
All rights reserved
Printed in the United States of America

02   5 4 3

Library of Congress Cataloging-in-Publication Data
Nishiyama, Matsunosuke, 1912–
Edo Culture : daily life and diversions in urban Japan, 1600–1868 /
Nishiyama Matsunosuke ; translated and edited by Gerald Groemer.
p.   cm.
Includes bibliographical references and index.
ISBN 0–8248–1736–2 (alk. paper). — ISBN 0–8248–1850–4 (pbk. :
alk. paper)
1. Japan—Civilization—1600–1868. I. Groemer, Gerald, 1957– .
II. Title.
DS822.2.N558   1997
952'.025—DC20   96–9710
CIP

University of Hawai'i Press books are printed on acid-free paper
and meet the guidelines for permanence and durability of the
Council on Library Resources.

Book design by Paula Newcomb

CONTENTS

HISTORICAL PERIODS

I have converted Japanese dates into their Western equivalents whenever possible, but in many cases Nishiyama's use of Japanese-year periods has proved to be more convenient. Beginning and ending dates of periods are provided in the text, but for the sake of convenience a list of all period names used in this volume is given here:

Heian (784–1185)
Kamakura (1185–1333)
Muromachi (1333–1573)
Edo or Tokugawa (1600–1868)
    Genna (1615–1624)
    Kan'ei (1624–1644)
    Keian (1648–1652)
    Meireki (1655–1658)
    Kanbun (1661–1673)
    Genroku (1688–1704)
    Kyōhō (1716–1736)
    Kan'en (1748–1751)
    Hōreki (1751–1764)
    Meiwa (1764–1772)
    An'ei (1772–1781)
    Tenmei (1781–1789)
    Kansei (1789–1801)
    Bunka (1804–1818)
    Bunsei (1818–1830)
    Kasei (Bunka and Bunsei: 1804–1830)
    Tenpō (1830–1844)
    Kaei (1848–1854)
    Ansei (1854–1860)
    Meiji (1868–1912)

1. Mutsu	28. Iga	55. Aki
2. Dewa	29. Ise	56. Suō
3. Sado	30. Shima	57. Nagato
4. Echigo	31. Yamato	58. Chikuzen
5. Etchū	32. Kii	59. Chikugo
6. Noto	33. Izumi	60. Buzen
7. Kaga	34. Kawachi	61. Bungo
8. Echizen	35. Settsu	62. Hyūga
9. Wakasa	36. Yamashiro	63. Ōsumi
10. Hitachi	37. Tango	64. Satsuma
11. Shimotsuke	38. Tanba	65. Higo
12. Kōzuke	39. Tajima	66. Hizen
13. Shimōsa	40. Harima	67. Iki
14. Kazusa	41. Awaji	68. Tsushima
15. Awa	42. Awa	
16. Musashi	43. Tosa	Chūgoku area: 46–57
17. Sagami	44. Iyo	Hokuriku region: 3–9
18. Kai	45. Sanuki	Kamigata area: western Japan
19. Shinano	46. Bizen	centering on Kyoto and Osaka
20. Hida	47. Bitchū	Kantō area: eastern Japan center-
21. Mino	48. Mimasaka	ing on Edo/Tokyo
22. Izu	49. Inaba	Kinai area: 31, 33–36
23. Suruga	50. Hōki	Kinki area: 27–29, 31–41
24. Tōtōmi	51. Oki	San'in area: 37–38, 49–53
25. Mikawa	52. Izumo	San'yō area: 46–48, 54–57
26. Owari	53. Iwami	Chichibu area: western part of 16
27. Ōmi	54. Bingo	

Premodern Provinces and Districts of Japan, 645–1868.

TRANSLATOR'S INTRODUCTION

Nishiyama Matsunosuke was born in 1912, during the last weeks of the Meiji period (1868–1912). He spent his childhood in the countryside around Akō, home of those most Japanese of heroes, the legendary forty-seven "loyal retainers" of the saga *Chūshingura*. After attending school in the city of Himeji (Hyōgo prefecture), Nishiyama went to Tokyo to enter Tōkyō Kōtō Shihan Gakkō (now Tsukuba University) to prepare himself for what he thought would be a career teaching elementary school in rural Japan. Here he found the lectures dry and uninspiring. Instead of attending classes, he frequently attended talks by the Rinzai Zen master Shaku Sōkatsu (1870–1954), whose ideas made a deep and lasting impression. As a result, Nishiyama decided to devote himself to the serious study and practice of Zen Buddhism. He joined a Zen meditation group in Tokyo and by 1937 had earned the Zen name Zōun.

All the while, Nishiyama continued his studies of Japanese history. His abilities in this field were soon recognized, and in 1944 he was appointed assistant professor. Several years later, he was named full professor, a position he held until retirement. Despite his impeccable academic credentials, Nishiyama's activities have never been limited to scholarship. An avid calligrapher, *katō bushi* performer, amateur botanist, carver of tea ladles, and connoisseur of nearly every form of Edo-period (1600–1868) art and culture, he has always tried to put into practice the suggestions for a "cultured life" that so often appear in his writings.

The 1950s and 1960s were one of the most exciting, fertile periods in Nishiyama's career. In 1959, his most influential work, the volume *Iemoto no kenkyū* (*Iemoto* Studies) appeared.[1] In the following years, he led a group of scholars known as the "Edo Chōnin Kenkyū-kai" (Edo townspeople study group). This team undertook a detailed examination of the social history of Edo's artisan and merchant classes (collectively known as *chōnin*, "townspeople"); the

1

results of this project were later issued as the five-volume *Edo chōnin no kenkyū* (Tokyo: Yoshikawa Kōbunkan, 1973–1975), which, along with *Iemoto no kenkyū*, is today recognized as a milestone in Edo-period historical studies.

In the 1980s the publisher Yoshikawa Kōbunkan issued a seven-volume set of Nishiyama's collected writings. Thus Nishiyama's writings, originally scattered throughout a number of journals and books, are now easily available to a large readership. Almost none of Nishiyama's work has been translated into a Western language, however. The studies translated here, written over some twenty years, have thus been selected to give a broad overview of some of Nishiyama's key concerns. Unfortunately, Nishiyama's work on botany, the pleasure quarters, and much else has had to be omitted, because his studies on these topics are either too long or too detailed for a nonspecialist readership. Nevertheless, I believe that the outlines of Nishiyama's approach can be easily discerned from the studies that follow.

A careful reading of any of these works will show that Nishiyama's main interests, and those of most of his disciples, are not so much Edo-period culture in general as the culture of the city of Edo itself. Although to Nishiyama "Edo culture" can mean the culture of the Edo period—that is, all Japan from the seventeenth to the mid-nineteenth centuries—it more often indicates the culture of Edo the city during this age. Other areas of Japan, especially the Kyoto-Osaka region, are frequently mentioned and occasionally studied in some depth, but the insights gained usually serve to highlight the uniqueness of the nation's capital. This "Edocentric" bias finds its roots in the fact that, as Nishiyama argues, after the middle of the eighteenth century the city of Edo led the land in cultural innovation and production. The culture of Edo the city in fact gradually became the hegemonic culture of the Edo period. This culture, it is often argued, was *daihyōteki*—usually translated as "representative" but in fact meaning "prominent" or even "outstanding." Other areas, both rural and urban, generally took more than they gave. The writings translated in this volume, too, reflect this bias, for with the exception of sections of Chapters 6 through 9, all studies center on the culture of the Edo metropolis. The reader is reminded, therefore, that a truly balanced picture of Edo-period culture would require more detailed discussion of the culture of provincial cities and rural areas.

In translating I have striven to remain faithful to the spirit rather than the letter of Nishiyama's prose. Some, therefore, may wish to label this book an adaptation rather than a translation. Nishiyama's writing style is stiff and often thrives more on a general tone of enthusiasm for the subject than on logical connections between sentences or paragraphs. Such a style, informed by the conviction that a good point bears repetition and that the relevance of an example need not be clarified until the very end of a section, entirely rules out literal translation. I have thus pruned judiciously, rewritten, rethought sentence and paragraph order, but refrained from adding anything substantially new to Nishiyama's writing. The only exceptions to this rule are a few brief definitions of terms unlikely to be known to a nonspecialist Anglophone readership and, moreover, the endings of Chapters 7, 8, and 9. In the original, these chapters simply stop when Nishiyama has run out of things to say. Such a writing style, common enough in Japanese academic prose, often irritates Western readers, who tend to prefer more synthetic conclusions. In these chapters, therefore, I have added summaries of Nishiyama's major points, thereby bringing the chapter to a smoother close while not adding anything new.

Since the studies translated here were not conceived by Nishiyama as forming one volume, much material is repeated. In some cases I have simply excised such duplication. The largest cut occurs in Chapter 6. Here I have eliminated or moved to other chapters most of the information that is presented in the first half of the original study, which repeats much of what has already been translated as Chapters 1 through 5. All major changes have been discussed with Professor Nishiyama, who himself occasionally suggested alterations and corrections.

Documentation in the original studies is often lacking and sometimes erroneous. In an effort to complete as many references as possible, I have started from scratch. Unless otherwise indicated, therefore, all notes are by the translator. Rechecking sources has allowed me to uncover several errors and misprints, which have been silently corrected after confirmation by the author.

The selection of illustrations and maps, the transcription of musical examples, and the production of the glossary are also my responsibility. Other editorial additions include dates and footnoted biographical information on individuals, details of geographical location of small towns and villages, variant names and performance dates of kabuki plays or musical works, and dates of publication of books. Names of individuals have presented a special problem, since Nishiyama endows the use of pseudonyms (*geimei*) with a special significance. Edo-period writers, actors, musicians, and artists often assumed a large variety of pseudonyms, forcing the translator to select one of several names for the sake of consistency.

I have generally selected the name most likely to appear in bio-graphical dictionaries.

Translating the titles of books or kabuki plays presents yet other obstacles. Titles of novels, plays, or collections of poetry are often the source of cryptic puns—and in cases where a work no longer exists, the exact reading and meaning of the title are anybody's guess. For extant books I have usually followed the reading of titles found in the *Kokusho sōmokuroku*. Kabuki titles are given in the ver-sion most likely to appear in kabuki dictionaries; alternative titles are given in the notes. A rough translation of a title's most obvious meaning follows the original in parentheses; when such a translation appears in italics, this indicates that the book has been published under this title in English. The reader should note that the names of Buddhist temples end with the syllables *ji, in, tera,* or *dera*; Shinto shrines often end with *sha, gū,* or *miya*.

Besides these problems, Nishiyama's idiosyncratic use of certain terms poses special difficulties for the translator. A few important examples deserve special mention. Nishiyama presumes, for exam-ple, that his readers have some knowledge of the *iemoto* system.[2] This system comprises a hierarchical, guildlike structure in which a ficti-tious household *(ie)* is organized so that the *iemoto* (the head of the *ie*) takes both responsibility and credit for transmitting to disciples the orthodox form of the house tradition. The position (and name) of the *iemoto* tend to be hereditary. When no son or daughter (real or adopted) is available, the best or most powerful disciple may be awarded the post. The process of transmitting an art within the *iemoto* system is usually a form of training that appeals primarily to direct experience and praxis. Transmission often involves a certain degree of secrecy, but students who after a period of apprenticeship have attained the appropriate rank (and paid the appropriate fees) may take on their own pupils and continue to pass on the art. The *iemoto,* however, continues to control the tradition by reserving the following rights:[3]

1. Rights regarding the art—for example, the right to secrecy, the right to allow or prohibit performances, rights over the reper-toire or the set forms *(kata)* of an art.
2. Rights concerning the teaching, transmission, and licensing of the art.
3. The right to expel or punish members of the school.
4. The right to dispose of costumes, ranks (pseudonyms), and the like.
5. The right to control equipment or properties used in the art.

6. Exclusive rights to the income resulting from the preceding five items. Since the Meiji period this right has included the copyright of all musical scores, nō texts, textbooks, scholarly writings, or journals issued by the school or family.

According to Nishiyama, the crucial period of the *iemoto* system's development occurred during the mid-eighteenth century. The contemporary proliferation of "town teachers"—mediators between the *iemoto* and the novice pupil—was in Nishiyama's view a result of the increase in the *chōnin*'s demand for cultural activity. This concern with culture was, in turn, premised on the *chōnin*'s great economic advance during this period. Nishiyama does not, however, interpret the *chōnin*'s desire for cultivation or the rise of the *iemoto* system as merely a "reflection" of economic or political forces. Instead he views the *iemoto* system's growth as part of a popular strategy in which *chōnin* attempted to break through the rigid framework of social rank and status that was strangling Edo-period society. When *chōnin* created cultural communities in which samurai and merchant, men and women, young and old, were nominal equals, or when they assumed *geimei* allowing them to hide their real social status, these individuals were creating a new world radically at odds with the feudal ethic that governed daily life. According to Nishiyama, this world of culture provided a sense of liberation, a sense of freedom, that was sadly lacking in contemporary social reality.

A related term that Nishiyama uses with particular emphasis is *yūgei* (leisure pursuits). *Yūgei* are cultural activities pursued only for the purpose of pleasure. Nishiyama contrasts *yūgei* to martial arts *(bugei)*, to popular performing arts *(taishū geinō)*, and to skills pursued solely for financial gain. *Yūgei* thus include most of Japan's best-known traditional arts: flower arranging, the tea ceremony, calligraphy, various forms of music and dance, bonsai and horticulture, poetry writing, and even card or board games.[4] The associations that formed around such cultural pursuits Nishiyama terms *bunka shakai* ("culture society"). This label, however, is also sometimes used to refer to the totality of all cultured individuals in Edo or elsewhere. I have thus rendered the term as either "cultural communities" or, in its broader sense, "cultured society."

Nishiyama's use of terms describing social strata or classes is often vague. *Kaisō* and *kaikyū* are employed more or less interchangeably with little concern for the overtones these words have acquired in Japanese sociological and historical (particularly Marxist) writings. Consequently, I have not attempted to maintain any strict differentiation between the terms "social stratum" and "social class."

I would like to thank Professor Nishiyama for spending much time with me discussing editorial changes, confirming errors and misprints, and helping me to determine likely readings of obscure names and titles. My gratitude goes also to the various libraries and museums that allowed me to reproduce illustrations from books and pictures in their possession.

I should like to thank Professor Ogi Shinzō and the staff at the Edo-Tokyo Museum for providing a comfortable and stimulating workplace and answering a constant stream of questions. Finally, I wish to thank my wife Sayuri, who provided invaluable help in preparing illustrations, and who urged me to go on at times when everyone else seemed to be telling me to give it up.

INTRODUCTION: THE STUDY OF EDO-PERIOD CULTURE

The writings collected here, written over a period of nearly two decades and appearing in various books and journals, lack a systematic unity. I would thus like to outline my views on how Edo-period culture should best be studied. To do this adequately would require a discussion of Japanese cultural history in general, but I shall employ a more limited strategy. First, I shall discuss the kind of historical perspective necessary for a correct assessment of Edo-period culture; second, I shall outline some methods for carrying out actual research, methods that make this historical perspective possible.

Approaches to Edo-Period Culture

Two basic historical perspectives are available to students of Japanese culture during the Edo period (1600–1868). One may compare the entirety of Edo-period culture to archaic, medieval, or modern Japanese culture; or one may focus on the question of what Edo-period culture is in and of itself. Historians who have taken the former approach have tended to dismiss Edo-period culture as the "vulgar" culture of the city of Edo. When, for example, I was at work on my university graduation thesis, which focused on the kabuki plays of Tsuruya Nanboku IV (1755–1829), I was often told that such a subject was inappropriate for a thesis in the Department of History. At the time, virtually no scholarly studies of *rakugo* (comic monologue), *kōdan* (storytelling), kabuki, or the arts of itinerant performers had yet appeared. Even in the 1960s I was still frequently advised to restrain my enthusiasm for the "vulgar" culture of Edo.

A few years ago, the still healthy Kagoshima Juzō looked over some of my work and remarked that it brought back old memories.[1]

When he was young, he recollected, he had gone to the house of a senior colleague to borrow some Edo-period books printed with woodblocks. On his way home, he met the poet Saitō Mokichi (1882–1953), who immediately took him to task for reading such "insipid Edo trash." Saitō's influence left its mark: Kagoshima was for many years unable to appreciate Edo-period culture. Only now, Kagoshima noted, was he finally able to see its true value.

Until the early years of the Taishō period (1912–1926) few Japanese showed much respect for Edo-period culture. As I have argued elsewhere, even men open and receptive to Edo-period culture—for example, the novelists Nagai Kafū (1879–1959) and Shimazaki Tōson (1872–1943)—were receptive only because they had come into contact with European evaluations of the subject.[2] These men were, in fact, almost entirely ignorant of Edo-period culture. Even thereafter, only a tiny minority, a few pioneers, showed some appreciation; the prevailing opinion within Japanese intellectual circles was similar to Saitō's. Even fairly recently, such bias had not completely disappeared.

What, then, are the true weaknesses of Edo-period culture? Certainly, Edo-period architecture, painting, or Buddhist sculpture did not attain the heights they achieved during the Heian (784–1185) and Kamakura (1185–1333) periods. No Edo-period painting equals the "Yellow *Fudō*";[3] nor can Edo-period swords rival the blades forged by the master smiths from the houses of Aoe or Osafune.[4] Much the same is true of Buddhist priests. Outstanding Japanese Buddhist priests are almost all from the Muromachi (1333–1573), Kamakura, Heian, and earlier periods. These priests contributed greatly to the establishment of Japan's superb Buddhist culture. Great Edo-period priests are rare: Jiun (1718–1804) and Hakuin Ekaku (1685–1768) are the exceptions that prove the rule. Edo-period culture did have its shortcomings; but the examples cited here are of an extremely limited nature and do not support the common view that Edo-period culture as a whole is weak.

The strength of Edo-period culture is not to be found in extant artifacts of the era. Rather, its strength lies chiefly in its spectacular breadth and diversity. This was a period of unprecedented cultural prosperity. Even the general public took part in leisure pursuits and played an active role in the creation of new cultural forms. The average commoner read books or visited the theater; some even wrote haiku verses and *senryū* (seventeen-syllable comic verse) or performed musical genres such as *gidayū, katō bushi, shinnai,* or *nagauta.* Others went on pilgrimages sponsored by religious associations *(kō)* and toured distant places. The Edo period saw a rise in the quality of culinary fare that commoners consumed; clothing and housing too showed marked improvement. Even the poor managed occasionally to indulge in the luxury of purchasing a "custom-made" comb or an ornamental hairpin. The demand for such cultural items fostered the development of a highly refined handicraft industry. Never before had there been such an extraordinary variety of hand-made cultural artifacts in Japan.

Even in remote areas in the countryside or on distant, isolated islands, inhabitants cultivated rare varieties of flowers and trees and marketed unusual rocks or curiosities. As Suzuki Bokushi (1770–1842) noted in his *Akiyama kikō* (Autumn Mountain Travelogue, 1831), people in every corner of the land were busy manufacturing local specialties. Such articles were being produced, one by one, by thirty million people. By the late Edo period this activity had stimulated an unprecedented development of the transportation network. Mountain roads, waterways, and sea routes were extended in all directions to every nook and cranny of the country. Indeed, the construction of footpaths during the late Edo period can be seen as a kind of symbol of this golden age of handicraft culture.

No doubt, Japan today boasts a high level of culture. But the price has been high as well: severe environmental pollution and the wholesale destruction of nature. Until the end of the Edo period, red-crested cranes could still be seen soaring through the skies over the city; swans and geese flocked to Shinobazu Pond in Ueno Park. Foxes and badgers were found everywhere, and cuckoos *(hototogisu)* flourished in such numbers that their song was considered a nuisance. Even during the late Meiji period the water of the Sumida River was clean enough to be used for brewing tea while boating. Human activity imparted only minimal damage to nature. Viewed in this way, Edo-period culture seems almost ideal.

Certain elements of the Edo-period cultural heritage were vulgar, no doubt, but a more comprehensive view of the period reveals an almost infinite number of admirable qualities. Nevertheless, after the Meiji Restoration of 1868, governmental policies of modernization and westernization dictated a wholesale rejection of the preceding feudal era. Even the best elements of Edo-period culture were deemed outdated and vulgar and were thought to require prompt and thorough extirpation. That the true value of Edo-period culture could not yet be properly assessed had much to do with the lack of any inquiry into its origins and actual conditions. Recent research, however, has shown that Edo-period culture was outstanding in its own way and not at all inferior to the culture of earlier or later periods.

Boating and moon viewing on the Sumida River. From *Tōto saijiki.*

Methods for Studying Edo-Period Culture

Research into the culture of the Edo period should have, I believe, three broad aims. First, this culture must be correctly evaluated and restored to its proper position. Past biases must be corrected; the actual conditions of this culture must be reappraised.

Second, the high level attained by handicrafts during this age must be explained. Edo-period handicraft culture developed throughout Japan, adapting itself to the natural conditions of each locality. Both Edo and Kyoto served as major cultural centers in which handicraft production was consolidated. In regional cultural centers such as Kanazawa or Kumamoto, diverse high-quality articles were also manufactured on a large scale.

Third, the relation of human beings and nature necessary for an ideal cultured life must be reconsidered. Something close to an ideal relation of production to consumption—that is, an ideal relation of people to nature—was, in fact, attained by the thirty million Japanese of the Edo period. Now I would like to outline some observations concerning the first two points.

Toward a Correct Appreciation of Edo-Period Culture

A lack of adequate records of cultural activities of individual families during ancient and medieval times makes these eras difficult to research. This is much less true of the Edo period. During this age many houses kept detailed diaries and registers that can shed much light on contemporary cultural life.

Though of great importance, the splendid culture of the Edo-period warrior class has been especially neglected. Yet detailed records provide the researcher with much useful information. The upper-level warrior stratum kept meticulous diaries: examples include the *Matsudaira Yamato no kami nikki* (Diary of Matsudaira, Governor of Yamato),[5] the *En'yū nikki* (Diary of Banquets and Amusements),[6] and the *Moriyama Takamori nikki* (Diary of Moriyama Takamori).[7] "Secret transmissions" *(hidensho)* such as the *Heihō kadensho* (Transmissions of the House Concerning Warfare) by Yagyū Tajima-no-Kami Munenori (1571–1646), the *Gorin no sho (Book of Five Rings)* by Miyamoto Musashi (1584–1645), or the works on gunnery by Inatomi Ichimu (d. 1611) also constitute important historical sources. Writings of daimyo, tea masters, and literati such as Furuta Oribe (1543–1615), Kobori Enshū (1579–1647), or Katagiri Sekishū (Sadamasa, 1605–1673) are useful as well.

Such documents exist in profusion, and their analysis requires much time and effort. Close reading, however, soon reveals a remarkable phenomenon: that from around the middle of the seventeenth century, the city of Edo was becoming a cultural center of Japan. It soon rivaled Kyoto, which had been the center of culture since Heian times. Two clearly differentiated types of culture were now recognized. One was the culture of Kamigata (the "upper region," the area including Kyoto and Osaka); the other was the culture of the city of Edo.

Kyoto continued to have an elite aristocratic cultural community. By contrast, the culture of Edo centered on a far larger upper-class warrior stratum. This cultured society included both daimyo stationed in the city and the upper echelon of warriors associated with the Tokugawa bakufu. Unlike the rootless, refined individuals of the Kyoto court, these warrior nobles of Edo ruled over innumerable lower-ranking warrior houses who were tethered to rural castle towns. Cultural exchange between Edo and rural areas was stimulated by a system of "alternate attendance" *(sankin kōtai)* that required daimyo to spend alternate years in their home province and in Edo. Incessant travel between Edo and the provinces, therefore, spread the influence of Edo upper-class culture throughout the land.

The developments of the city of Edo had important cultural consequences. Many artistic pursuits that had existed since the Heian period—martial arts *(bugei)* as well as leisure pursuits *(yūgei)*—were now reorganized as a *geidō,* an artistic "Way." No less important, the Japanese language itself underwent changes. A lingua franca spoken by people throughout the land gradually arose. In addition, many customs and forms of etiquette that were to become the basis of a nationwide style of everyday life were born at this time.

A good example of warrior culture can be seen in handicrafts associated with the martial arts. This topic has been left largely unresearched; in fact it has almost been consigned to oblivion. Nevertheless, careful study reveals that corresponding to the demand for swords—the samurai's favorite possession—designs on scabbards and fittings developed remarkably. When a new sword was ordered for occasions such as the ceremony accompanying the attainment of manhood *(genpuku)* or the acquisition of an official post, everything, including the design on the scabbard, was specified in great detail. Scabbards were adorned with an infinite variety of lacquer designs. This great diversity, one of the hallmarks of Edo-period culture, was the result of individual production of most articles. Scabbard designs show that Edo-period culture was not just varied but also highly refined and innovative.

Scabbard designs are by no means the only phenomenon that has received inadequate scholarly attention. In the past, for example, the kabuki and puppet theater were often portrayed as pointless, low-brow, and crude forms of theater. Strolling performers of *shinnai* and other genres of *shamisen* and vocal music were also seen as tainted by the sultry mood of the brothel areas. Even the tea ceremony, flower arranging, and other traditional arts have often been portrayed as somewhat less than truly artistic. When, for example, a school of fine arts was founded in Tokyo's Ueno Park during the Meiji period, the Japanese government established a department of Western music but made no provisions for the study of traditional Japanese music. Today hardly anyone would agree with this policy, but it took many years before Japanese traditional music began to be regarded as equal in value to Western music. And it was not until after World War II that Japanese music was made part of the official public school curriculum.

During the Edo period the world of culture, with its many schools or styles *(ryū)* and its *iemoto* system, played a large role in providing the Edo-period populace with a sense of liberation. The outlines of this cultural world can be pieced together from sources that have been handed down in each house *(ie):* lists of disciples, accounts of secret transmissions, and extant licenses issued to students. In the past, cultural historians simply tossed such sources aside, judging them unworthy of serious consideration. Such a disdain for Edo-period culture was still common after the war, when I began to collect and copy many records of disciples. Nevertheless, during the Edo period such registers, secret transmissions, and licenses had a profound significance. For these documents list artists' names *(gei-mei)*, haiku poets' names *(haimei)*, and other pseudonyms that were used by Edo-period citizens when they wished to achieve an imaginary transformation.

The discovery of this process of imaginary transformation, which has profound implications for Edo-period cultural history, did not result from a use of traditional research methods. It was, instead, the fruit of a thorough and stubborn investigation utilizing a broad range of hitherto unused historical sources. Such documents are available in nearly limitless abundance. Unearthing and carefully inspecting such sources opens up entirely new fields of inquiry.

There is yet another reason why Edo-period culture has not been properly appreciated: the influence of Chinese culture has not yet

Chinoiserie, Edo style. From *Tōshisen ehon,* 1791. (In the possession of the translator.)

been properly understood. During the Edo period Chinese culture was highly venerated. Its deep and lasting influence was important, not just for Japanese Confucianism and Confucian scholarship, but for a whole range of other pursuits as well. The effect of Chinese poetry and literature, or of Ming and Qing dynasty art and scholarship, can hardly be overestimated. For example, the book *Tianxia yitong zhi* (Records of All the World) greatly influenced the *fudoki* (gazetteers) produced throughout Japan. This volume was published as *Dai Min ittō-shi* (Records of the Ming Dynasty) at the beginning of the Genroku era (1688–1704) by a warrior from the Wakayama domain.[8] Similarly, the volumes *Gai yu cong kao* (*Gaiyō sōkō* in Japanese) by Zhao Yi (1727–1814) were also profoundly influential. The respect for things Chinese lasted until the Sino-Japanese War (1894–1895), but thereafter the fact that Chinese culture had once been of great importance faded from memory.

Similarly, "Dutch learning" (that is, Western learning, *rangaku*) was also highly important during the Edo period. Over one hundred times throughout the Edo period, the chief of the Dutch settlement at Dejima in Nagasaki came to Edo to receive an audience and present gifts to the shogun. For some twenty or thirty days during the spring, the chief and his retinue stayed at the Nagasaki-ya, a lodge at Hongoku-chō. From around the middle of the Edo period, a number of cultured individuals made use of these few weeks to engage in unfettered cultural exchange with the Dutch. Japanese were strictly forbidden to enter the Dutch outpost of Dejima in Nagasaki, but within Edo much free activity was possible. After the Meiji Restoration, however, the diplomatic relations maintained by the Tokugawa bakufu with the Dutch were overshadowed by the Meiji government's policy of strengthening ties with England, France, Germany, and the United States. In turn, much that concerned *rangaku* was forgotten. Although cultural exchange with the Dutch was once of great significance, its conditions and historical role have only recently begun to receive scholarly attention. Such examples show that Edo-period culture demands reevaluation. The type of historical perspective suggested here should begin to make a correct appraisal possible.

Edo-Period Culture and Handicrafts

Let us now turn to another area of inquiry: the sophisticated and widespread handicraft culture of the Edo period.[9] Throughout its long history, Edo-period popular culture maintained a remarkably high standard. This is obvious, for example, in books of famous artworks by Ogata Kōrin (1658–1716), published by Sakai Hōitsu (1761–1828) under the title *Kōrin hyakuzu* (One Hundred Drawings After Kōrin). Sakai transferred to woodblocks some two hundred of Ogata's paintings, privately publishing the first volume of one hundred pictures for the 1815 Ogata centennial, the Buddhist ceremony of which he was in charge. The second volume followed eleven years later in 1826. Although Ogata was a highly respected artist at this time, publication of these books seems to have taken place with no concern for public demand. Yet a look at the preface written by Kameda Hōsai (1752–1826) for the first volume, or the preface written by Tani Buncho (1763–1840) for the second, reveals that these men greatly praised "Saint Hōitsu" for making two hundred of Ogata's pictures available to the public at large.

An outstanding example of Edo-period handicraft design is Katsushika Hokusai's *Imayō sekkin hiinagata* (Modern Comb and Pipe Designs, published in 1822). This work presents one hundred and fifty designs for combs and an equal number of designs for the metal fittings of pipes. The publication of these marvelously detailed drawings demonstrates that Hokusai (1760–1849), in this way no different from Kōrin and Hōitsu, was not an artist who sought to produce museum pieces but, rather, a craftsman who lived in close contact with the common people. In other words, just as the general public could purchase and enjoy inexpensive *ukiyo-e* (woodblock prints) by Suzuki Harunobu (1725–1770), Kitagawa Utamaro (1753–1806), Tōshūsai Sharaku (fl. 1794–1795), and Utagawa Kunisada (1786–1864), it could also savor the drawings of Kōrin and Hōitsu and order such illustrations transferred onto combs and pipes, fans, screens, and sliding doors. During this age of handicrafts and custom-made articles, volumes by Hokusai and others functioned as catalogs that showed the public what was available. Collections of designs for small-sleeved kimono *(kosode)* had also been published since the early part of the Edo period.[10] Similar catalogs existed for other articles as well. From these volumes, the public selected designs to be executed by highly skilled artisans, most of whom are not known to us by name today.

In the past, the study of much Edo-period culture was relegated to dilettantes, hobbyists, and collectors. But some collectors and so-called dilettantes have made important discoveries. Let me give a few illustrations. Takao Ryōichi was a highly cultured man who served as an administrator in the Imperial Household Agency and painted many wonderful sets for the kabuki. Since his student days he worked on a detailed study of the tens of thousands of *senryū* in the *Haifū yanagidaru* collection, filling over one hundred notebooks

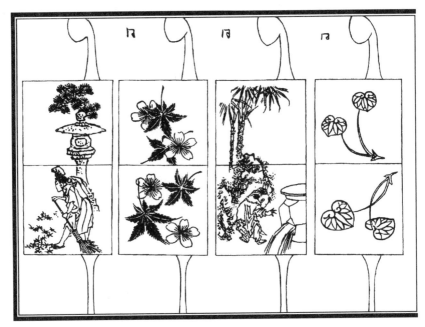

Pipe designs by Katsushika Hokusai, as seen in *Imayō sekkin hiinagata*. From
Hokusai no e-tehon, vol. 5 (Iwasaki Bijutsusha, 1986).

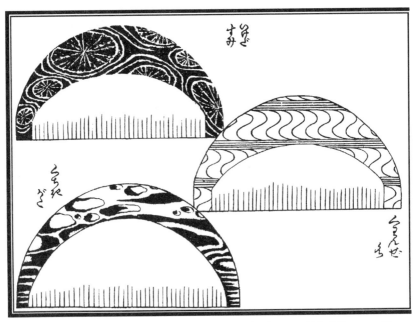

Comb designs by Katsushika Hokusai, as seen in *Imayō sekkin hiinagata*. From
Hokusai no e-tehon, vol. 5 (Iwasaki Bijutsusha, 1986).

 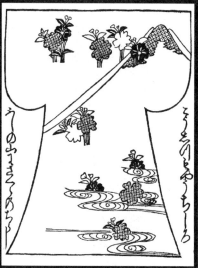

Kosode kimono designs. From Asai Ryōi, *Shinsen ohiinagata* (published in 1666). The design on the left is a rebus: *kasa* (sedge hat) plus *sagi* (snowy heron) equals *kasasagi* (magpie), a bird associated with the seventh-month Tanabata Festival. The design on the right features Mount Fuji and cherry blossoms.

with commentary. As a result, the meaning of only about a dozen of these comic verses remains obscure. Yet this great work of scholarship, the fruit of a lifetime of painstaking research, remains almost entirely unknown. We must look with humility upon such unpublished works from which we have much to learn.

Two other scholars who have taught me much are Iwasa Ryōji and Watanabe Yoshitaka. Iwasa is an expert in Edo-period gardening; Watanabe has studied the cultivation of hybrid morning glories. A result of my visits to these two men was my study *Kaei bunka shiron* (An Examination of Kaei-Period [1848–1854] Culture). Although my study deals only with the development of the hybrid morning glory, I discovered that the culture of the 1840s and 1850s—the time from the Tenpō Reforms to the opening of Japanese harbors—was the high point of Japanese handicraft culture.

The development of hybrid morning glories was just one element of a refined and broadly based culture in which a high premium was placed on handmade articles. This culture included *ukiyo-e* woodcuts, flyers and chapbooks, the kabuki, storytelling, clothing, gardening, and much else. That this culture has often been labeled "decadent" merely reflects bias or sloppy and myopic research meth-

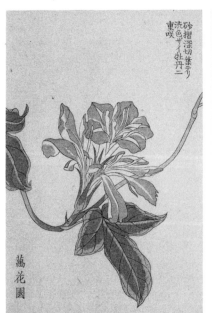

Morning glories cultivated during the late Edo period. From *Asagao san-jūrokkasen.* (In the possession of the Tokyo Metropolitan Central Library.)

ods. Decadence can of course be found here; but the creative urge of the common citizenry of this era was nothing if not sound and healthy.

Finally, I must mention the so-called folk and popular performing arts. Today many Edo-period folk and popular arts survive only as shadows of their former selves. Their present inferior and debilitated versions have little of the vigor the originals once possessed. Since they lack the permanence enjoyed by works of pictorial or literary art, past forms of performing arts have been lost and their earlier states forgotten. Cultural history can breathe new life into such vanished forms only with great difficulty. Few scholars have recognized that many of these arts, though perhaps mediocre today, were in the past quite remarkable.

In sum, then, a proper evaluation of Edo-period culture calls for broad perspectives. Today there seems to be more reason than ever to review the possibilities latent in Edo-period culture. For this culture was made possible by two hundred years of peace and isolation, conditions entirely at odds with Japan's history of war since the Meiji period. Perhaps now, at last, times of peace will once again prevail. This respite should allow us to rethink the conditions necessary for leading cultured lives.

PART I

EDO: THE CITY AND ITS CULTURE

CHAPTER 1

EDO: THE WARRIOR'S CITY

Topography and the City's Layout

When Tokugawa Ieyasu (1542–1616) came to Edo in 1590, he inherited little more than the vestiges of a castle built long before by Ōta Dōkan (1432–1486). With the implementation of Tokugawa political rule, this sleepy, historic area was destined to become the capital of all Japan. By the start of the eighteenth century, roughly one century after the establishment of the Tokugawa bakufu, the city of Edo already boasted a population of around one million inhabitants. The appearance of a city of such size was an event unprecedented in Japanese history.

The city's development commenced in earnest once Edo became the castle town of Ieyasu, then merely the daimyo of the eight Kantō provinces. This era lasted for roughly a decade, ending with Ieyasu's decisive victory at the Battle of Sekigahara (1600) and his subsequent promotion to the position of shogun. When the Tokugawa bakufu was established in 1603, plans were drawn up for constructing a castle worthy of the nation's capital and a city for the general populace.

Today Tokyo bristles with skyscrapers, and one can hardly imagine the city's original geographical position. After the air raids of World War II, however, Tokyo was reduced to a charred wasteland, and the impregnable position of Edo castle once again became visible. Topographically speaking, the Musashino Plateau, on which Edo stood, was a diluvial plain with deep valleys carved away by erosion. Five adjacent terraces remained, spread out like the fingers of the hand. The ends of these terraces were named the Ueno Terrace, the Kanda Terrace, the Kōkyo (Palace) Terrace, the Shiba-Atagoyama Terrace, and the Shinagawa-Goten'yama Terrace. The central Kōkyo Terrace was itself partitioned into five smaller terraces: from the west, the Kioi-chō Terrace, the Sannō-Hie Shrine

23

Terrace, the Kasumigaseki Terrace, the Nishinomaru ("western enclosure") Terrace, and the Honmaru ("main enclosure") Terrace. Ōta Dōkan had built his castle on the Honmaru Terrace; Ieyasu was to follow suit, supplementing the main enclosure with a shrine (the Momijiyama Tōshōgū) and a "western enclosure" on the Nishinomaru Terrace. Edo castle was thereby ensconced in a nearly invulnerable position. A further advantage of this site was that unlike the other four major terraces, which extended to the Musashi Plain, the Kōkyo Terrace bottlenecked around the Yotsuya Approach (mitsuke), isolating it from the surrounding areas.

To ensure the unassailability of its stronghold, the bakufu skillfully utilized the Sumida and Kanda rivers to serve as large-scale moats. Tremendous construction projects were carried out. The Sumida and Kanda rivers were joined by moats excavated from around Iidabashi to Shōheibashi, passing through the waters of what is now Ochanomizu. A particularly deep trench was dug at the Yotsuya Approach, the only point where the Kōkyo Terrace was connected directly to the Musashi Plain. The strategic use of the Sumida

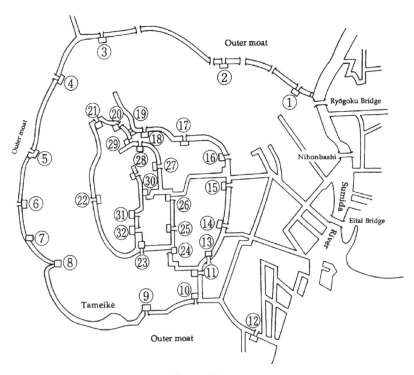

Map of Edo.

and Kanda rivers caused the Edo castle moats to describe an unusual spiral shape, drawing ever nearer to the castle. Moving in the direction from the Sumida River to the center, the moats began around Ryōgokubashi and proceeded to Asakusa-gomon (at Asakusabashi) (1), Sujikaibashi (2), Koishikawa-gomon (3), Ushigome-gomon (4), Ichigaya-gomon (5), Yotsuya-gomon (6), Kuichigai-gomon (7), Akasaka-gomon (8), Toranomon (9), and Saiwaibashi (10).[1] From Saiwaibashi a deep moat ran from Yamashita-gomon (at Soto-hibiya) (11) through Sukiyabashi (13), Kajibashi (14), Gofukubashi (15), Tokiwabashi (16), Kandabashi (17), Hitotsubashi (18), Kijibashi (19), Shimizu-gomon (20), and Tayasu-gomon (21). From here to Hanzōmon (22) the moat was called Chidorigafuchi. Next came Soto-sakuradamon (23), Hibiya-gomon (24), Babasakimon (25), Wadakuramon (26), Ōtemon (27), Hirakawa-gomon (28), Takebashi (29), Uchi-sakuradamon (30), Sakashita-gomon (31), and finally Nishinomaru-ōtemon (32). From Saiwaibashi (10) a moat extended past the Hamaōte-gomon (12) all the way to the ocean.

The inner area of Edo was designed to lie between the Yotsuya–Akasaka–Tameike–Toranomon–Saiwaibashi–Hamōte-gomon line of castle moats, on the one hand, and the segment of the Sumida River extending from Ryōgokubashi to the river's mouth on the other. This was the most important area of the city, and its significance increased as one moved inward. At the very center, encircled by the inner and outer enclosures, stood the castle. Inside the Yotsuya Approach, the one spot where the castle could be reached directly overland, three great allies of the bakufu—the daimyo houses of the Kii, Owari, and Ii—were placed as guards. Accordingly, this location was later known by a combination of the first ideograph of the names of each of the houses: Kioi-chō. At the outer side of the Yotsuya Approach, along the highway to the north, official sentinels were stationed; immediately to the rear lay the great estate of the Owari family. The Kii house was also granted property at the outer side of the Akasaka Approach; the Mito house was put in charge of guarding the outer side of Koishikawa-gomon. The Mito house had its "upper residence" *(kami-yashiki)* here and was required to watch over both the Ōshū and Nakasendō highways. The Maeda house of the Kaga (Kanazawa) domain, with a wealth rated at over one million *koku* (1 *koku*=approximately 180 liters) of rice, was placed at what is now the Hongō area around Tokyo University. The area around the university's Department of Agriculture was once taken up by the Mito family's "middle residence" *(naka-yashiki)*. The road that now passes between this area and the Department of Engineering was at the time only a hedge: thus the powerful Maeda house could be observed year-round by the Mito house, a branch family of the Tokugawa.

As the largest *tozama* daimyo house, the Maeda was checked from the east by the Kan'eiji, a temple from which it was separated by nothing more than Shinobazu Pond. To the immediate south and west stood the "middle" and "lower" residences of the Sakakibara and Honda, two of Ieyasu's four most loyal supporters. Moreover, behind the Honda residence was the spacious "middle residence" of the Abe family, a house that had functioned for generations as senior councillors *(rōjū)* in the bakufu.

This is how things stood in the 1660s. The location of daimyo residences in Edo was in fact a miniature version of the position of the various daimyo within the country as a whole. By such means, the bakufu shrewdly stationed the forces of the *tozama* and *fudai* daimyo houses in ways that worked to its advantage. The bakufu governed the daimyo with an iron hand. Until the time of the fifth shogun, Tsunayoshi (r. 1680–1709), the bakufu frequently ordered fief transfers or confiscations.[2] As a result, daimyo residences were often moved within the city. Incessant changes in city planning also required construction of new wards or forcible relocation of old ones. Such changes can be seen in Table 1.1, which gives the number of residences the bakufu bequeathed to its vassals, calculated at five-year intervals.[3] The figures of the first and second columns reveal the number of new and relocated wards *(machi)* in the city. Table 1.1 does not take into account the size of residences. Daimyo residences and domiciles of smaller holders have not been differentiated, for example, and residences of such lesser figures as assistant magistrates *(yoriki)* and low-ranking peace officers *(dōshin)* have also been included.

For an idea of relocations experienced by daimyo, one can turn to the descriptions found in the registries of military households *(bukan)*. Table 1.2 presents the relevant figures for the large daimyo houses of the Owari Tokugawa, the Hikone Ii, and the Kaga Maeda. This table shows that during the early Edo period, the residences of the great daimyo houses were frequently moved. Locations stabilized during the Kanbun period (1661–1673); by the Genroku period (1688–1704) each daimyo had established an "upper," "middle," and "lower" residence. Later yet, by the first years of the eighteenth century, the only observable change is the addition of the Owari Tokugawa's middle residence at Kōjimachi. The placement of residences had clearly stabilized. Although one often hears that the system of upper, middle, and lower residences resulted from bakufu grants of alternate residences after the great Meireki fire (1657), this

Table 1.1. Number of Wards and Official Residences in Edo

YEAR	NUMBER OF NEW WARDS	NUMBER OF RELOCATED WARDS	NUMBER OF RESIDENCES GIVEN TO DAIMYO AND OFFICIALS
1620–1624	37	4	3
1625–1629	75	0	8
1630–1634	37	10	16
1635–1639	49	1	67
1640–1644	58	1	48
1645–1649	34	3	131
1650–1654	36	3	32
1655–1659	40	2	4
1660–1664	65	23	416
1665–1669	29	7	189
1670–1674	14	1	58
1675–1679	5	12	303
1680–1684	30	15	154
1685–1689	7	8	381
1690–1694	29	42	1,009
1695–1699	68	62	2,835
1700–1704	46	2	1,536
1705–1709	18	1	1,663
1710–1714	17	6	1,187
1715–1719	2	0	1,095
1720–1724	6	4	1,380
1725–1729	5	2	1,048
1730–1734	8	3	758
1735–1739	12	1	701
1740–1744	2	2	678

system was in fact established during the Genroku period. In both the *bukan* and the maps of Edo, one finds little change in the location of residences for the remainder of the Edo period.

The four-digit figures in the fourth column of Table 1.1 also point to a concentration of activity from the Genroku to the Kyōhō periods (1688–1736). The era of major transformations within the bakufu-fief order lasted until this age. As a result, drastic changes took place in the layout of the city. New wards were constructed, old wards were relocated, land was sequestered, and daimyo estates were reorganized. Changes also resulted from the bakufu's tendency to split official positions into increasingly narrowly defined posts and to award a residence to any vassal who obtained even a minor government appointment. Fires, too, provided a perfect opportunity to rebuild and rearrange residences. Records show, for example, that in the eighteen-year period from 1703 to 1721 the two largest Edo theaters,

Table 1.2. Relocation of Edo Daimyo Residences

YEAR	OWARI TOKUGAWA	HIKONE II	KANAZAWA MAEDA
1655	Kōjimachi Tsuchi-bashi no uchi	Sannō Minamidai	around Tatsu no kuchi
1669	Ichigaya Tamachi	Sannō Minamidai	Kanda Myōjin shita
1672	Ichigaya-gomon soto	(1679) Sakurada-gomon	Hongō 5-chōme
	Yotsuya-gomon soto	Gohoribata-nishi	
1698	u: Ichigaya-gomon soto	u: Sakurada Gohoribata	u: Hongō 5-chōme
	m: Yotsuya-gomon uchi	m: Akasaka-gomon	m: Somei
	l: Takada Anahachi-man	l: Sendagaya	l: Fukagawa
	l: Kobiki-chō Tsukiji	l: Hatchōbori	l: Itabashi
1705	u: Ichigaya-gomon soto	same as above	same as above
	m: Yotsuya-gomon no uchi		
	m: Kōjimachi 11-chōme		
	l: Takada Anahachi-man		
	l: Kobiki-chō Tsukiji		

u = upper residence *(kami-yashiki)*
m = middle residence *(naka-yashiki)*
l = lower residence *(shimo-yashiki)*

the Nakamura-za and the Ichimura-za, burned to the ground no fewer than eight times. Close by, in the Nihonbashi area, lay many warrior residences, which often went up in smoke as well. (See Table 1.3.)[4]

By the Kyōhō period (1716–1736), daimyo were only rarely shuffled from one fief to another. The placement of daimyo residences gradually stabilized, and the layout of Edo changed but little. The city had matured to become a metropolis with a population of around a million people, divided roughly equally between warriors and townspeople *(chōnin)*.

The Consequences of Warrior Rule

The warrior population contributed much to the uniqueness of Edo. A large number of "bannermen" *(hatamoto)*—direct vassals and

Table 1.3. Edo Fires

DATE	WARDS DESTROYED BY FIRE	NUMBER OF TIMES THE TWO MAJOR THEATERS BURNED DOWN
1620–1629	40	
1630–1639	37	
1640–1649	331	
1650–1659	736	1
1660–1669	422	1
1670–1679	74	1
1680–1689	282	2
1690–1699	640	
1700–1709	278	2
1710–1719	1,008	4
1720–1729	447	2
1730–1739	164	
1740–1749	73	1
1750–1759	223	1
1760–1769	179	3
1770–1779	758	1
1780–1789	318	3
1790–1799	143	
1800–1809	567	2
1810–1819	104	2
1820–1829	314	3
1830–1839	1,367	2

guardsmen of the bakufu—lived in the environs of the castle. A system of "alternate attendance" *(sankin kōtai)* required daimyo and their retainers to spend alternate years in the capital and at their domains. Daimyo wives and children resided permanently in the capital. Thus at any given time, a large part of the military force of the nation was stationed in Edo. No matter how distant a daimyo's domain lay from Edo, he took part in regular grand processions between his home area and the capital.

The concentration of warriors in the city stimulated the emergence of a unique Edo economy. The presence of a large stratum of newly enfranchised warrior nobles required the procurement of a tremendous quantity of consumer goods. Supplying such goods was the responsibility of official merchants and artisans who streamed to the capital from all parts of the country. Edo thus became a consumer capital.

Forced to live in the city, the daimyo, along with their retainers and families, enthusiastically set about developing their own culture.

Both the ancient Kyoto court traditions and the warrior culture of the Kamakura bakufu (1185–1333) developed rapidly among the aristocratic warrior stratum. The habits and lifestyle of the daimyo and the high-ranking officials—their food, housing, and clothing, their furnishings and utensils, even their styles of seating and deportment—were in fact all warrior-style variations of the ancient customs, practices, and etiquette of the Kyoto court.

In the hands of the warriors the ancient system of court ranks, which had degenerated into little more than empty formality, was consolidated into legal form. The bakufu decreed in Article 7 of the "Rules for the Palace and the Court" (*Kinchū narabi ni kuge sho-hatto,* 1615) that "court ranks and offices of members of the military houses are to be treated separately from those held by court nobility."[5] This law transformed the traditional system of ranks at a stroke. Titles issued to warriors included "Governor" (*kami* and *jō*), "Minister of the Right" (*udaijin*), "Major Counselor" (*dainagon*), and "Minor Counselor" (*chūnagon*).

In 1603 Tokugawa Ieyasu had already revealed his longing for the culture of the imperial court when he made Emperor Goyōzei (r. 1596–1611) appoint him "Minister of the Right," "Great Barbarian-Subduing General" (*Sei-i tai shōgun*), "Head of the Minamoto Clan" (*Genji chōja*), and "Superintendent of the Junna and Shōgaku Institutes" (*Junna shōgaku ryōin bettō*). Ieyasu was also given permission to use an oxcart; in addition, he was granted a retinue of attendants. Ieyasu was in fact emulating his cherished medieval predecessor Minamoto no Yoritomo (1147–1199). For Yoritomo had possessed the titles of both shogun and "Minister of the Right" and was called "Head of the Palace Guards" (*udaishō*). Like Yoritomo, Ieyasu was determined to become the most powerful man in the imperial court. Such actions were to set the tone of Tokugawa bakufu policy in the long years to come.

As medieval warrior culture began to be revived, high importance was placed on the traditions outlined in the *Azuma kagami* (Mirror of the East; a history of the Kamakura bakufu), the *Jōei shikimoku* (Jōei Code; promulgated in 1232),[6] and the legitimacy of Minamoto family rule. The latter claim resulted in the production of numerous genealogies—a practice that then spread to all the daimyo houses. The compilation of genealogies was brought to completion in the *Kan'ei shoka keizuden* (Kan'ei-Period [1624–1644] Genealogies of All Daimyo Houses).

A stress on things martial now led to the creation of a system differing radically from that accompanying the rule of Toyotomi Hideyoshi (1536–1598). The bakufu's basic policy was codified in the

Buke sho-hatto (Laws Governing the Military Households, 1615).[7] Bannermen and household retainers were actually put to work as guards in charge of fortifying the surroundings of Edo castle; daimyo wives and children were required to live in the capital; daimyo themselves were given no choice but to accept the system of alternate attendance. The Ogasawara house, which had traditionally regulated the warriors' two basic skills of archery and horsemanship, benefited greatly from the bakufu's new priorities. By governing the protocol of these two arts the Ogasawara house succeeded in controlling the code of decorum of the entire warrior stratum. Eventually, principles of warrior etiquette filtered down to Japanese society at large.

Warrior culture sought to regulate both the temporal/historical dimensions and the spatial/geographical dimensions of the land. History was codified by compiling the family lineages and codes of etiquette cited earlier. For example, Hayashi Razan (1583–1657) was ordered to compile the *Honchō tsugan* (A General Mirror of Japan; compiled 1644–1670), a book that sought to establish the lineages and norms of behavior of the shogun and the daimyo and justify the institutions and ranks that had arisen throughout Japanese history. Control over the spatial/geographical dimensions of the land required meticulous land surveys and the drafting of accurate maps of the nation. These maps, said to have been among the best in the world at the time, were collected in the *Shōhō kuni ezu* (Shōhō-Period [1644–1648] Maps of the Provinces); surveys were compiled in the *Kanbun inchi-shū* (Collection of Kanbun-Period [1661–1673] Land Surveys).

Principles of warrior rule governed the rank or status of individuals and families in the feudal hierarchy. Rules were drawn up stipulating the forms a daimyo was required to follow. Social rank determined the shape and size of a daimyo's Edo residence, the scale of his processions, and the kind of vehicles, furnishings, and clothing he was allowed to use. Distinctions of feudal rank were displayed to be immediately visible. These included the colors and designs of clothing, styles of architecture and materials used in buildings and gardens, and the methods and ingredients employed in manufacturing various goods consumed by the warrior. Even the borders of straw floor mats *(tatami)* in Edo castle varied according to the rank of the officials who sat on them. For this reason feudal culture—at its most typical, Edo warrior culture—is often said to be a predominantly visual culture.

Principles that are nearly unimaginable today governed society in rigid, unchanging ways. Each rank of the feudal hierarchy was allotted clearly defined limits above or below which it was impermissible to pass. The principle of "knowing one's place" was of paramount importance: it was the iron law of feudal ethics. Today, "knowing one's place" generally implies not rising above what is deemed appropriate. But during the Edo period, falling below one's station was also prohibited. This ethic and the social order that supported it were firmly established during the century that followed the founding of Edo.

With the arrival of an age of permanent peace, a decisive change occurred in the nature of the concept of the "martial" *(bu)*. The crucial period of these conceptual transformations lasted from the latter part of the reign of the third shogun Iemitsu (r. 1623–1651) to the age of the fourth shogun Ietsuna (r. 1651–1680). The emergence of a concept of "martial arts" *(bugei)* reflects such changes. Archery, horsemanship, and the use of firearms had been treated as martial arts for some time, but the most advanced combat techniques—the use of the long and short sword, lances, halberds, and poles, rock throwing, the arts of stealth, judo, naval techniques, and swimming—were hitherto regarded as little more than military techniques of murder. From the 1570s, however, the word *kenjutsu* (swordsmanship) begins to appear; and from the 1620s until the time of the fourth shogun Ietsuna, the term martial arts gradually included the use of the sword and spear, judo, and techniques of stealth.

The Ogasawara house had for many years set the standards for archery and horsemanship; principles for the use of firearms were then modeled after those of archery. Soon schools *(ryū)* of marksmanship, such as the Inatomi-ryū, the Nakanishi-ryū, the Tsuda-ryū, and the Tatsuke-ryū, began to appear. These schools taught the techniques of slaughter as an abstract, theoretical martial art, something resembling a sport in which murder found no place. The Ogasawara family's supreme authority in such matters was unrelated to any achievements this house had shown in archery and horsemanship on the battlefield. Its position as the highest authority on martial arts stemmed from its codification of what had become the rules of a sport. These abstract rules and practices were then turned into "secret transmissions" *(hidensho)*, which often took the form of a precious scroll.

Martial arts were greatly developed by Yagyū Tajima-no-Kami Munenori, head of the shogun's official house of swordsmanship. Munenori based his teachings on the military techniques described in the book *Shin-kage-ryū heihō mokuroku no koto* (Catalog of the Military Techniques of the Shin Kage School), written in 1601 by his father, Yagyū Muneyoshi (1526–1606). By the late 1630s Munenori had completed a remarkable systematization of swordsmanship in a volume entitled *Heihō kadensho* (Transmissions of the House Regarding Military Techniques). This book was a tripartite secret transmission consisting of sections entitled *Shinrikyō* (A Bridge for Progress), *Setsunintō* (The Murderous Blade), and *Katsuninken* (The Sword of Life). Though written as a manual of military technique, it testified to the establishment of swordsmanship as a martial art. Munenori's invention of the bamboo sword, an example of which is still in the possession of the Yagyū family today, shows unambiguously that swordfighting had evolved from a military technique to a martial art.[8]

Another outstanding book concerning martial arts was the *Gorin no sho* (*A Book of Five Rings*), written by Miyamoto Musashi (1584–1645), the greatest swordsman of the land. This volume, too, testifies to the great advances the martial arts were making throughout Japan. And unprecedented progress—both artistic and technical—was made in the production of beautiful, handcrafted weapons as well.

Warrior Culture and Court Culture

Ieyasu's vassals were elevated to high position by the rise of their master. Like Ieyasu himself, many of these vassals stemmed from a class of wealthy provincial landowners and peasantry of the Mikawa area. Only a few—the Satsuma Shimazu, Hirado Matsura, and Buzen Ōtomo families in the south or the Satake and Nanbu in the north—had been warrior families since Kamakura days. Many of Hideyoshi's chief vassals had also been erstwhile peasants from Owari. When these former provincials found themselves propelled to the highest social stratum of the land, their cultural abilities hardly matched their new official status. Undaunted, these nominal aristocrats soon exploited all means at their disposal to ennoble themselves. Since attempts to strengthen one's military prowess was sure to evoke displeasure from the bakufu, many warriors instead built huge gardens or absorbed themselves in leisure pursuits. Within three or four generations, both the daimyo and the shogun were no longer country bumpkins: they had become a true upper-class nobility in both name and deed.

Vestiges of gardens as they existed at Edo daimyo residences can still be found in Tokyo today. Examples include the Kōrakuen of the Mito house, the Hama Rikyū of the Kōfu Tokugawa, and the Rikugien at the Komagome villa of the daimyo Yanagisawa Yoshiyasu. These parks, as well as maps of ponds and gardens at residences of the Togoshi Hosokawa, show that construction took place on a grand scale. Residents of such estates could enjoy leisurely strolls within the grounds or ride in pleasure boats on the large ponds. The style of these gardens was in fact a restoration of the ancient style of the grand imperial *shinden-zukuri* manner—a style entirely at odds with the waterless rock and sand *(kare sansui)* garden of the middle ages. At such villas the Edo warrior nobility sought to revive the cultural life of Heian-period courtiers, who valued natural beauty and lived in natural surroundings.

The upper warrior stratum reinstituted many other elements of court culture as well. Warriors might wear tall black lacquered hats *(eboshi)* or broad-sleeved upper garments and cloaks *(suō, suikan)*. The ceremonial court music *(gagaku)* ensemble of the "three directions"—Kyoto, Osaka, and Nara—was systematized and used for performing musical offerings at Shinto ceremonies. In addition to the ensemble at the Kyoto palace, *gagaku* musicians were also stationed at the Momijiyama Tōshōgū at Nishinomaru (within Edo castle) and at Ieyasu's mausoleum at Nikkō. Many warriors learned instruments of the *gagaku* ensemble: the *biwa* (a four-stringed lute), the *shō* (a mouth organ), the *hichiriki* (a double-reed wind instrument), and the *fue* (transverse flute). The shogun and daimyo danced the dances of the nō drama, thereby continuing a tradition that had existed since the Muromachi period. Warriors also engaged enthusiastically in traditional leisure pursuits such as calligraphy, painting, the tea ceremony, flower arranging, linked poetry, and *kemari* (kickball). These activities were all based on Kyoto traditions developed by the Ashikaga shogunal house and the imperial court. Because of the efforts of the warriors, Edo soon stood on the leading edge of developments of these traditional arts.

The upper warrior stratum, moreover, enjoyed courtly pleasures together with Kyoto courtiers. In 1626, for example, the retired shogun Hidetada (1579–1632) and the third shogun Iemitsu (1604–1651) traveled to Kyoto with an entourage of daimyo. On this trip, the Sendai daimyo Date Masamune (1567–1636) staged an incense appreciation party at a lodge along the way. This gathering took place on the twenty-fourth day of the seventh month; many courtiers and cultured men were invited: the Konoe Regent *(kanpaku)*, the Ichijō Minister of the Right *(ushōfu)*, the poet and courtier Karasumaru Mitsuhiro (1579–1638), the Premier *(saishō)* Nishinotōin Tokiyoshi (1552–1639), and the linked-verse *(renga)* poet Satomura Genchū (1578–1638).

On another occasion Kobori Enshū (1579–1647), an outstanding daimyo tea master of the time, headed a group that received the retired Emperor Gomizunoo (1596–1680). The emperor was treated to a tea ceremony in which a gold teakettle was used. Enshū, who served many daimyo, engaged in much cultural exchange with the imperial court. Examples of such cultural exchange can easily be multiplied. The famous Zen priest Takuan (1573–1645), who had close connections with the imperial court, was welcomed to Edo by the shogun. And the earlier-mentioned Kyoto courtier and poet Karasumaru Mitsuhiro was also invited to Edo to serve as the shogun's cultural adviser.

Cultural exchange with the court allowed the Edo warrior population to create many new cultural forms. Eventually the customs and lifestyles of the top warrior stratum came to represent Edo as a whole. With the passage of time, these habits spread throughout the land, defining the style of behavior appropriate for special occasions in general.

Warrior Culture and the *Chōnin*

Today's standard Japanese is said to be the language of middle-class Tokyoites from the uptown area, a region once the site of countless samurai residences. Those who dwelled there—the bannermen, the household retainers, and the families of the daimyo—had all grown up in Edo. They were well versed in the ways of the upper warrior class, often having been stationed in the castle itself. From their early youth these people had thoroughly mastered the styles of speech and behavior expected of them in official situations. Strict training in the appropriate modes of conduct was socially indispensable, for all intercourse took place in person.

Person-to-person contact also occurred at gatherings for leisure activities: at nō drama performances, at tea ceremonies, or at meetings devoted to incense discrimination, linked verse, or *haikai* composition. Manners, customs, and cultural practices were refined and polished over decades. As a result, a new upper-class language appeared as well. This language was neither the dialect of Osaka or Kyoto nor the dialect of any specific province. Nor was it the speech of Mikawa, the home province of the Tokugawa family. Instead, it was a kind of lingua franca spoken by the daimyo from throughout the land and by retainers of the shogun.

Chōnin daughters sought avidly to be placed in the service of upper-class warrior households, since this was a prerequisite of a good marriage. These girls must all have been true Edo-born natives, for the Edo branches of provincial merchant houses were staffed exclusively by men. By frequenting the houses of the upper stratum of warriors, the *chōnin* and their daughters gradually learned the upper-class language. By the eighteenth century the city's middle classes—the so-called *Edokko chōnin*—had begun to speak a unique Edo Japanese. This language was entirely different from the provincial dialects used by employees of Edo branches of provincial businesses. Nor was it identical to the language of country samurai, whose stay in Edo was limited to a year by the alternate attendance system. Rather, it was a style of speech created by the city's upper-class warriors. From such origins this language spread throughout the land. Eventually it would become the standard language of modern Japan.

The warriors' presence had yet other effects on the *chōnin*. Until the early eighteenth century, the construction of Edo castle, fire prevention policies, and the previously mentioned relocations of warrior residences required constant relocation of *chōnin* homes. The experience of one house is recorded in the *Machikata kakiage* (Records of Town Officials).[9] Here one finds the story of Matatarō, one of a line of ward representatives *(nanushi)* from Yotsuya Nakachō (Samegahashi). Since the early days of the city, Matatarō had made his home in the vicinity of Momijiyama Fukiage. With the construction of Edo castle, however, his house was sequestered, forc-

Street scene at Naitō-Shinjuku (Yotsuya). From *Edo meisho zue.*

ing him to move to Hanzōmon-soto. Soon thereafter, this area
became official property for the construction of a castle moat. Thus
he moved again, this time to the area around the Hirakawa-chō and
the fifth block of Kōjimachi. But this area too soon became official
property; and he fared no better at Yotsuya-gomon-soto, which also
became the site of moat construction projects. Next Matatarō moved
to Yotsuya Nakadono-machi, but here his property was soon needed
for the site of Toda Oribe's residence. Thus he moved to the south-
east of Samegahashi, but during the Meireki period (1655–1658)
this land was required for the construction of the residence of the
lord of Kii. This time Matatarō shifted his home to Hakkenchō. But
this area was swampy and so unsalutary that he preferred once again
to move back to the north of Samegahashi. Then, in 1664, this property was granted to officials known as *Igamono;* and thus Matatarō
moved to a corner house at the entrance to Kitamachi. Only in 1685
was he finally able to settle down at Yotsuya Nakachō. Hence, within
about one century, this headman family was relocated some eight
times. Matatarō's case may have been extreme, but property confiscations and forced relocations were the order of the day.

Fires were another source of flux. Unlike the warriors, who lived
in spacious mansions, merchants and craftsmen operated their businesses from cramped quarters in the downtown area or along major
roads, or from shops squeezed between warrior residences and temple compounds. Fires, many the result of arson, thus easily spread to
nearby buildings. The son of Edo could count with certainty on losing his property and merchandise to frequent conflagrations.

Edo: City of Men and Conflict

Many characteristics of the city of Edo were the result of demographic factors. Building the metropolis had required a tremendous
number of individuals with traditional skills and knowledge: house
builders, plasterers, *tatami* makers, carpenters, tailors, armorers, sur-
veyors, draftsmen, scholars, and legislators. Anyone with an outstanding ability sought his fortune in Edo. Competition was fierce,
and fighting instincts surged to the fore.

The majority of the Edo population was male. Male apprentices
and clerks staffed the Edo branches of provincial stores. Most of
these men returned to their home area after finishing their stint in
Edo. Male laborers were required by daimyo for constructing Edo
branches of local shrines and family temples. Samurai stationed in
Edo were of course also exclusively male. In addition, Edo boasted a

huge population of priests. Some of these saw to the operation of the Kan'eiji, a temple constructed by the bakufu. Priests were found at major temples throughout the city, as well, or at the graveyard of the Zōjōji in Shiba.[10] Temporary laborers streaming in from the countryside to help out in construction projects—whether planned or necessitated by yet another fire—were all male as well. According to a census taken by the city magistrate's office during the Kyōhō era (1716–1736) the *chōnin* population stood at approximately half a million, with men outnumbering women two to one.

Close relations existed among members of the warrior class, between warriors and *chōnin,* and between merchants and artisans. For example, the Iami family of straw *tatami* makers had served many shoguns since the days of Ieyasu. Hence this family became the most powerful *tatami* manufacturer of Edo. Other large official merchant houses included the house of Gotō Shōzaburō, with its connection to the gold mint, the house of Gotō Nuidonosuke, with its control of dry goods, and the house of Daikoku Jōze, which was associated with the silver mint. The needs of each domain were met by yet other official merchants, who used the authority of the bakufu or their lord to gain an advantage over competitors. The world of merchants and artisans was rife with conflict; eventually, this disharmony spilled out onto the city's streets. During its early years Edo retained much of the atmosphere of the period of civil wars. Incessant conflict left little room for human warmth and kindness.

Masterless samurai *(rōnin)* and the self-styled "street knights" known as *kyōkaku* contributed greatly to conflicts in the city. With the end of civil wars and with the peasantry under tight administrative control, *rōnin* could no longer ramble freely about the villages. They too began to search for new forms of employment. A few members of this vast population went abroad; but many more slipped into Edo to become merchants, craftsmen, flute-playing monks *(komusō),* or *kyōkaku.*

A famous example of a street knight was the *hatamoto yakko* Mizuno Jūrōzaemon (d. 1664), who was in fact a retainer of the bakufu. His rival was the *machi yakko* Banzuiin Chōbee (1622–1657). The feud between Mizuno and Banzuiin showed that disputes between warriors and *chōnin,* or among the *chōnin* themselves, were often settled by the use of force. Social justice in Edo usually meant violence; minor squabbles often ended in a bloodbath. Edo's social structure and demography virtually guaranteed that violent disputes would arise constantly.

Rivalry extended even to the pleasure quarters of Yoshiwara. This was a world apart, a district in which men could for once free themselves of distinctions of social rank. But here too fights broke out among "chivalrous" rowdies known as *otokodate*. Rivalries in love might result in *saya-ate*—"scabbard brushing," a term that denotes both sword fights and contentions in love. *Saya-ate* even became the title of popular kabuki plays, versions of which are still performed today.[11]

Swaggering through the streets of Edo were members of the "six gangs of Edo" and the so-called *kabukimono* with their distinctive speech and outrageous dress. Such street knights with their distinctive machismo may perhaps have been "men about town," but many of them were little more than gangsters and hoodlums—the dregs of Edo society. With its jumble of a million assorted inhabitants, Edo provided a convenient home to such forms of scum.

On the whole, Edo was a metropolis tinged with something of a soldierly, bleak atmosphere. Nevertheless, one also finds a naive ebullience—a human quality that served as a basis for genres such as the recitation style known as *Kinpira jōruri* or the "rough style" or "bravura" acting style *(aragoto)* of Ichikawa Danjūrō. Yoshiwara, the center of Edo social life, also contributed greatly to the city's vigor.

The "big spender" Kibun finds pleasure in tossing gold coins around the room. From *Kinsei kiseki-kō*, 1804. (In the possession of the Tokyo Metropolitan Central Library.)

Here merchants could meet wealthy customers such as bannermen, household retainers, or daimyo and their vassals. Here too the "big spenders" *(daijin)*, personified by business magnates such as Kibun (Kinokuniya Bunzaemon, d. 1734?) and Naramo (Naraya Mozaemon, d. 1714), found their special place.

Let us turn next to these and other commoner inhabitants of Edo. For as we shall see, the prototypical townspeople, known as *Edokko,* gave the culture of the city many of its most unique characteristics. We must seek to understand not only what these characteristics were, but what kind of social context made their emergence possible.

EDOKKO: THE TOWNSPERSON

Characteristics of the *Edokko*

As we have seen in Chapter 1, the center of Edo was the shogun's castle. At least until the Genroku period (1688–1704) the city was primarily the capital of the warrior. It was a teeming metropolis, a million strong, with men outnumbering women by more than two to one. Edo bustled with warriors, craftsmen, merchants, and performers from throughout the land. The upper class amused itself at the kabuki or in the Yoshiwara pleasure quarters; the activities of the big spenders captured the public imagination.

The shogun, daimyo, and their retainers spent almost all their money in the city; Edo was a center of consumption. Originally, very little was produced there, neither daily necessities nor high-grade cultural artifacts. Instead, articles were imported from Kamigata, that is, from the Kyoto and Osaka area. Such goods were called *kudarimono*—quality products that had "come down" from Kamigata. Wares that had not "come down" were considered inferior: thus the origin of the word *kudaran* ("not come down"), meaning uninteresting or worthless. The sale of imported goods netted great profits for Edo branches of stores headquartered in Ise, Ōmi, or other provinces. From around the Genroku period these businesses, known as *Edo-dana* and located at Nihonbashi, Denmachō, and elsewhere, expanded greatly. This expansion signaled the rise of the Edo *chōnin*'s economic power.

As mentioned earlier, *Edo-dana* were staffed exclusively by men who had come to Edo only to work. These men even saw to their own cooking, cleaning, and laundry. Unable to sink their roots in the city, *Edo-dana* employees remained perennial outsiders. During the latter half of the eighteenth century, however, a new type of individual appeared: the *Edokko,* a pure Edo *chōnin*, who was rooted in the city itself. The first recorded usage of the term *Edokko* occurs in a *senryū* of 1771,[1] and thereafter the word was used by many authors. Around 1788 Santō Kyōden (1761–1816) perfectly defined the character of the *Edokko* in a *sharebon* ("smart book," witty novelettes mainly about the licensed quarters) entitled *Tsūgen sō-magaki* (Grand Brothel of Connoisseur Language) and a *kibyōshi* ("yellow-covered book," illustrated satirical fiction) entitled *Nitan no Shirō Fuji no hitoana kenbutsu* (Nitan no Shirō Views the Cave of Mount Fuji). According to Kyōden,[2] the *Edokko chōnin* is typified by the following five qualities:

1. He receives his first bath in the water of the city's aqueduct; he grows up in sight of the gargoyles on the roof of Edo castle.
2. He is not attached to money; he is not stingy. His funds do not cover the night's lodging.
3. He is raised in a high-class, protected manner. He is quite unlike either warriors or country bumpkins.
4. He is a man of Nihonbashi (the downtown area) to the bone.
5. He has *iki* (refinement) and *hari* (strength of character).

In my reading of contemporary books I have found forty-six examples of the term *Edokko,* all illustrative of the pride *Edokko* took in their identity. The main points of pride can be summarized by the five noted here by Kyōden.

Kyōden's five characteristics have, however, been subjected to much ridicule: it was Nagoya castle, not Edo castle, that was decorated with gargoyles; the aqueducts had only dirty water; the supposed "high-class" upbringing of the *Edokko* was nothing but an imaginary inversion of a childhood spent in poverty. Some have said that the *Edokko*'s vanity was merely a product of his feelings of inferiority toward the wealthy Kansai-based *Edo-dana* merchants; that the *Edokko* was merely a low-class, poor, uncultured *chōnin* with neither strength nor guts.

Documents of this age, however, demonstrate otherwise. *Edokko* had lived in this city from its early years and considered it home. With the passing of the Genroku and Kyōhō periods, and with the shogunal house going into its eighth and ninth generations, the true sons of Edo from Kanda, Kyōbashi, Ginza, Shiba, and the rest of the *shitamachi* (downtown) area were in fact accumulating great wealth. It was these pure-bred Edo *chōnin* who were the true *Edokko.* These men operated riverside fish markets, worked as *fudasashi* (rice brokers and financial agents) at the bakufu's Asakusa rice granary, dealt in lumber at Kiba, or acted as receiving agents for *kudarimono* at Shinkawa or Reigan-jima.

The *Edokko* was branded as "mediocre" and "low-class" only because he was mistaken for a mediocre type of individual who appropriated this label for himself after the Kasei period (1804–1830). Later yet, around the turn of the century, rural inhabitants thronged to what is now the Bunkyō ward of Tokyo. A modern version of the "insider" and "outsider" arose; within this context a modern, inferior type of *Edokko* was able to attract attention. Such people were doubtlessly also a type of *Edokko,* but they should hardly be confused with the real *Edokko* of an earlier era. For the real *Edokko* had strength of character, economic power, and a highly developed culture. In fact, *Edokko* covertly wielded much authority in Edo society.

One finds no label corresponding to the *Edokko* in Osaka and Kyoto. No concept of an "Osakakko" or a "Kyotokko" exists; nor is there any parallel in Nagoya, Kanazawa, or Hiroshima. Thus we must ask why the idea of such a native arose solely in Edo. The answer to this question is simple. In Osaka, Kyoto, and other cities, almost the entire *chōnin* population corresponded to what the *Edokko* was in Edo. In the capital, however, a huge number of unassimilated provincials remained "outsiders," providing a contrast to the distinctly native *Edokko.* During the city's early years, this heterogeneous population grew larger and developed evenly; but by the second half of the eighteenth century a marked contrast between natives and nonnatives begins to appear. This contrast was not entirely missing in other large cities such as Osaka or Kyoto, but in Edo a much larger part of the population remained nonnative.

Within Edo there existed yet another distinction: the sharp contrast between the uptown *(yamanote)* and the downtown *(shitamachi)* areas. These terms can already be found in the *hanashibon* (storybook) known as *Eda sangoju* (Beads of Coral) published in 1690.[3] The *yamanote* area was a diluvial terrace packed with warrior residences; the *shitamachi* area was an alluvial area with a concentration of *chōnin* dwellings. Since the *chōnin* class was further split between *Edokko* and a large population of *Edo-dana* "outsiders," *Edokko* were constantly confronted with a large number of people unlike themselves. The unmistakable character of the *Edokko* developed within this social context.

The *Edokko*'s sense of nativeness that emerged during the second half of the eighteenth century fostered the efflorescence of *Edokko* culture. This unique culture was, however, not created by *Edokko* alone. Instead, it resulted from the interaction of three groups, each of which complemented the others: the warriors, the provincial *chōnin* "outsiders," and the *Edokko.*

Edokko culture was rooted in the Edo language. But it went far beyond this language. It included, as we shall see in Chapter 3, the aesthetic of *iki* (refinement) and *tsū* (savoir faire) as elaborated in the Yoshiwara pleasure quarters. This aesthetic was also displayed on the kabuki stage. Another example of *Edokko* culture was the *ukiyo-e* woodcut—also known as *Edo-e* (Edo pictures) or *azuma nishiki-e* (eastern brocade pictures). Such prints were produced in tremendous quantities and circulated throughout the land. *Edokko* literature blossomed with the production of *kibyōshi, sharebon,* and *yomihon* ("reading books," usually historical novels). Illustrated books known as *akahon* ("red books") were a significant innovation in children's literature. *Edokko* issued many collections of comic poetry in both Japanese and Chinese. In addition, a tremendous number of *chōnin* participated in the great *senryū* craze, and many more learned various narrative or musical genres. Let us examine some of these phenomena in more detail.

Edokko Culture and the Japanese Language

As mentioned earlier, *Edokko* culture had at its base the Edo language, which became not just one city's dialect but the core of today's standard Japanese. Early examples of Edo *chōnin* speech appear in Jōkanbō Kōa's *Imayō heta dangi* (Clumsy Modern Sermons), published in 1752. This work, highly regarded in its day, offers penetrating commentary on numerous fads and social issues. Another remarkable work in the Edo language is the drama *Shinrei yaguchi no watashi* (Spirits at the Yaguchi Ferry), written for the Edo Geki-za puppet theater in 1770 by Hiraga Gennai (1729–1779). Both Jōkanbō and Hiraga were "outsiders" originating from other parts of Japan. Yet they observed Edo impartially, shaping what they saw into literary or dramatic works. That this was possible shows that the *Edokko*'s social life, cultural forms, and creative activities had undergone tremendous development since the city's early days.

Families of daimyo, forced to lead lives of hostages within the city, played a particularly important role in the formation of the language used both by warriors and the townspeople. The language of the aristocratic warrior class was fully formed by the Genroku period. By the end of the eighteenth century this language had spread throughout *Edokko* society.

According to Ogawa Kendō's *Chirizuka dan* (A Mound of Dusty Tales, published in 1814), from the 1760s to the 1780s the everyday language of the *shitamachi* merchants was changing dramatically. *Chōnin* began to address their wives with the respectful term *goshinzō-sama* rather than the hitherto usual *okamisama;* even the children of day laborers added the honorific prefix *"o"* to the terms used in addressing their parents and elder siblings. The wealthy rice brokers and financial agents of the Asakusa area, imitating the stiff formalities of the warrior houses, were also calling their wives *goshinzō-sama* and their daughters *ojō-sama.* Ogawa interprets this usage as the baneful influence of the merchant, who needed to show deference to even the lowliest customer.[4]

Here one witnesses the emergence of, not just another dialect, but a language that would eventually become the common tongue of the entire land. *Chōnin* women played an especially large role in disseminating this language. For after the 1750s it was highly fashionable to send one's daughters into the service of an influential warrior family as a precondition for a good marriage. In such surroundings, young women were initiated into upper-class etiquette and culture. *Chōnin* daughters with such experience often became the wives of influential Edo merchants and assumed important positions in social life. Such an education was limited to the wives and daughters of the *Edokko,* for the provincially based *Edo-dana* merchants usually did not bring women with them to the city.

Edokko Culture and the Spirit of Cooperation

Cultural production was often a collaborative effort—and the heterogeneity of the Edo population allowed disparate social groups to complement each other. Edo-period comic poetry, both in Japanese and Chinese, is a good example of collaborative efforts taking place within a cultural community of bakufu retainers, samurai from various domains, and Edo *chōnin.*

Associations for writing the thirty-one-syllable comic poems known as *kyōka* figured largely in contemporary society. Such groups, known as *kumi* or *ren,* appeared during the Meiwa period (1764–1772) when Karakoromo Kitsushū (1743–1802) established the Yotsuya-ren. Meetings of this group were attended by Yomo no Akara (Ōta Nanpo, 1749–1823), Tobuchiri no Batei, Hezutsu Tōsaku (Tatematsu Tomo, 1726–1789), Ōya no Urazumi, Ōne no Futoki, and others. During the An'ei period (1772–1781), when the *kyōka* movement was in full swing, many more *kyōka* groups appeared in rapid succession. Some of these groups are listed here along with the individuals around whom they gathered:

The *kyōka* poets Akera Kankō, Yomono Akara, Yadoya no Meshimori, and Shikatsube Magao. From *Azumaburi kyōka bunko* (A Collection of Eastern-Style *Kyōka*). Drawings by Santō Kyōden, published in 1786. (In the possession of the Tokyo Metropolitan Central Library.)

Akera-ren   (Akera Kankō)
Asakusa-ren
Bakuro-ren   (Yadoya no Meshimori [Ishikawa Masamochi], 1753–1830)
Funamachi-ren
Gohyakuzaki-ren
Hiyoshi-ren
Honchō-ren   (Ōya no Urazumi and Harakara no Akindo [Nakai Tōdō], 1758–1821)
Misuji-ren
Mokuzai-ren
Ochikuri-ren   (Moto no Mokuami)
Shakuyaku-ren
Shiba-ren   (Hamabe no Kurohito)
Shinba-ren
Sukiya-ren   (Shikatsube no Magao)
Yamanote-ren   (Yomo no Akara)
Yoshiwara-ren   (Kabocha no Motonari)

Kyōka parties were also highly fashionable. One of the most lavish parties was a moon-viewing *kyōka*-fest, lasting five days and five nights, held by Moto no Mokuami in 1779. Another example of a *kyōka* group was the association surrounding Ichikawa Danjūrō V (1741–1806), the top star of the Edo kabuki. This group extended its influence to lovers of *kyōka* throughout the country. Danjūrō, the model *Edokko* and pride of the city, thereby found himself supported by cultured individuals throughout the land.

Groups devoted to other forms of light verse also flourished during this age. In particular, the genre of seventeen-syllable comic verse known as *senryū* constituted one of this era's most noteworthy creations. These highly refined verses depicted all the faults and foibles of humanity with extreme sensitivity and piercing wit. One finds no languorous depictions of mountains, no nostalgic impressions of the sea or pastoral villages. Instead, *senryū* thrive on portrayals of human differences and contrasts, on sharp thrusts at political corruption, and on flashes of insight.

The originator of this genre of comic verse was Karai Senryū (1718–1790), who came to Edo in 1757. Karai functioned as a ward representative *(nanushi)* in Asakusa. Not long after arriving in the city he became a teacher and judge *(tenja)* of comic verse. Disciples presented their work to him for assessment and correction; he then published anthologies of his students' best efforts. Every ten days, during summer and fall, Karai collected verses for evaluation. From these "collections of ten thousand verses" Karai selected the best and awarded prizes to their authors.

The *senryū* fad peaked during the 1770s and 1780s, when participants formed groups throughout the city. *Senryū* associations included the Sakuragi-ren at Nakachō in Yamashita (Ueno), the Hōrai-ren at Onandomachi in Ushigome, the Takasago-ren and Ume-ren at Kōjimachi, the Ryūsui-ren at Azabu, and the Chikudo-ren at Ushigome. Karai Senryū was by no means the only *senryū* teacher in Edo at the time; some twenty other renowned masters were active as well, judging and improving the verses offered by disciples.[5] Most *senryū* poets were from the Edo *chōnin* class; but some were warriors from the *yamanote* (uptown) area.

Edo cultural groups often spread their influence over a broad geographical area. A typical example is found in Chiba Ryūboku's Genji school of flower arranging *(ikebana).* Since the mid-eighteenth century, this school had found many adherents in the Asakusa area. In 1784 the Genji school staged an elaborate exhibition of several hundred flower arrangements at the Baion'in, a temple in Asakusa. To commemorate this event a stone monument was erected at the Akiba Shrine, near Ryōgoku, listing the names of all the students who had taken part in the exhibition. This list was reproduced in the *Genji sōka himei sho* (Record of the Names on the Monument of Genji School Flower Arrangers), a publication printed with woodblocks. Here one finds a record of 1,147 students from various Kantō provinces (listed by time of entry into the Genji school), as well as 154 members from more distant areas, for a grand total of 1,301 individuals. The Genji school, of course, had no monopoly on the teaching of flower arranging. Schools such as the Ikenobō and the Senke-ryū had existed for generations; newcomers such as the Senke-shinryū, Koryū, Enshū-ryū, Yōken-ryū, Enchūrō-ryū, Doku-ryū, Shōfū-ryū, Shōgetsudō-koryū, Mishō-ryū, and Hachidai-ryū also earned widespread support.

Such examples show that by the eighteenth century Edo cultured society had expanded tremendously and was attracting a broad range of followers, especially members of the *chōnin* class. An almost infinite variety of arts was pursued by contemporary cultural groups. A 1775 publication presents an inventory of no fewer than seventy-four types of leisure activity: acting, martial arts, *shakuhachi* (an end-blown bamboo flute), *shōgi* (Japanese chess), *kowairo* (mimicry of kabuki actors' lines), various styles of vocal music, appraising *(mekiki),* fortune telling, genres of street music and performance, and much else.[6]

Edokko Culture and the Spirit of Resistance

> The people of Edo wish to be rude; showing respect seems to them a
> shame. The worst offenders are those of the lowest rank. Some Edo
> people even make malicious remarks that one mustn't be afraid of
> samurai and lice. Such people lack all discretion.[7]

Thus lamented Jōkanbō Kōa in his *Kyōkun zoku heta dangi* (Didactic
Clumsy Sermons, Continued) of 1753. Here "Edo people" *(Edo-shū)*
could only have meant the Edo *chōnin.* Jōkanbō's observation that
the *chōnin* lacked respect and were generally rude implies that they
displayed a spirit of resistance, a desire to strike back at their
oppressors.

This spirit of resistance began to emerge during the middle of
the eighteenth century. Its appearance can to some degree be attrib-
uted to the peculiar nature of the city of Edo. Most early modern
Japanese cities were castle towns centered on a feudal lord. Strong
master/servant bonds and feelings of solidarity marked the relation
between the lord and the commoners. In Edo, however, little solidarity existed within the highly heterogeneous population. *Edokko* felt
themselves opposed by the warriors, the provincials, or even the
whole of the Kamigata area. Such a social structure greatly fostered
the desire to resist.

The spirit of resistance is incarnated in the *aragoto* acting style of
the kabuki. This "muscular" style appeared during the Genroku
period in the bravura acting of the first Ichikawa Danjūrō (1660–
1704). *Aragoto* style can be seen in the play *Shibaraku* ("Wait a
Moment!" first performed in 1697) and in plays depicting the deeds
of the Soga brothers. Both *Shibaraku* and the Soga plays were tales of
revenge that were produced annually until the very end of the Edo
period. New Soga plays were performed at the start of each year by
all three major Edo theaters. That such long runs were possible demonstrates that the deeply held antiauthoritarian sentiments of the
commoners here found their ideal expression.

Yet another *aragoto* play perfected at an early time was *Sukeroku.*[8]
This play also gave a subtle rendition of the *Edokko*'s temperament.
The character of Sukeroku, created by the Ichikawa family, was none
other than the younger of the two Soga brothers, costumed as a
swashbuckling dandy. In scenes in which Sukeroku argues with his
rival, the wealthy samurai Ikyū, or in which Sukeroku's courtesan
lover Agemaki heaps scathing abuse on Ikyū, the *Edokko*'s spirit of
resistance is transformed into the very essence of kabuki. In fact, the

play *Sukeroku* may have put on stage the style of the prototypical *Edokko*—the *fudasashi* rice brokers and financial agents of the Asakusa Kuramae area. Some scholars, however, hold the opposite to be true, claiming that Ichikawa Danjūrō's portrayal of Sukeroku itself influenced the *fudasashi*'s bold style. In any case, *Sukeroku* appealed greatly to *Edokko* associated with the pleasure quarters of Yoshiwara and the Nihonbashi fish market.

That *Sukeroku* and other plays could become vehicles for expressing defiance rested on the existence of strong cultural groups that had absolute control over "house arts" or family traditions *(iegei)*. In Edo, almost all artistic traditions surrounding the kabuki were passed down for generations. Even Edo theater managers—Nakamura Kanzaburō of the Nakamura-za, Ichimura Uzaemon of the Ichimura-za, and Morita Kan'ya of the Morita-za—all passed on their names to their descendants. Hereditary actor names included Ichikawa Danjūrō, Ichikawa Danzō, and Iwai Hanshirō. *Nagauta* musicians included the hereditary name Kineya Rokuzaemon; kabuki instrumental music, Tanaka Denzaemon; dance, the names Shigayama, Nishikawa, and Fujima; stage settings, Hasegawa Kanpei. Even signboard art was hereditary and monopolized by the Torii family.

Most of these traditions were established at the time of the

The Nihonbashi fish market. From *Edo meisho zue.*

Edokko's first appearance. Edo practices differed markedly from those of the Kamigata area. In Kyoto and Osaka the families of theater managers and actors showed little continuity, for people were hired on a one-year contractual basis. In Edo, however, the strength of tradition allowed a spirit of independence and ultimately of resistance to emerge from the kabuki theater.

An attitude of defiance appeared in Edo literature as well. Baba Bunkō (1718?–1758), for example, who was active during the 1750s, was savagely critical of contemporary political authority. The authorities rewarded his efforts by sentencing him to death by crucifixion. Later, in the 1780s, Santō Kyōden also contributed to the spirit of resistance. In the previously mentioned book *Nitan no Shirō Fuji no hitoana kenbutsu,* Kyōden satirized the social and political reforms of the bakufu elder Matsudaira Sadanobu (1758–1829). During the same year Kyōden wrote a volume entitled *Jidai sewa nichō tsuzumi* (Two Drums: Contemporary and Ancient Events) in which he modeled his plot on the murder of Tanuma Okitomo (1749–1784), another bakufu official. Again in 1789 Kyōden cleverly mocked Matsudaira Sadanobu's policies in a *kibyōshi* entitled *Kōshi-jima toki ni aizome* (Blue Stripes in Tune with the Times). During the same year another writer, Koikawa Harumachi (1744–1789), also criticized Matsudaira's reforms in a *kibyōshi* entitled *Ōmugaeshi bunbu no futamichi* (Parroting the Ways of the Pen and the Sword). Then, when Santō Kyōden drew the illustrations for Ishibe Kinkō's *kibyōshi* entitled *Kokubyaku mizu-kagami* (Black and White Reflected in Water), the authorities struck back and sentenced Kyōden to a heavy fine. Undaunted, Kyōden published three more satirical books three years later; this time he found himself manacled for fifty days. Increasingly severe censorship in the following years put a temporary damper on the *Edokko*'s critical spirit; but by the 1830s stinging political satire had again found its way into the drawings of Utagawa Kuniyoshi (1797–1861). Even when defiance did not appear in print, wild rumors and slander were rampant in the streets. This was as true of Edo in the 1780s as it was true of the city in the 1840s and 1850s.

Paralleling such strong feelings of defiance were new, more passive trends arising within various Edo cultural communities. Practitioners of countless contemporary artistic endeavors assumed "artist's names" *(geimei)* that allowed them to transform themselves into cultured members of an artistic world with no distinctions of feudal rank or wealth. Such freedom made it possible for initiates to devote themselves fully to the pleasures of calligraphy, writing, or other leisure pursuits.

Many other notable achievements of *Edokko* culture remain to be explored: phenomena such as fashion and culinary trends; the opening of new sights and scenic spots; a "culture of activity" in general, including pilgrimages to various temples and shrines; and, finally, developments in popular performing arts. These topics and others are the subjects of the chapters to follow.

CHAPTER 3

IKI: THE AESTHETIC OF EDO

Iki seems to be a specifically Japanese form of aesthetic consciousness. Pinpointing where or how a person embodies the quality of *iki* may be difficult, but its presence is felt by every Japanese. The aesthetic of *iki* is, in this sense, the common property of the Japanese people.

An adequate definition of *iki,* however, remains elusive. *Iki* may be quite easily grasped experientially, but verbalizing this experience is difficult. Parallels may be found in the performing arts: here too direct (and often secret) transmission, not verbal explanation, provides the surest means for attaining true mastery of details in speech or movement. Since verbal description cannot fully convey a culture of feeling, no generally accepted theory of *iki* has yet been established. Although I too shall write of *iki,* the reader must bear in mind that a truly satisfactory explanation remains elusive.

First I want to present a critical summary of two outstanding studies of *iki:* the treatises of Kuki Shūzō and Asō Isoji. Then I shall consider the relation of *iki* and *tsū,* two concepts that are often discussed together. Finally, I shall try to determine why the aesthetic of *iki* is a specifically Japanese form of aesthetic consciousness.

Theories of *Iki*

For the reasons just mentioned, writings on *iki* invariably lack clarity. No study has yet succeeded in elucidating *iki* in a way that endows the reader with a sure grasp of the subject. Nevertheless, Kuki Shūzō's " 'Iki' no kōzō"[1] (The Structure of *Iki*) and Asō Isoji's "Iki/tsū" are two outstanding studies that have earned a high reputation and are written in an authoritative manner. Kuki's work is particularly detailed and filled with numerous examples. It presents the concept of *iki* in a well-organized, logical, and systematic fashion.

Even so, although Kuki offers many insightful observations, the realm of sensibility that comprises *iki* remains difficult to grasp.

Kuki and Asō's conclusions can be summarized as follows. From around the Genroku era (1688–1704) the word *iki* gradually came into common use. The term was written with a variety of Sino-Japanese ideographs that cover a wide range of meaning and have complex implications. By the middle of the Edo period, however, the aesthetic consciousness crystallized in the word *iki* had come to center on three elements: a strength of character called *hari;* the allure referred to as *bitai;* and the urbanity known as *akanuke.*

Hari was a sharp, straightforward, coolly gallant manner that resisted all compromise, conciliation, and undue social adroitness or tact. In Edo, the capital of the warrior, cold and brusque human relations confronted one at every turn; quarrels and sword fights were the order of the day. But in the egalitarian world of the Yoshiwara pleasure quarters, samurai were required to lay down their swords; *hari* then became the ideal of behavior. *Hari* was also esteemed as the very essence of Yoshiwara courtesans, who behaved in such a manner until quite recently.

Bitai implied a kind of eroticism; but more important was the maintenance of a sense of charm. Any feigned high-class demeanor or uprightness was strictly taboo. Flirtatious allure and a light coquettishness were allowed so long as they remained untainted by any vulgar or wanton feeling.

The quality of *akanuke* demanded an unpretentious air, a thorough familiarity with all aspects of life, and an unconcerned, unassuming character. Cosmetics, when used at all, remained light. The ideal beauty was not overwrought; it still appeared pleasant when no longer in perfect shape. Designs with stripes were favored over elaborate floral patterns; colors tended toward smoky light-browns.

This summary does not exhaust all the qualities of *iki* as analyzed in various scholarly works, but its main aspects are more or less covered. These qualities are gleaned mainly from Kasei-period (1804–1830) novelettes *(sharebon)* about the pleasure quarters and *ukiyo-e* woodblock prints. Indeed, *iki* as described here strongly reflects the aesthetic consciousness of the courtesans and geisha of Edo.

Hari, bitai, and *akanuke* were in fact developed chiefly in Edo, in an environment quite at odds with productive labor. *Iki* developed in a social context in which one found no faces blackened by the sun, no tough palms or stout, strong-jointed fingers, no conversations shouted in broad dialect. The rough behavior that might accompany tilling, logging, fishing, or salt making was entirely out of place. Indeed, any activity taking place in fields, forests, or waters—activities in which efforts were directed at the nonhuman—were incompatible with *iki*. *Iki* emerged entirely from the subtle tensions in human relationships. Tensions between people were not entirely lacking at sites of material production, of course, but here *iki* did not appear.

Instead, *iki* was an aesthetic of the metropolis, where men and women entered into relations subtly tensed with *hari*, *bitai*, and *akanuke*. The young wife of an urban merchant could embody the ideal of *iki* only with great difficulty. Her allure *(bitai)*, an essential ingredient of *iki*, was to be directed at only one man; the feeling of *iki* was thereby destroyed. Young married women, therefore, rarely embodied a sense of *iki*. Indeed, any situation lacking a balanced tension in male/female relations was devoid of *iki*.

An outstanding example of a fictional character with the quality of *iki* is the geisha Yonehachi in Tamenaga Shunsui's novel *Shunshoku umegoyomi* (Spring Love: A Plum Blossom Almanac, 1833–1834). Yet another illustration can be found in the kabuki play *Osome Hisamatsu* (The Scandal of Osome and Hisamatsu).[2] Let us examine this play for a moment. Osome is pregnant with Hisamatsu's child, but Hisamatsu has been forced to return to his native Nozaki. In this village Hisamatsu's bride to be, Omitsu, has long been awaiting her betrothed's return. Though overjoyed by the reunion, Omitsu senses the presence of Osome and Hisamatsu's strong bond. She guesses that if Osome cannot marry Hisamatsu, a suicide will surely result. Consequently, Omitsu abandons her dream of marrying Hisamatsu: she cuts her black tresses and becomes a nun. This figure of the nun symbolizes Omitsu's deeply moving, intense passion for her lover. Earlier in the play, Omitsu is outfitted in a fresh, sprightly, floral-patterned kimono befitting a young country girl. Now, however, she dons a beautiful light blue costume, a color similar to that worn by Hayano Kanpei when he prepares for his suicide in the sixth act of the play *Chūshingura*. Omitsu, though forced to renounce her pure love, thus radiates a burning, powerful passion, a love that is of an entirely different order than that of the pregnant Osome.

The cathartic beauty of the drama that arises at the crucial point—where tension in the relations between men and women comes to a head—seems to be entirely unrelated to the feeling of *iki*. Yet the stylizations of the kabuki endow both Omitsu and Kanpei with undeniably *iki* qualities. Moreover, a powerful effect of *hari* can be sensed when Osome and Hisamatsu bring their young lives to an early end, while Omitsu lives on. Osome, however, is already with child, and her ponderous, cloying affection is anything but *iki*. Perhaps the only element detracting from the sense of *iki* in Omitsu is the lack of coquettish *bitai.* Some may therefore object to describing Omitsu (or Kanpei of *Chūshingura*) as *iki.* In any case, this drama provides a good example of the subtle tensions suffusing male/female relations.

In his work " 'Iki' no kōzō," Kuki Shūzō explains *bitai* as follows:

> *Bitai,* in its most perfect form, must absolutize as potentiality the dual, dynamic possibilities between the sexes. True *bitai* is known only by vagabonds who perpetuate an "endless finitude," evildoers who enjoy a "bad infinity," or an Achilles who never stumbles in his eternal pursuit. This kind of *bitai* regulates the erotic charm *(iropposa)* that provides the foundation of *iki.*[3]

Bitai arises when a man and a woman strive to achieve the imaginary goal of subjugating each other; but the essence of *bitai* requires that this purpose remain unachieved. When marriage realizes and terminates such potentiality, *bitai* vanishes. Thus at the very moment that Omitsu, who has remained in the realm of pure potentiality, becomes a nun, she absolutizes this potentiality and exudes *bitai.* Osome, however, has relinquished her possibility long before; in contrast to Omitsu's *iki* beauty, her pregnancy expresses only boredom, slovenliness, and despair.

The aesthetic consciousness of *iki* was perfected within the world of the potential. A young wife might be beautiful in a charming, graceful manner, but, though highly attractive, she lacked *iki.* An example of such a woman can be seen in a famous picture by Uemura Shōen (1875–1949). This work, now in the possession of the Tokyo National Museum of Modern Art, portrays a beautiful young wife holding a child. With her eyebrows shaved and her blackened teeth barely visible, this young woman radiates the essence of happiness. A mysterious sensuousness emanates from the faint traces of her shaved eyebrows, a mere hint of color. This color too has much in common with the *akanuke* color of the costumes of Omitsu or Kanpei cited earlier. But the attractiveness here is that of a woman whose life has already been brought to fulfillment; consequently, her sensuality contains no *iki.* Attractiveness or erotic charm can become *iki* only if remaining within the realm of the potential. *Iki* requires a type of *bitai* that remains in the realm of possibility, a realm in which relations between men and women maintain a subtle vibrating tension, appearing and vanishing, at once weak and impassioned, both intimate and distant.

If *iki* is clearly a type of aesthetic consciousness, the claim that *akanuke* is such a form is somewhat more problematic. Following the

Uemura Shōen, "Mother and Child." (In the possession of the Tokyo National Museum of Modern Art.)

lead of Kuki and Asō, I have defined *akanuke* as an unpretentious air, a thorough familiarity with all aspects of life, and an unconcerned, unassuming character. The problem of whether or not to consider *akanuke* a form of aesthetic consciousness stems, I believe, from an inadequate differentiation of the concepts of *iki* and *tsū*.

Iki and *Tsū*

The aesthetic consciousness of *iki* is part of a refined culture of sensation; *tsū* is this aesthetic consciousness put into practice. In other words, *tsū* is the behavior brought forth by *iki*. Asō, however, interprets the relation of *iki* and *tsū* as the inside and outside of the same thing or the relation of waves to water. He claims that if something is to be *iki* it must also be *tsū* and up-to-date. *Tsū* thus becomes a condition for *iki*. Asō's conceptualization of *tsū* is, of course, only one theory of the subject. Nakamura Yukihiko, Mizuno Minoru, Uzuki Hiroshi, and others have also produced quite useful treatises on *tsū*.[4] Here I would like to consolidate these writers' views and then reinterpret the relation of *iki* and *tsū*.

According to *Hitome tsutsumi* (A Glance over the Riverbank, 1788), the word *tsū* came into use around 1769–1770. The term *daitsū* (grand connoisseur) was in great vogue around 1777. From this time on, many books designed to enlighten the public contained the word *tsū* in the title: *Fūzoku-tsū* (Guide to Ways of the World, 1800), *Ryōri-tsū* (Cooking Know-How, 1823–1835), and the like. The use of Chinese-sounding words such as *tsū* and *daitsū* represented a trend of the day. Chinese-influenced "literary men's painting" *(bunjin-ga)* also peaked at the time the term *tsū* became fashionable, and Chinese scholarship was all the rage. The popularity of the notion of *tsū* seems to have been another element of contemporary sinophilia.

Tsū emerged from the context of the pleasure quarters, the theater, restaurants, and the musical world. These were realms accessible to nearly everyone, worlds of play, which in their most common form had nothing to do with notions of *tsū* or *daitsū*. But when play develops to an inordinate degree, a surprisingly elaborate lawlike quality may emerge. Rules of behavior, formalities, sensibilities, or ways in which money is handled may become increasingly intricate. Once such detailed procedures are carefully codified, the number of people sufficiently proficient to truly enjoy themselves drops to virtually nil. In Edo-period Japan, those who felt entirely at ease with such rules and could enjoy themselves fully were labeled *tsū* or *daitsū*.

The *tsū* individual was necessarily an amateur. Although he might well garner public acclaim and achieve some degree of renown, professionals were excluded.. A famous *tsū* individual might wish to engage in egocentric behavior, but to remain *tsū* he had to conform to other standards. He was required to have discretion, the ability to remain somewhat aloof, and a certain flexibility and perspicacity that allowed him to accommodate himself to circumstances. He was not arrogant and did not display a feigned highbrow tone. The *tsū* individual was not cynical or vulgar; his use of money was neither too lavish nor too stingy; his thoughts were never narrow-minded or deviant. He did not speak ill of others or engage in pretentious behavior. And he was a keen judge of human character: he showed a deep understanding of the inner workings of the human psyche.

The opposite of the *tsū* individual was the boor *(yabo)* or the phony *(hankatsū)*. The phony desired to parade the fact that he was *tsū*, but by doing so merely demonstrated his ignorance. While showing that he lacked any true knowledge or understanding, he engaged in absurd or ridiculous behavior, all with utter seriousness. The boor, however, did not even attempt to behave like the *tsū*. When, for example, a rustic bungler entered the *tsū's* territory and behaved in a blatantly barbarian way, he thereby exhibited an almost charming naïveté. The phony, by contrast, did not.

Aside from the depiction of the boor, which is my own addition, the foregoing descriptions are distilled from recent studies that seem to me correct. Nevertheless, in these works one finds no serious consideration of whether *tsū* is a form of aesthetic consciousness or a mode of behavior. Attempts to shed light on the relation between *iki* and *tsū* have limited themselves to the kind presented by Asō: *iki* and *tsū* are related like waves to water. Such a description appears to me inadequate. Indeed, *tsū* seems to be a style of behavior, an attitude toward behavior, or a specific behavioral pattern that is an expression of such a style or attitude. To investigate the meaning of *tsū* further we must turn to the historical context within which the notion of *tsū* emerged. *Iki* and *tsū* are no doubt intimately linked; both arose during the latter half of the eighteenth century, an age with a dazzling urban culture. Thus we must ask: to what historical forces can this appearance be credited?

The Social Context of *Iki*

As we have already noted, *iki* and *tsū* were developed within the world of play. *Iki* evolved as a kind of aesthetic consciousness; *tsū* was a typically Edoesque principle of behavior. On the most general level, *iki* was the aesthetic consciousness typified by courtesans *(yūjo)* and female geisha; the model of *tsū,* by contrast, was found among pleasure seekers who actively fostered the development of *iki*—that is, the men who frequented the pleasure districts. *Tsū* was their model of cultivation and their principle of behavior. In the world of play, *iki* represented the utmost refinement of the allure that women used to captivate men; *tsū* was the principle of behavior typified by men who best understood the *iki* qualities of such women. These men thoroughly enjoyed play but did not lose themselves in it. Of course, there were many *iki* men—for example, Sukeroku—as well. Conversely, trustworthy women with understanding, women who exhibited characteristics of *tsū,* were also to be found. Nevertheless, on the whole, *iki* and *tsū* arose from the differences in the social position accorded to men and women.

Yoshiwara, where *iki* was perfected, began to undergo alterations during the Kyōhō period (1716–1736); then, after the Hōreki period (1751–1764), drastic transformations took place. The nō stages of the better-known brothels were removed. Frequent fires radically transformed the physical environment. During the first 111 years after Yoshiwara was moved from Nihonbashi to Asakusa, only one major fire is recorded. But in the ninety-eight-year span from 1768 until 1866 the area burned to the ground no fewer than eighteen times.

Changes were not limited to physical structures. From the Kyōhō period the head family of Yoshiwara lost its position of leadership and was replaced by lesser headmen representing each of the five wards. From the Hōreki period the high-ranking courtesans known as *tayū,* along with the intermediary houses *(ageya)* where they met their guests, gradually vanished. Female performing artists (geisha) appeared; now both males and females entertained guests with parlor games and amusements.

From the early eighteenth century, the population of Yoshiwara prostitutes gradually increased. According to *Yoshiwara saiken* (Guides to Yoshiwara), published during the Kyōhō period, the contemporary population of Yoshiwara prostitutes at the time stood at around 1,800 to 2,100. By the Tenmei period (1781–1789) this figure had risen to 2,800 or 2,900. During the time of the Kansei Reforms (1787–1793) many unlicensed prostitutes were forcibly sent to Yoshiwara, increasing the population to over 4,000. By 1799 some 4,972 prostitutes labored there; and with the Tenpō Reforms of the early 1840s the population rose dramatically again. By 1846 it had increased to 7,197.

What is one to make of these changes and their relation to *iki*? Certainly fires or natural calamities cannot be held responsible for the disappearance of the nō stages or the decline in the number of *ageya* and *tayū,* for these had already largely vanished during the Hōreki period. Instead, these changes resulted from the fact that the *chōnin* had replaced the warriors as the main clients of Yoshiwara. Members of the warrior class, of course, still wielded considerable economic power and continued to utilize Yoshiwara for their social life. But as the bakufu and the various domains increasingly came to face an economic impasse, such activity declined dramatically. Instead, the *chōnin* became the main patrons of the pleasure quarters. Yoshiwara was thus transformed into a site where *chōnin* culture could be nurtured. As a result, Yoshiwara became the favorite setting for *sharebon, kibyōshi, ukiyo-e, senryū,* kabuki plays, and much else.

From the Hōreki period a standard format was given to the *Yoshiwara saiken,* the guide booklets that evaluated and minutely described the attributes of Yoshiwara courtesans. New guides were published annually and sold on the streets of Edo. The inconvenience of frequent fires was overcome by constructing "temporary houses" *(karitaku).* The culture of *bitai, akanuke,* and *hari* within the brothels was reinforced by using young girls as assistants *(kamuro).* As these girls grew up, they perfectly mastered the language and practices of this world.

Brothel owners devised intricate schemes to spur on the women, whom they subjected to severe working conditions. Courtesans were forced to muster all their knowledge and ability to refine their *bitai.* The owner of the Gomyōrō brothel (more commonly known as the Ōgiya), which appears in Santō Kyōden's *sharebon* entitled *Keiseikei* (Buying a Courtesan, published in 1788),[5] seems to have gone to particular lengths to pressure the women who worked for him. Wishing both to rebuke and motivate Takigawa, a courtesan whose rival was the highly popular Hanaōgi, he had a gorgeous present intended for Hanaōgi "mistakenly" delivered to Takigawa's room. Only after Takigawa had seen Hanaōgi's present was it taken away and given to its intended recipient.[6]

Such trends all contributed to the creation of the concept of *iki* in Yoshiwara from the 1760s to the 1780s. During the years of the Kansei Reforms (1787–1793), severe restrictions on this world of play led to a period of stagnation. Only during the peaceful and liberal era of the Bunka and Bunsei periods (1804–1830) did the aesthetic of *iki* undergo further development. Now it moved beyond Yoshiwara to become the hallmark of the unlicensed "town geisha" *(machi geisha),* in particular the geisha of the Fukagawa area.

By the Meiwa period (1764–1772) restaurants were established in the Fukagawa area, especially at popular spots around Suzaki and

Tatsumi (Fukagawa) geisha as depicted in Tamenaga Shunsui's *Shunshoku umegoyomi* (Spring Love: A Plum Blossom Almanac), published in 1833–1834. (In the possession of the Tokyo Metropolitan Central Library.)

along the banks of the Sumida River. These restaurants hired many "town geisha" and the aesthetic of *iki* began to develop here as well. At these spots there was little of the indiscriminate sale of sexual favors that typified Yoshiwara. A woman's *bitai* was kept within the realm of the potential, in an atmosphere of "service." Here the sexes retained an unusually tense relationship; and this tension heightened the feeling of *iki*. Eventually the geisha of the Fukagawa area became the outstanding representatives of *iki*.

The aesthetic consciousness of *iki* was created and refined by people who, though living in the last century of a feudal age, were alert, undeceived, and in many ways quite modern. Nevertheless, whatever modern tendencies may have been present, contemporary society was severely constricted by the boundaries of feudal rank and status. In order to surmount such barriers, people swarmed to the world of play, the realm of *iki* and *tsū*. These qualities exemplified the ultimate refinement of the world of play. *Iki* and *tsū* thus quickly caught the public imagination. Eventually these notions became the shared cultural property of the nation at large.

Today the pressures of feudal society have disappeared from social life, and the aesthetic consciousness of *iki* is unlikely to undergo further development. Nevertheless, the aesthetic of *iki* continues to be a vital element in the Japanese sensibility. Even in the future, things that are experienced as *iki* will probably continue to move the Japanese people.

CHAPTER 4

EDO PUBLISHING AND *UKIYO-E*

The great majority of woodcuts known as *ukiyo-e* were produced and marketed in the city of Edo. These prints were bought for the purchaser's own enjoyment or to be taken back to the provinces as souvenirs for friends and family. Mass production of *ukiyo-e* first took place in Edo during the Kyōhō period (1716–1736). Morishima Chūryō (1757–1809) noted that the golden age of the beautiful polychrome *ukiyo-e* known as *azuma nishiki-e* (eastern brocade pictures) or *Edo-e* (Edo pictures) lasted until the final decade of the eighteenth century.[1]

Ukiyo-e emerged from a social milieu that centered on publishers and groups of cultured individuals who lived in the *shitamachi* area, particularly around Nihonbashi. From the mid-eighteenth century, a time when Edo was becoming the cultural center of Japan, this area functioned as the hub of cultural activity not just of Edo but of all Japan.

Edo Publishers

By the Genroku period (1688–1704) the most important features of the Edo metropolis were firmly set in place. Sources such as the *Edo meisho-ki* (Records of Famous Sites in Edo, 1662), the *Edo suzume* (The Sparrows of Edo, 1677), and the *Murasaki no hitomoto* (A Purple Thread, 1683) provide precise descriptions of the city during the late seventeenth century. These guides to famous spots in Edo placed a heavy emphasis on the shogun's castle before moving on to portray the Nihonbashi area. As time went on, such guides became increasingly detailed. Excerpts from registries of military households *(bukan)* are usually presented, but the center of attention invariably shifts to the *chōnin*, whose activities are recorded meticulously.

A few years after the appearance of these three works, two

Nihonbashi. From *Edo meisho zue.*

important books entitled *Edo ka no ko* (A Dappled Cloth of Edo, 1687) and *Kokka man'yōki* (Records of Japanese Efflorescence, 1693) were published. These two volumes were an entirely new type of book, documenting with extraordinary accuracy *chōnin* society and the details of each block in the city. From the *Edo ka no ko* and *Kokka man'yōki* one learns that block cutters *(hangiya)* of the day were concentrated around Nihonbashi-minami, Sakai-chō, and Tōriabura-chō. Picture-book shops could be found at Muramatsu-chō, where the artists Hishikawa Moronobu, Hishikawa Kichizaemon, and Hishikawa Sakunojō were active. Prose volumes were sold at some twenty shops in Nihonbashi-minami, Tōrinorimono-chō, Tōrishirogane-chō, Koku-chō, Moto-ryōgae-chō, Shiba Shinmei-mae, Kyōbashi, and Kanda Kaji-chō. Fashionable books of *jōruri* narratives were sold on the third block of Ōdenma-chō by Yamamoto Kyūzaemon and Urokogataya Sanzaemon, at Hasegawa-chō Yoko-chō by Matsue Sanshirō, at Tōriabura-chō by Tsuruya Kiemon and Yamagataya Ichirōemon.

At the start of the Edo period, the Edo publishing world was monopolized by branch shops of Kyoto book dealers. Gradually, however, Edo *chōnin* began to publish their own popular books and prints. Publications included *jōruri* books, erotic "pillow books" *(makura-ehon),* and the *ukiyo-e* of Hishikawa Moronobu, Torii Kiyomasu (active 1700–1720), and Torii Kiyomitsu (1735–1785).

Bookseller and customer. From *Jinrin kinmōzui*, 1690.

Eventually, large wholesalers of illustrated storybooks appeared. Nevertheless, until the middle of the eighteenth century bookshops linked to Kyoto and Osaka were still a formidable force. Thereafter, however, Edo publishers gained enough strength to compete with their Kamigata rivals. The opening salvo in the move for independence was launched by Maekawa Rokuzaemon, who ran a shop named Sūbundō on the third block of Nihonbashi-minami. In the middle of the eighteenth century Maekawa refused to acknowledge Kamigata book dealers' traditional copyrights and began to reprint their books. The Suwaraya, which from this time on was the outstanding Edo publishing house, was also powerful enough to contend with its Kamigata counterparts. Other Edo publishing houses expanded rapidly as well; by the latter half of the eighteenth century, Edo branches of Kyoto bookshops were in a steep decline.[2]

By this time, the Edo publishing industry was issuing many bestsellers and amassing great fortunes. These successes mobilized a large number of cultured individuals. A good example is provided by the Suwaraya, which comprised a chain of bookstores located at Nihonbashi Tōri-itchōme, Tōri-nichōme, and elsewhere in Edo. During the Kan'en period (1748–1751) six Suwaraya shops were in operation; by the Bunka period (1804–1818) there were twelve, making the Suwaraya one of the top Edo publishing houses.

At Tōri-nichōme stood the "Suzanbō," a Suwaraya shop run by Kobayashi Shinbee. Kobayashi had achieved renown by publishing many works of scholars and literati such as Ogyū Sorai (1666–1728), Dazai Shundai (1680–1747), and Hattori Nankaku (1683–1759). Of Sorai, he printed the *Gakusoku* (School Regulations, 1727) and much else; of Shundai he issued *Seigaku mondō* (Dialogue on the Wisdom of the Sages, 1733), *Shisho koden* (Transmissions Concerning Chinese Poetry, 1758), and other volumes; of Nankaku he published the best-selling *Nankaku sensei bunshū* (Collection of Writings by Professor Nankaku, published in 1727–1758) and *Tōshisen* (Selected Tang-Dynasty Poetry, first published in 1724). The *Tōshisen* was particularly popular; it was probably the number one bestseller of the entire Edo period. The first printing of one thousand copies was immediately sold out; thereafter two or three thousand additional copies were issued annually.

Kobayashi Shinbee was closely linked to Sorai's school of ancient learning. This school advocated a fresh and thoroughgoing study of Chinese classics. Sorai felt that without an ability to read the classics in the original, true understanding of Chinese thought and culture was impossible. His school also placed much emphasis on statesmanship and the writing of Chinese poetry. Such pursuits required the student to maintain a broad interest in political science, economics, and culture in general. Sorai's school captured the public imagination and earned a large following among both the warriors and the commoners. The Suwaraya was sensitive to these new trends. By quickly publishing relevant materials it succeeded in boosting Sorai's school to prominence and making it one of the leaders of the age.

The largest bookshop of the Suwaraya chain was Suwaraya Mohee's store at Tōri-itchōme. Mohee was an outstanding man in the publishing world who had many close acquaintances among contemporary literati. Mohee's shop held a monopoly on publishing *bukan* and illustrated guides to Edo. It was his business that, together with Suwaraya Ihachi, published Saitō Gesshin's mammoth *Edo meisho zue* (Illustrations of Famous Sites in Edo, published in 1834–1836).

Another outstanding Suwaraya shop was owned by Suwaraya Ichibee. During the Hōreki period (1751–1764) Ichibee's shop was located on the third block of Kita-muromachi in Nihonbashi. Rather than focus on the Chinese learning of Sorai's school, Ichibee turned his attention to Western learning. By placing himself at the forefront of the contemporary intellectual world, he rapidly succeeded as a publisher. During the latter half of the eighteenth century, Ichibee's shop published many significant volumes: *Butsurui hinshitsu* ([Natural] Objects Categorized, 1763), *Fūryū Shidōken-den* (A Humorous Tale of Shidōken, 1763), *Kakanpu ryakusetsu* (Asbestos: An Outline, 1765), and *Shinrei yaguchi no watashi* (Spirits at the Ferry of Yaguchi), all by Hiraga Gennai; *Minkan bikōroku* (Public Preparations for Famine, 1775) by Tatebe Seian (1712–1782); *Kaitai yakuzu* (Anatomical Charts, 1773) and *Kaitai shinsho* (1774, a translation of Johann Kulmus's *Tabulae Anatomica*) by Sugita Genpaku (1773–1817); *Sangoku tsūran zusetsu* (Illustrated Survey of Three Nations [Korea, the Ryūkyū Islands, and Hokkaidō], 1785–1786) by Hayashi Shihei (1738–1793); *Bankoku zusetsu* (Illustrations and Explanations of Myriad Nations, 1785–1786) by Katsuragawa Hoshū; *Kōmō zatsuwa* (Miscellaneous Tales of Barbarians, 1787), *Bankoku shinwa* (New Tales of Myriad Nations, 1789), and *Ryūkyū-banashi* (Stories of the Ryūkyū Islands, 1790) by Morishima Chūryō; *Naika sen'yō* (Summary of Western Theories of Internal Medicine, 1792), translated by Udagawa Genzui (1755–1797); and many new literary works by Ōta Nanpo and Hezutsu Tōsaku.

The expansion of the Suwaraya family business is symbolic of the remarkable developments in book publishing and marketing that

Music and dance from the Ryukyu Islands. From *Ryūkyū-banashi* (Morishima Chūryō), published in 1790. (In the possession of the Tokyo Metropolitan Central Library.)

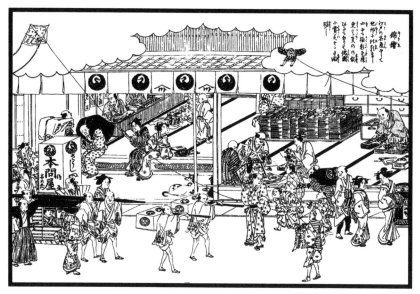

Tsutaya Kihee's bookshop. From *Edo meisho zue.*

had occurred in the Nihonbashi area. The Suwaraya was, of course, by no means unique. Other businesses, such as the previously mentioned Urokogataya, which specialized in *joruri* books, or the Tsuruya, Yamagataya, and Yamamotoya, were also active at this time. These shops frequently published woodcuts of famous kabuki actors. From the second half of the eighteenth century, the age of the Suwaraya's rapid growth, *ukiyo-e* quickly rose in popularity. Illustrated fiction also developed rapidly and was published in ever increasing quantities.

One of the most important publishers of *ukiyo-e* was Tsutaya Jūzaburō (1750–1797). Jūzaburō first opened his business outside the main gate of the Yoshiwara pleasure district, but later he moved to Tōriabura-chō, where he continued to be highly active, publishing many *ukiyo-e* by Sharaku and Utamaro as well as works of Santō Kyōden. Although Tsutaya Jūzaburō was a newcomer to the publishing world, he was instrumental in producing many woodcuts by famous *ukiyo-e* artists of the day.

Cultural Groups and the Birth of *Nishiki-e*

As mentioned earlier, shops of Suwaraya Mohee and Suwaraya Ichibee stood in close contact with literati and scholars of Western

learning. In fact, publishers and writers of the downtown area constituted a type of cultural community. For example, Hiraga Gennai's
Nenashigusa (Floating Weeds, published in 1763–1768), a highly
original work that includes a discussion of Torii Kiyonobu's (1664–
1729) actor prints, was published by Okamoto Ribee, whose shop
stood at Kanda Shirakabe-chō. Gennai too lived in Kanda. Not far
away, at the fourth block of the Tōrichō in Nihonbashi, lived his
friend Sugita Genpaku, who practiced Dutch-style medicine and
surgery. Near Genpaku's home resided the artist Sō Shiseki (1716–
1786, real name Kusumoto Sekkei). Close by, at Mizuya-chō in
Kyōbashi, stood the Shirandō, the academy of Western learning of
Ōtsuki Gentaku (1757–1827). These men met constantly, enjoying
various diversions, eating meals together, even throwing "Western-
style" New Year's parties.

A famous example of a collaborative effort by such individuals is
Sugita Genpaku's *Kaitai shinsho*, a pathbreaking translation of a
Western anatomical manual. This volume was illustrated by Gennai's
student, Odano Naotake (1749–1780) from the Akita domain; the
publisher was Suwaraya Ichibee. Ichibee was probably informed of
Sugita's translation by Gennai and then asked Sugita for the publication rights. Odano's function as illustrator was most likely decided in
a meeting of the cultural coterie just mentioned, although the exact
nature of these processes remains obscure. No matter what actually
took place, however, publishers, authors, and illustrators remained
in close contact.

Calendar-picture printing events known as *daishōkai* were another
fashionable activity enjoyed by cultured men of the downtown area.
At these gatherings participants competed to produce the best pictures for calendars indicating the small months (twenty-nine days)
and large months (thirty days) of the coming year. *Daishōkai* were all
the rage during the latter half of the eighteenth century and were visited by almost every important *ukiyo-e* artist of the time.[3] Participants
also included literati and artists such as Mitsui Shinna (1700–1782)
and his son Shinkō, Shiba Kōkan, Sawada Tōkō, Kubo Shunman
(1757–1820), and Morishima Chūryō. It was at a 1765 *daishōkai*
staged by the Ushigome bannerman Ōkubo Jinshirō Kyosen that
Suzuki Harunobu first produced polychrome Edo *nishiki-e*. Harunobu was undoubtedly a pioneer of Edo *nishiki-e*, but his work was not
undertaken in isolation. Much of the credit for the birth of Edo *nishiki-e* must go to Ōkubo, the leader of these gatherings. Hiraga Gennai was yet another participant in the early *daishōkai*. Gennai, who was
well versed in Western art and painted in oils himself, was surrounded by a cultural group whose role in Edo-period culture can

hardly be overestimated. Gennai's coterie included scholars of Western learning, doctors practicing Dutch-style medicine, scholars of Chinese literature, calligraphers, and many others. The interaction of these men led to the creation of a number of *ukiyo-e* and books.

Nishiki-e were an artistic development that stood in sharp contrast to earlier Japanese prints. In Japanese painting before the age of *nishiki-e*, empty space was charged with great meaning. Use of blank areas was deeply related to the Buddhist notions of emptiness *(kū)*, to specifically Japanese ideas of space *(ma)*, and to Japanese philosophies of nature. These concepts are in turn related to the idea of nothingness *(mu)* found in Eastern thought in general. From the time of Harunobu's *nishiki-e*, however, virtually the entire surface of the picture was filled with color. Moreover, many *nishiki-e* employed Western techniques of perspective. This denial of the Eastern concept of *mu* and departure from the design and coloration of previous Japanese pictorial art was in part the result of a familiarity with Western techniques of oil painting and copperplate etching. Not everything was taken from these sources, but the works of Harunobu, Haruaki, Sharaku, Utamaro, and Hokusai unambiguously show such influence. These men (with the possible exception of Sharaku) often attended the *daishōkai* and were good friends with Hiraga Gennai, Shiba Kōkan, and Gennai's outstanding disciple Morishima Chūryō.

The establishment of *nishiki-e* with perspective within the context of traditional "flat" Japanese painting was an epoch-making event in the history of Japanese pictorial art. Western techniques had here been completely absorbed into Japanese culture. Although the roots of these techniques could be traced back a century and a half to Western influence at the start of the Edo period, Western procedures now reemerged as something entirely new. *Nishiki-e* met with such unusual acclaim by the Japanese commoner population because Western techniques had been so thoroughly assimilated.

This process of assimilation also led to the *nishiki-e* fads in Europe and the United States. From the end of the Edo period to the early years of the Meiji era, a tremendous number of *nishiki-e* masterpieces were sold to foreigners. The works of Hokusai, which were perhaps the most Western in tone, were especially prized and often became the subject of scholarly studies.

Chōnin Culture and Handicrafts

The production of woodcuts required the services of expert craftsmen of the kind listed in such number and variety in the *Kokka*

man'yōki and *Edo suzume*. Recently I searched out aging craftsmen
and recorded their stories of bygone times. When these artisans are
asked about their apprenticeships, they often recall stories of masters who lived in the old artisan quarters of Nihonbashi or Kanda.
"Most of the better craftsmen of the old days lived here," they often
say. "Some lived in Shiba and Asakusa, or in Fukagawa, but a true
Edo craftsman resided in the Nihonbashi vicinity."

During the eighteenth and nineteenth centuries, the *shitamachi*
area of Edo was home to a huge number of anonymous but highly
skilled artisans. Competition among these artisans gave rise to a special artisan temperament and sense of pride. The master craftsmen
of Edo staked their entire self-esteem on their technical ability and
their almost superhuman speed and precision. The skill of such artisans was often put to use in creating advertisements. Edo advertising
flourished from around the Meiwa period (1764–1772). One example is the *senjafuda*, a votive slip that serves as a symbol of religious
faith. Names and addresses of stores were attractively printed on
these slips, which were pasted all over famous temples and shrines.
Senjafuda existed in great variety and were highly popular. Edo-
period signboards and shop curtains, too, were designed and manufactured by nameless craftsmen. Such artifacts exhibit extraordinary
originality, boldness, and freedom in design.

Stencils of fine-patterned fabrics *(komon)* are yet another out-

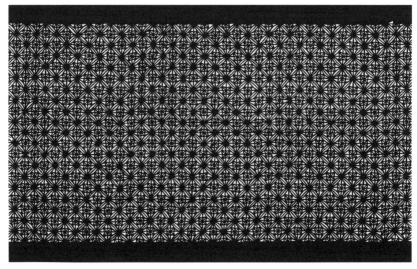

Edo *komon* stencil featuring a pattern consisting of a sequence of interlock-
ing shapes. From *Some no katagami: Edo-gata no hakken* (Kōdansha, 1984).

standing example of Edo handicrafts. It has always been thought that the production of such stencils was monopolized on a national scale by the village of Shiroko near Ise. But recently over a thousand Edo stencils were discovered, proving that many stencils used by Edo *komon* dyers were produced in the city itself. Almost all Edo *komon* stencils appear to have been manufactured in the Kon'ya-chō area of Kanda. From the mid-eighteenth century, stencils were produced here under a special license agreement with Shiroko. The stencils used in Edo *komon* were of outstanding quality. Compared to contemporary stencils from Shiroko or Kyoto, the Edo varieties exhibit a greater sense of *iki*, elegance, and sobriety. When these stencils were used for actual dyeing, the selection of colors further contributed to Edoesque characteristics of the resulting *komon*.

The exact nature of the cooperation among artisans, publishers, and artists remains unclear. Yet one may venture to guess how *ukiyo-e* production might have taken place. Let us imagine the scenario for the manufacture of, say, Utamaro's *ōkubi-e* (portraits from the waist up)—prints that were to capture perfectly the spirit of the day. The publisher, Tsutaya Jūzaburō (more compactly known as Tsutajū), might have sent an errand boy to summon the artist. Tsutajū and Utamaro then perhaps took a swift rowboat to Yoshiwara or to a restaurant where they leisurely discussed the new project. Next, Utamaro drew the pictures, while Tsutajū called block cutters and printers, whose workshops stood nearby. Details of coloration or the powdered mica background were now debated, probably in the presence of Utamaro. All the steps in the printing process were probably the subject of careful deliberation among members of a team that included the artist, publisher, block cutter, and printer.

Books and the Edo Reading Public

Around the start of the year wholesalers such as Tsutaya Jūzaburō and Tsuruya Kiemon of the Tōriabura-chō produced and sold large numbers of new books. Most of these were easy-reading material such as small illustrated satirical fiction of the *kibyōshi* kind. Takizawa Bakin noted in his *Kinsei mono no hon Edo sakusha burui* (Catalog of Recent Edo Authors, 1834) that these dealers could expect to sell some ten thousand copies of two- or three-volume sets of light fiction by the end of the first month. Bestsellers might achieve sales of twelve or thirteen thousand copies, selling out as soon as they were issued. In addition, three or four thousand copies of other types of books "conforming to the taste of the times" were placed in individ-

A block cutter at work. From *Jinrin kinmōzui,* 1690.

ual pouches and sold.[4] In short, fiction published by Tsuruya and Tsutaya sold like hotcakes during the golden age of *ukiyo-e*.

An interesting demonstration of the high level of Edo *chōnin* culture is provided by the record of an official award presented in 1795 to one Iwa, the daughter of Denbee on the third block of Hongō Haruki-chō. The *Kōgiroku* (Records of Filial Piety),[5] a fifty-volume work ordered written by Matsudaira Sadanobu (1758–1829) and printed with woodblocks during the Kansei period (1789–1801), records that Iwa's aged father was bedridden with palsy. To support him, Iwa sold tofu. Since her father was fond of "reading books" *(yomihon)*, Iwa borrowed such volumes from the residents of her block and read them to the sick man. After some time she had exhausted all the books available within the block, but nearby residents lent Iwa books borrowed from people who lived farther away. A similar case involved Iwajirō on the second block of Haruki-chō, who was awarded an honor for filial piety in 1801. Iwajirō too won his award for borrowing books and reading them to his father. Iwa and Iwajirō were residents of the city's edge, but even the lower-class *chōnin* of this area seem to have read *yomihon* and other literature borrowed from book lenders.

Not all citizens of Edo did this, of course. But the age in which Utamaro, Santō Kyōden, and hundreds of other *ukiyo-e* artists and literati were active was also an era in which Edo-period culture drew its strength from a broad lower-class urban public. The intellects necessary for cultural production, the craftsmen who had the skills to realize it, and the *chōnin* recipients had succeeded in forging close ties. Time and again, broad-based cultural communities were established. These groups engaged in modern and progressive ventures that produced some of the outstanding art, literature, and scholarship of the age.

CHAPTER 5

EDO TEMPLES AND SHRINES

The history of Japanese religion is a vast subject that I shall not attempt to cover here. Instead, I should like to focus on the religious activities of the Edo populace. Many questions need to be answered: How were Edo-period temples and shrines established? What kind of religious beliefs were associated with these institutions? And how did the function of temples and shrines change historically?

Yet another important issue concerns pilgrimages undertaken by the Edo citizenry. Pilgrimages often occurred within the city; at times, however, pilgrims traveled to the outskirts of Edo or even to distant temples and shrines throughout the land. Conversely, Shinto and Buddhist images or sacred treasures from remote provincial temples and shrines were transported to Edo where they were unveiled at temple fairs *(kaichō)*. Such fairs were also a popular destination for the Edo populace.

Temple Construction and Relocation

The system of alternate attendance established during the early years of the Edo period required all daimyo to assemble in the city at regular intervals and to build residences there. As the city grew, however, daimyo were often required to relocate their residences. Temples and shrines fared no better. During the city's early years, such religious institutions were also moved and rebuilt at frequent intervals. Statistics on these movements are given in Table 5.1.[1] Figures in columns 1 and 2 document the founding and relocation of Edo temples and shrines over a period of some two centuries. Column 3 gives statistics on the establishment of new quarters located near temples and shrines *(monzenmachi)*. Columns 4 and 5 show that temples and shrines commonly leased land or built and managed houses for which rent was collected.

Table 5.1. Establishment and Relocation of Edo Temples and Shrines

YEAR	NUMBER OF TEMPLES AND SHRINES FOUNDED	NUMBER OF TEMPLES AND SHRINES RELOCATED	NUMBER OF NEW MONZENMACHI	NUMBER OF TEMPLES AND SHRINES LEASING LAND	NUMBER OF TEMPLES AND SHRINES LEASING HOUSES
before 1599	131				
1600–1609	97	9			
1610–1619	128	26			
1620–1629	201	37	31		
1630–1639	91	122	25		
1640–1649	76	49	38		
1650–1659	57	154	31		
1660–1669	42	40	24		
1670–1679	21	21	6		
1680–1689	25	67	14		
1690–1699	27	57	12		
1700–1709	4	22	15		
1710–1719	4	19	3	20	
1720–1729		6	2	34	
1730–1739		5	13	36	26
1740–1749	2	7	9	44	26
1750–1759		7	8	46	24
1760–1769		3	4	37	49
1770–1779		4	3	41	50
1780–1789		3	6	35	47
1790–1799		1	1	33	35
1800–1809	2			30	30
1810–1819	1	1		35	36
1820–1829		2		38	31

From Table 5.1 one can see that most temples and shrines were founded during the early decades of the Edo period. Construction of new temples and shrines continued until around the Genroku period (1688–1704); then such activity decreased rapidly. Relocations peaked between the 1630s and the 1660s, and they continued until the Genroku period. Some stability was reached by the second decade of the eighteenth century.

Most Edo temples and shrines were branches of temples and shrines located in a daimyo's home province. Construction of such buildings took place largely during the first century of the city's existence. Besides building temples and shrines in Edo, daimyo also funded the construction of temples or shrines in their home domains or in the old capitals of Kyoto or Kamakura. New buildings were also commonly added to famous older temples. For example, Lord Ikeda Mitsumasa (1609–1682) of Okayama (Bizen domain) ordered the construction of Tenkyūin Hall at the Myōshinji, a temple in Kyoto; Lord Hosokawa of Kyūshū (Kumamoto domain) had a memorial hall built at the Myōhōji in Kamakura for his daughter Kō.

To enshrine Ieyasu as the "Great Incarnation Shining over the East" *(tōshō dai gongen),* the bakufu built a mausoleum and grand shrine at Nikkō. Smaller shrines deifying Ieyasu and modeled after the Tōshōgū at Nikkō were built at Momijiyama (within the precincts of Edo castle) and at Ueno. The Zōjōji at Shiba and the Kan'eiji at Ueno functioned as family temples of the Tokugawa house. Construction of major Edo temples and shrines was begun in the following years:

Zōjōji: 1598
Denzūin: 1608
Gokokuji: 1615
Kan'eiji: 1624
Tōshōgū: Kan'ei period (1624–1644)

Each of these projects required huge expenditures over a long period of time.

Until the Edo period, government policy regarding temples and shrines had been very conservative. The basic approach of the Kamakura bakufu was codified in the *Jōei shikimoku* (Jōei Code, promulgated in 1232). Article 1 of this code stipulated that shrine upkeep and the maintenance of ceremonies be given high priority; Article 2 required Buddhist temples to be kept under repair and Buddhist services to be held. The Muromachi bakufu continued this policy. The Tokugawa bakufu, however, revised this tradition.

Tokugawa Ieyasu himself was deified at the Tōshōgū, and new Tokugawa family temples and shrines were built. Provincial daimyo imitated this practice and built shrines honoring the founder of their domain. Such shrines were often constructed at scenic spots within castle compounds. A branch shrine might then be built within the grounds of a daimyo's Edo residence. Some daimyo even built a Tōshōgū in their home province. In addition, branches of famous local temples and shrines were often erected within a daimyo's Edo residence. These activities took place mainly during the seventeenth century. Relocations, however, continued somewhat longer, lasting until the first decades of the eighteenth century. This phenomenon is closely related to movements in Edo daimyo residences, which in turn were prompted by the confiscation of old fiefs and the establishment of new ones.

The construction of new *monzenmachi*—quarters around temples and shrines—was a result of the dearth of land available to *chōnin.* According to a survey conducted during the first years of the Meiji period, 69 percent of the city of Edo was warrior land, 16 percent belonged to the *chōnin,* and 15 percent belonged to temples and shrines. In other words, land owned by religious institutions almost equaled that owned by the *chōnin.* As the *chōnin* population increased, temples and shrines began to permit the construction of new quarters on ecclesiastical property. Eventually temples and shrines built rental dwellings on such land themselves. Even today, temples and shrines often own and lease apartment buildings.

Religious Activities in the City

The large temples and shrines mentioned earlier were not, of course, constructed for the Edo citizenry. They were the institutions of a privileged stratum of warriors and often enshrined a single shogun or a specific daimyo. The daimyo and even the bakufu did not, however, prohibit commoners from worshiping at temples and shrines such as the Zōjōji, Kan'eiji, Tōshōgū, and Gokokuji. The Asakusa Sensōji, which had already earned great public support from before the Edo period, was also open to the public for worship.

Edo-period guides such as the *Tōkaidō meisho-ki* (Famous Sites on the Tōkaidō, 1662) or the *Edo meisho-ki* (Records of Famous Sites in Edo, 1662) show that temples such as the Kan'eiji, Zōjōji, and Sensōji and shrines such as the Sannō Hie Shrine, the Kanda Myōjin Shrine, and the Yushima Tenjin Shrine were highly popular spots for the Edo citizenry. Directories of Edo such as the *Edo suzume* (The

Sparrows of Edo, 1677), the *Edo ka no ko* (A Dappled Cloth of Edo, 1687), the *Edo sunago* (Grains of Edo Sand, 1732), and the famous *Edo meisho zue* (Illustrations of Famous Sites in Edo, published in 1834–1836) also allot much space to temples and shrines in their pages.

The *Edo meisho zue* describes the temples and shrines of Edo and their attendant religious events in greater detail than any other Edo-period source. This book was compiled by Saitō Gesshin, a ward representative *(nanushi)* of Kijichō in Kanda. Saitō continued the research that his father and grandfather had already carried out for two generations. The resulting twenty-six-volume guide to Edo, the product of three generations of intensive labor, was based largely on on-site inspections of the locations depicted and includes many detailed illustrations by Hasegawa Settan (1778–1843).

Besides this tremendous work, Gesshin also composed the *Tōto saijiki* (Records of Annual Events in the Eastern Capital, published in 1838) and a detailed diary in thirty-eight fascicles.[2] The latter work records Gesshin's activities in great detail and contains much information on his visits to temples and shrines throughout the city. Here I should like to introduce sections of the diary that are concerned with popular religious faith and with annual events.[3] Gesshin's comments provide considerable insight into the religious life of the Edo citizenry during the last part of the period.

On the day after New Year's, Gesshin went to worship the Kannon at Asakusa and then paid his respects to the Shōden deity at Matsuchiyama.[4] Such a pilgrimage was undertaken almost every year. On the third day of the new year, he paid obeisance to the shogun at Edo castle; thereafter he often went with friends to the Bishamonten ceremony at the Atago Gongen.[5] The Edo citizenry usually visited this deity at various locations on the "first day of the tiger" *(hatsu tora)* of the first, fifth, and ninth months.

On the "first day of the rabbit" *(hatsu u)* of the year, Gesshin invariably went to the Tenjin Shrine at Kameido.[6] Then, on the tenth day of the first month, he made a pilgrimage to the Konpira at Toranomon.[7] This was a branch shrine of a major shrine located in the Kyōgoku family's domain in Kotohira (Sanuki). The Kyōgoku family had funded the construction of the Edo branch of the shrine within the premises of the family's Edo residence. Every month, on the tenth day, Gesshin came here to worship. When he was prevented from doing so by urgent business, he sent someone to worship in his place; but on the following day he always visited the shrine in person. Occasionally Gesshin also worshiped at the Konpira enshrined at the lower residence of the Kyōgoku house at Roppongi in Azabu.

The "first day of the rabbit" at Kameido. From *Tōto saijiki.*

One may thus assume that shrines were often built at lower, middle, and upper daimyo residences.

On the eleventh day of the first month, Gesshin paid homage to the Sanja deity at Asakusa where he also watched a horseback archery exhibit. On the sixteenth he went to the Tenmangū in Kameido for the "seventy-five dish" *(shichijūgo-zen)* ceremony, a rite in which seventy-five varieties of food were offered to the gods. Then he made the rounds to the Matsuchiyama and Akiba shrines, after which he went to Kuramae to worship Enma, god of the underworld.[8]

On the seventeenth Gesshin went by boat to the star festival of the Myōken deity at Yanagishima;[9] on the night of the twenty-third he sometimes went to a moon-watching festival, for it was believed that wishes were sure to be granted if one waited for the moon to rise on this night. Then, on the twenty-fifth, he went to the Kameido Tenjin Shrine for the ritual known as *usokae* (bullfinch exchanging). A figure of a bullfinch was exchanged for a new one each year, for placing this figure on the family altar was thought to bring good luck.

During the second month, Gesshin's schedule included attending the festival of the "first day of the horse" *(hatsu uma)*, visiting six temples in which the Amida Buddha was enshrined, making a tour of thirty-three Kannon temples, going to view plum blossoms,

Biwa performance at the Bentendō at Honjo Hitotsume. From *Tōto saijiki*.

attending the "Nirvana Festival" *(nehan-e)*, and hearing a lute *(biwa)* recital by blind priests at Hitotsume. Gesshin also worshiped at temples at Asakusa, at Matsuchiyama, and at the Konpira at Toranomon. Inari (the god of grains) was enshrined at Gesshin's house, and on the "first day of the horse" a ritual dedicated to this god was performed. Many children of the neighborhood gathered on this occasion and received presents. The enshrinement of this god at Gesshin's residence and at many other households was a by-product of the Inari crazes that periodically swept the city. Crowds thronged to Inari shrines, especially the ones at Ōji and Karasumori. Gesshin noted that at Karasumori, floats were sent off and huge lanterns with pictures of scenes from the kabuki were arranged in rows. All these events drew tremendous crowds of spectators. Gesshin also visited Inari at the Kasamori Shrine in Yanaka, where he donated a tablet depicting a troupe of children acrobats *(kakubee-jishi)*.

The Nirvana Festival on the fifteenth day of the second month took place everywhere in grand style. In 1855 on this occasion Gesshin went to the Ginsōin, a temple at Atagochō, to worship the depiction of Buddha's attainment of nirvana as painted by Hanabusa Itchō (1652–1724). For the Nirvana Festival, paintings of this motif by various artists were displayed publicly: at the Jōgyoin of the Kan'eiji one could inspect a painting by Kanō Tsunenobu (1636–1713); the Yōgyokuin in Shitaya featured a work by Hasegawa Tōun; at the Gokokuji a depiction by Kanō Yasunobu (1613–1685) was put on display; and at the Chifukuji in Shiba worshipers could see a work by Chō Densu (Kichizan Min Chō, 1352–1431). The picture by Kanō Yasunobu shown at the Gokokuji was so large that steps for viewing were set up in the back of the main temple hall. The Nirvana Festival was also the source of highly popular "nirvana prints" purchased by the Edo public.

The tour of the six Amida temples, which even found its way into a humorous book by Jippensha Ikku, existed in several versions throughout the city.[10] An old circuit took the pilgrim to the Jōrakuin at Shitaya, the Yorakuji at Tabata, the Muryōji at Nishigahara, the Saifukuji at Toshima, the Enmeiji at Shimo-Numata, and the Jōkōji at Kameido. Another course covered temples in the Yamanote area; yet another was located in the western part of the city. Similar tours of thirty-three Kannon were established around the city. At some temples, such as the Gangyōji at Hongō, all thirty-three Kannon were assembled in one place, allowing the pilgrim to worship all of them simultaneously.

On the fifteenth day of the third month, Gesshin took a stroll on the banks of the Sumida River on his way to the great Amida invoca-

Kanbutsu-e. A small statue of the Buddha is doused with tea. From *Tōto saijiki.*

tion *(dai nenbutsu)* at the site marking the death of Umewaka.[11] Then, a few days later, on either the seventeenth or the eighteenth, Gesshin went to see the Sanja Festival at Asakusa.

Buddhist images from provincial temples were often put on display at various Edo temples and shrines. Fairs *(kaichō)* held on such occasions at the Ekōin at Ryōgoku and the Tenjin Shrine at Yushima were particularly popular. Gesshin often visited such displays: on the seventeenth and twenty-fifth of the third month and the thirteenth and twenty-fifth of the fourth month of 1838, he went to *kaichō* at Ryōgoku; on the fourth day of the sixth month he visited fairs at Honjo; and on the sixteenth, twentieth, twenty-seventh, and twenty-ninth of the same month he went to such events at Ryōgoku.

On the eighth day of the fourth month, Gesshin set out to participate in the "Buddha ablutions" *(kanbutsu-e)*, a festival in which hydrangea tea is sprinkled on an image of the infant Buddha to celebrate his birthday. On the seventeenth he made a pilgrimage to the Takada Hachiman Shrine, popularly known as Anahachiman. He also paid a visit to the Kishimojin Shrine.[12]

During the fifth month Gesshin began preparations for the Kanda Festival; at the end of the month he made a pilgrimage to Mount Fuji. Fuji pilgrimages were highly popular during the Edo period. The gospel of the Fuji religion was the transmission of the hermit Jikigyō Miroku (1671–1733), who engaged in Buddhist meditation on top of Mount Fuji. This religion found many believers, who were subsequently organized in numerous associations *(kō)*. Indeed, small versions of Mount Fuji were built throughout Edo. According to the *Morisada mankō* (Morisada's Miscellany, 1830s–1860s):

> On the last day of the fifth month and the first day of the sixth month, crowds of visitors go to the "Fuji mountains" in Edo: at Asakusa, Komagome, Takada, Fukagawa, Meguro, Yotsuya, Kayabachō, and Shitaya Onoterusaki. At each of these eight spots a model of Mount Fuji has been constructed for worshiping at a Sengen Shrine. Normally, climbing these model mountains is prohibited; it is allowed only on these two special days. The main Edo spot of this type is the one at Komagome.[13]

The model Fujis at Komagome and Takada had existed for many years, but those at the other locations were not built until the early nineteenth century.[14] Many more Fuji replicas are listed in Gesshin's *Tōto saijiki:* at Asakusa-jariba, Morishita-chō Shinmeigū, Teppōzu Inari, Ikenohata Shichiken-chō, Yanagi no mori Inari, Kanda Myōjin, Matsushita-chō Fudō, Koami-chō Tōkabori Inari, Takanawa Sen-

A Fuji replica at Tomigaoka. From *Edo meisho zue.*

gakuji and Nyoraiji, and Honjo Mutsume.[15] According to Miura Ieyoshi, sixty-eight such sites in the Edo vicinity still survive today.[16]

The opening of each of these mountains on the last day of the fifth month and the first day of the sixth month was accompanied by a well-attended service. Gesshin made pilgrimages to the Fuji at

Komagome, Kayachō (in Shitaya), and Yanagihara. Women were prohibited from climbing the real Mount Fuji, but they were allowed to scale the miniature versions; indeed, here women were held in high regard. The citizens of Edo, both believers and nonbelievers, assembled at these spots and enjoyed themselves throughout the night. This phenomenon was unique to Edo; it cannot be found in Kyoto or Osaka.

During the sixth month Gesshin decorated the outside of his house with hydrangeas *(ajisai-tsuri)*, went to the festival of the god Gozu,[17] and visited the Hikawa Shrine at Akasaka. Finally, he attended the Shogun Festival *(tenkasai)* at the Sannō Hie Shrine. *Ajisai-tsuri* was a practice that Gesshin continued well into the Meiji period. This event took place on the first day of the sixth month of the lunar calendar, the start of the most severe summer heat. Many pictures of *ajisai-tsuri* have been drawn by Kaburagi Kiyokata (1878–1972), who had a special liking for hydrangeas. Kaburagi even named his personal residence the "Hydrangea House." The connection between the sacred nature of this flower and daily life seems to have been felt strongly by downtown residents during the Edo and Meiji periods.

During the seventh month Gesshin took part in the Tanabata Festival;[18] on the ninth or tenth day he made the "46,000-day pilgrimage" or what was commonly known as the "thousand-day pilgrimage" *(sennichi mōde)*. It was believed that if one went to one of several Edo shrines on this day, one received the indicated number of days of benefit. On the thirteenth Gesshin went to worship Inari at the Ōji Inari Shrine and the god Fudō.[19] On the fifteenth there was the mid-year celebration *(chūgen)* in which many temples aired their prized treasures to guard against mold and insect damage. Gesshin often made the rounds to worship these holy artifacts. On the twenty-sixth he sometimes went to the "moon festival of the twenty-sixth day" *(nijūroku-ya machi)*.

The "first day festival" *(hassaku)* of the eighth month was celebrated in Edo with much enthusiasm and commotion. On this day Gesshin participated in a celebratory occasion at Edo castle. The autumnal equinox occurred during this month, and Gesshin again made the circuit of the six Amida temples and the thirty-three Kannon just as he had done in the spring. On the fifteenth there was an extremely lively ceremony at the Tomioka Hachiman. Twice—during the Shōtoku period (1711–1716) and again during the Bunka period (1804–1818)—so many spectators crowded to this affair that the Eitai Bridge collapsed and many people drowned in the river below.

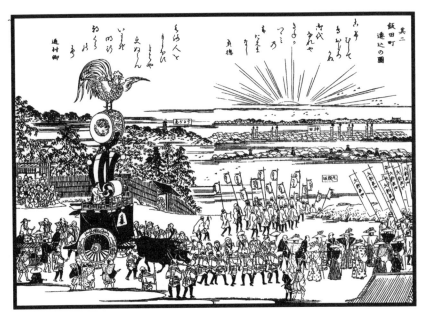

The Kanda festival. From *Tōto saijiki.*

The ninth month was the time of the Kanda Myōjin (the "gracious deity of Kanda") festival. Gesshin, a Kanda ward representative, expended much energy to make this event a success. Preparations for the festival called for a surprising amount of time and effort.[20] Also during this month nurserymen from Somei gathered at Komagome to display elaborate chrysanthemum arrangements. Gesshin and innumerable other spectators thronged to these annual exhibits. This outing provided yet another opportunity for visiting various temples and shrines.

Gesshin's chronicle from the eighth day of the tenth month in 1864 records this excursion in some detail. With his wife and child, he departed early in the morning, first making a pilgrimage to temples and shrines at Kagurazaka, Iwatochō, Yakimochizaka, and the Anahachiman Shrine at Takada. Then, passing Jariba and Omokage Bridge, the family paid its respects to the Kishimojin deity and then stopped at a teahouse called the "Myōgaya" for lunch. From there the three went to worship at the Gokokuji and then to view the chrysanthemums at Komagome. On their way home they stopped for refreshments at Kobinata-Suidōchō and finally arrived home around four o'clock in the afternoon. This leisurely trip thus lasted the entire day. In some years Gesshin went on such a chrysanthemum viewing tour twice.

Chrysanthemum viewing at Somei. From *Tōto saijiki*.

During the eleventh month Gesshin viewed "face showing" *(kaomise)* performances at the kabuki theater. These performances, which took place at all three Edo kabuki theaters, introduced to the public the cast of stars that had been hired for the coming year. During this month Gesshin also attended the sumo tournament. On rare occasions he participated in religious ceremonies of Kinoe-ne Day or the Hattengū deity.[21] On the first "day of the rat" *(hatsu ne)*, rice boiled in tea was served at Gesshin's house and the Rat Festival was celebrated.[22] Also during this month Gesshin, together with several friends, went to the "day-of-the-cock fair" *(tori no ichi)* at the Ōtori Shrine in Asakusa. Gesshin showed great enthusiasm for this event, attending it on the first, second, and third "cock days" of this month.[23] On the day of the Star Festival during the winter solstice, Gesshin also made a pilgrimage to various Myōken deities located around the city.

During the twelfth month Gesshin went to the Sensōji Temple at Asakusa and its year-end market *(toshi no ichi)*. At the end of the year he also customarily paid his respects at the graves of his ancestors.

Besides engaging in all these activities, Gesshin often attended performances at nō and kabuki theaters or variety halls *(yose)*. He also worshiped at the Sensōji and Ekōin temples and the Yushima Tenjin Shrine, and he visited the temple at Matsuchiyama to offer dumplings made of rice flour and sesame to the god Shōden. While paying visits to temples and shrines he enjoyed stopping off at various restaurants for lunch and dinner. Indeed, with all these excursions and meals it is surprising that he remained financially solvent.

Edo: City of Many Gods

Since ancient times, Japanese religion has been pantheistic. During the Edo period temples and shrines continued the ancient tradition of combining Buddhist and Shinto elements. Both types of gods were often worshiped on the same premises and the two religions were not considered to conflict with each other. A typical example of such syncretism was the Asakusa Sensōji, a Buddhist temple that contained a branch of the Ise "Crown Prince Shrine" (Kōtai Jingū). This temple, which functioned as a grand repository of gods and spirits, attracted many devotees who sought solace in worship.

Often certain gods would suddenly attract the fanatical devotion of a great number of believers. Examples of such typically Edoesque fads include the Kasei-period (1804–1830) crazes for the Tarō Inari and the Seishōkō deity (enshrined on the premises of the Hosokawa residence at Hamachō).[24] A temple fair displaying a holy image from the Saga Seiryōji, a temple in Kyoto, was also wildly popular for some time. On yet other occasions, a large portion of the Edo populace suddenly worshiped the god Fudō at Narita or Aizen Myōō of the Saidaiji, a temple in Nara. The latter two crazes arose because the *aragoto* play *Narukami Fudō kitayama-zakura* was staged at the kabuki and because Yanone Gorō, the hero of the kabuki play *Yanone,* was said to be an incarnation of Aizen Myōō.[25]

In conclusion, then, Gesshin's Buddhist and Shinto practices indicate that the Edo citizenry conducted a highly varied religious life, worshiping Inari, Konpira, Hattengū, and many other gods. Not everyone was as pious as Gesshin. But compared to today, many Edo-period individuals often visited temples and shrines and felt the deep communal bonds conferred by religious faith.

PART II

THE TOWN AND THE COUNTRY

CHAPTER 6

PROVINCIAL CULTURE OF THE KASEI
PERIOD (1804–1830)

The Rise of Provincial Culture

The Center and the Provinces

Any discussion of provincial culture during the late Edo period must first address the question of whether the city of Edo was truly the center of Japanese culture. Japanese historians have usually agreed that from the middle of the eighteenth century the center of Japanese culture gradually moved eastward, from the Kamigata area to the city of Edo. As we have seen in previous chapters, from the mid-eighteenth century Edo was indeed the site of many new creative forces. Nevertheless, the Kamigata area, especially Kyoto, which had been the most important center of Japanese culture until the Edo period, remained influential as well. Rather than speak of Edo as the cultural center of the land, therefore, it would better reflect contemporary reality to speak of two centers: one in Edo and another in Kyoto.

Even during the late Edo period, creative activity in Kyoto had by no means stopped or stagnated. During the nineteenth century Kyoto still played an important role in the production of many cultural artifacts and in the transmission of artistic techniques. Outstanding and innovative examples of Kyoto culture can be found in "literary men's painting" *(bunjinga)* and poetry or, somewhat later, in musical works such as *Godan-ginuta* (Cloth-Beating Music in Five Sections) and *Akikaze no kyoku* (Autumn Breeze Music), two instrumental compositions of Mitsuzaki Kengyō (d. 1853).

Discussion of the relation of urban to provincial culture is further complicated by the major differences that existed between large provincial castle towns, such as Sendai, Nagoya, and Kanazawa, and isolated small towns or farming villages. To begin to understand the complex relation of urban to provincial culture let us first examine several Kasei-period cultural communities with members spread throughout a broad geographical region.

Cultural Communities in the Provinces

One such cultural community was the Shōfū Enshū-ryū (orthodox Enshū school) of flower arranging. A glance at this school's 1814 register shows a total of 845 members, 501 of whom resided in Edo. Of the remaining 344 provincial members, 300 lived in the Kantō area. Twenty-eight resided in Shinano, six in Hizen, two in Ōmi, two in Ise, one each in Echigo, Owari, Suruga, and Tanba, and two elsewhere. The 300 Kantō members were distributed over a large area. As can be seen in Figure 6.1, domiciles of Enshū-ryū flower arrangers were concentrated around three types of sites: highways such as the Nakasendō, Kōshū-kaidō, Kawagoe-kaidō, Nikkō-kaidō, and Sakura-kaidō; important shipping sites on the Shingashigawa, Tonegawa, and Kinugawa rivers; and textile manufacturing centers in the Chichibu area or at the foot of Mount Akagi in Kōzuke province.

This map also shows the distribution of members of the Tachibana school as recorded in the *Tachibana-ryū shogei monjin denju-roku* (Record of Disciples of Various Arts of the Tachibana School). This document was drafted by Nara Teruaki, the leader of the school. Nara had studied in Kyoto; during the Kasei period he was active in Fujimi village (Seta county, Kōzuke province). The Tachibana-ryū practiced reading, writing (calligraphy), painting, flower arranging, and physiognomic divination. Some 145 members are listed for the period from 1789 to 1813. The greatest number of students came from around Fujimi; others stemmed from an area that extended from Kuragano and Tomioka in Kōzuke province all the way to Karuizawa and Oiwake in Shinano province. One member even came from distant Hitachi; yet another lived even farther away in Dewa. Most of these disciples seem to have been members of a stratum of wealthy local gentry residing in textile-producing regions. These students were thus intimately linked to the markets in Kiryū and Maebashi. Other members were upper-class *chōnin* from the post-station villages along highways that led to these markets.[1]

Statistics for another cultural community are given in Table 6.1. These figures show the distribution of two schools of *kyōka* poetry. The first column gives figures for the school of Rokujuen (Yadoya no Meshimori) and is based on the *Kyōka gazō sakusha burui* (Illustrated Catalog of *Kyōka* Poets) published in 1811; the second column gives figures for the school of Shikatsube Magao and relies on a document

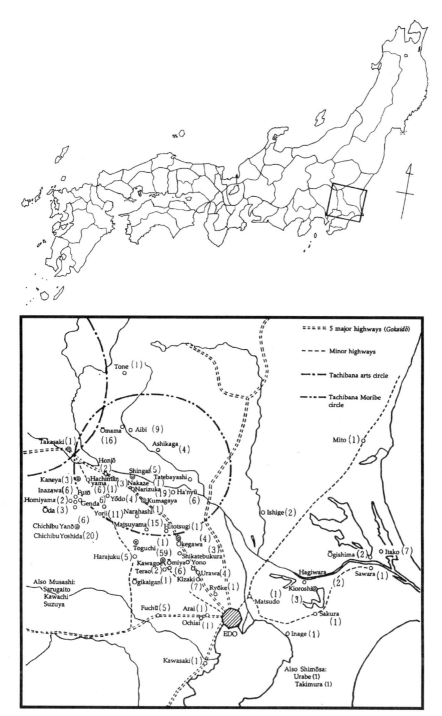

Members of the *Kadō shachū renmei* in the Kantō area (Shōfū Enshū-ryū flower arrangers). ◎ indicates the presence of a master teacher *(shihan)* or an assistant.

entitled *Haikaika mitsudomoe* (A Friendly Gathering for Light Verse), published in 1828.[2] From Table 6.1 one can see that members of these two *kyōka* poet communities lived in many of the same areas as students of the Shōfū Enshū-ryū. Most disciples lived in the Kantō area, but the community extended from the Kai-Shinano-Echigo region to the Mino, Owari, and Kinki areas. Artisans and merchants outnumbered warriors two to one. After warriors came peasants, followed by *sake* brewers, doctors, priests, literati, weavers, booksellers, pawnbrokers, and hostlers.

An example of a cultural community centered on Kyoto is the Yabunouchi school of tea as it existed from the Kasei period to the end of the Edo period. Most disciples resided in Kyoto; but many students made their homes in Echigo, the Kinki area, the San'in area,

Table 6.1. Number of Pupils of Rokujuen and Magao

PROVINCE	ROKUJUEN (1811)	MAGAO (1828)
Mutsu	43	52
Dewa		27
Edo	206	73
Hitachi	5	17
Kōzuke	81	2
Shimotsuke	27	14
Musashi	19	9
Kazusa	5	12
Shimōsa	21	6
Sagami		1
Kai	13	
Shinano	1	27
Echigo	1	16
Suruga	5	1
Tōtōmi	3	
Mikawa	1	1
Owari	28	3
Mino	30	2
Kaga		1
Ise	4	9
Ōmi		3
Kyoto	2	2
Osaka	12	
Izumi	1	
Settsu	6	
Harima	5	
Aki		1
Awa (Shikoku)	1	
Total	520	279

and the Inland Sea area in Shikoku and Kyūshū.[3] By far the most pupils were *chōnin;* far behind them trailed Buddhist priests.

An example of a group whose center shifted to Nagoya after earlier activity in Kyoto was the Hachiya family of the Shino school of incense discrimination. A list of students of the Hachiya family shows that few disciples lived in the Kantō area; unlike the Yabunouchi school, members were distributed fairly evenly throughout the country.[4]

The provincial cultured population grew rapidly during the Kasei period. This growth was the result of several factors: an increase in the cultivation of cash crops; the attendant rise in commodity production; and the development of means of commodity circulation and routes of transport. *Chōnin* and peasants who took part in cultural pursuits were usually members of an affluent upper stratum. Many made a fortune from *sake* brewing or by shipping goods purchased from local smallholder peasants to Edo and Kyoto. Such merchants returned to the provinces loaded with various urban wares, which were sold in the countryside. As we shall see again later, however, membership in such cultural groups was not limited to those who had recently become wealthy. The Yabunouchi school, for example, was tightly linked to long-extant, broadly based religious groups associated with the Nishi Honganji, a temple in Kyoto.

An idea of conditions in the countryside can be gained by examining the diffusion of the "national learning" *(kokugaku)* of Motoori Norinaga (1730–1801), Hirata Atsutane (1776–1843), and Tachibana Moribe (1781–1849). In Kiryū (Kōzuke province), a long-established circle of poets was influenced by the "national learning" of Tachibana Moribe. Even after Moribe left for Edo, he remained in close contact with the Kiryū-based group. The leader of the Kiryū group was Yoshida Akinushi, who stemmed from a family of weavers. Akinushi had an income of 30 *koku* of rice and owned over fifty looms. As an employer of nineteen workers he was a powerful local figure. When Tachibana Moribe went to Edo, the Kiryū group paid for his stay; Moribe in turn investigated new trends in Edo fashion and relayed this information to Akinushi, who was able to make use of it in his weaving business.

Somewhat earlier a group of wealthy provincial poets in the Yoshida area of Mikawa province was sufficiently inspired by Motoori Norinaga's writings to join his "Suzunoya" school of national learning. Somewhat later this group then switched to Hirata's school. Such a switch was not at all uncommon. As upper-class members of rural cultural groups sensed a crisis befalling the farm village, Motoori's philosophy was increasingly felt to be an inadequate response to this increasingly urgent problem. Atsutane's learning, by contrast, contained a pragmatic element that was much more appealing. But Atsutane's thought, too, had limits, which were painfully exposed by the case of Ikuta Yorozu (1801–1837). Ikuta had stood in Atsutane's favor; he had even served as the head of the Hirata school. But Ikuta eventually cut his ties to his master and led a peasant uprising in Echigo. He thereby took a stance diametrically opposed to that of Atsutane's provincial followers, who found themselves the victims of such uprisings. The basic difference between Ikuta and Hirata can thus be interpreted as a disagreement over how best to disseminate a form of learning. The limits of provincial cultural development from the Kasei period to the end of the Edo period were thereby exposed: for Ikuta's thought was ineffectual, whereas Hirata's continued along the same lines and greatly expanded its following.[5]

Provincial Culture and Commodity Production

"Commodity production," as I use the term, does not refer only to the kind of production that later turned into modern capitalism. Rather, it is the general phenomenon of production for the market as it occurred throughout Japan during the Edo period.

Commodity production is not easily linked to culture in any fixed manner. Progress in production often requires an introduction of culture from advanced areas. Increased production of raw materials requires not only new types of seeds and fertilizers, but also a knowledge of the latest techniques of cultivation, farm management, and processing. Without such knowlege, major agricultural reforms are doomed to failure. Similarly, progress in the production of manufactured goods requires up-to-date knowledge, modern techniques and facilities, and of course capital.

Culture, in turn, can be stimulated by agricultural production and manufacture. In Japan, production had stimulated interest in botany *(honzōgaku)* and pragmatic learning *(jitsugaku)* since early times. Toward the end of the Edo period, authoritative books devoted to farm management and to cash crop cultivation and processing were published in rapid succession. For example, Ōkura Nagatsune (1768–1860), who wrote prolifically, authored a book entitled *Kōeki kokusan-kō* (Furthering National Production, 1844). Satō Nobuhiro (1769–1850), too, wrote many similar treatises. Unlike such practical culture, rural "high" culture had to await the appearance of an affluent rural social stratum. Let us turn to some

examples of provincial culture and examine the interaction of commodity production and cultural activity.

Suzuki Bokushi (1770–1842), the son of a merchant from
Shiozawa in Echigo province, was renowned as the author of
Hokuetsu seppu (Album of Echigo Snow, published in 1835–1836)
and as a highly cultured individual. Bokushi was a prosperous *chōnin*
who associated with a number of literati and artists of his day.
Bokushi's father Bokusui (Kōemon) had made a fortune dealing in
the valuable ramie textile known as Echigo *chijimi*. Production of this
cloth peaked between the 1750s and the 1780s. In the 1780s annual
output reached a volume of 200,000 *tan* (1 *tan* = about 30 feet). This
textile thereby outpaced the earlier market leader, a bleached bast-
fiber cloth from Nara (Nara *zarashi*). Official marketplaces were
established in Ojiya, Tōkamachi, and Horinouchi (Echigo province)
to serve as centers for collecting and marketing Echigo *chijimi*.
Bokusui was associated with the latter two markets. From the end of
the third month, these three official markets opened for fifty-seven
days each. The Horinouchi market came first, followed by the Ojiya
and Tōkamachi markets. These markets were visited by merchants
from Edo, Osaka, Kyoto, Nagoya, and elsewhere. On such occasions,

Preparing a stage for theater in the snow (Echigo province). From *Hokuetsu
seppu,* 1835–1836. (In the possession of the Tokyo Metropolitan Central
Library.)

considerable cultural exchange took place between provincial and urban areas.

Strong ties were gradually forged with Edo.[6] The Ojiya Nishiwaki house, for example, operated a store on the third block of Motoginchō in Edo. Peasants who resided on level terrain constituted a good part of the labor force that went to Edo for part-time work during the agricultural slack season. As the local economy boomed, even inhabitants of remote mountainous regions around Shiozawa began to take part in *chijimi* production. To circumvent the limitations of the three official markets, modes of collection and delivery were devised by freight-collection associations. Transactions could thus be undertaken with Edo directly. Within such a context Bokusui became a wealthy merchant. In fact, he had already given up working as a *chijimi* merchant and had become a pawnbroker before activity in Shiozawa peaked. This allowed him to extend the scope of his financial transactions even further.

From an early age Bokusui's son, Bokushi, devoted himself to painting, calligraphy, prose, *haikai*, and Chinese poetry. In his twenties Bokushi worked for the family business as a *chijimi* merchant. This occupation required him to make frequent trips to Edo. With Bokusui's death in 1807, Bokushi took charge of the house, all the while vigorously continuing his cultural activities. Indeed, Bokushi wrote over a dozen works, including travel diaries, surveys, and research reports. The geographical range of his activities can be witnessed in the *Harimaze byōbu kokusho shōmei-chō* (Register of Authors and Places from a Screen of Miscellanies, 1822). The original poems from this collection, gathered since Bokusui's days, were written on narrow colored strips of paper and pasted onto a screen. A total of 221 poets were included: 55 from Echigo and 166 others from Edo, Osaka, Kyoto, and twenty-four other provinces. Edo is represented by such writers and artists as Santō Kyōden, Santō Kyōzan (1769–1858), Santō Kyōsui (1816–1867), Takizawa Bakin, Jippensha Ikku, Ōta Nanpo, Yadoya no Meshimori, Ōshima Ryōta (1718–1787), Natsume Seibi (1749–1816), Suzuki Fuyō (1749–1816), Tani Bunchō (1763–1840), Katsushika Hokusai, and Utagawa Toyokuni; the Confucian scholars Sawada Tōkō (1732–1796) and Kameda Hōsai; the author of Chinese poetry Ōkubo Shibutsu (1767–1837); the actors Ichikawa Danjūrō and Iwai Hanshirō; and the courtesan Hanaōgi.[7] Many of these luminaries had traveled to Echigo and called upon Bokushi in Shiozawa. Even the priest Ryōkan supposedly wrote a tribute praising Bokushi's artwork.[8]

In 1801 Bokushi and the wealthy trade agent Inoue Mokei sponsored the production and publication of the *Jippyō hokku-shū* (Collection of Verses Judged by Ten Critics), a collection of short poems offered to the god Tamonten in Urasa (Echigo). The verses of this anthology were gleaned from a huge number of examples collected throughout the *chijimi* sales district. Ten master poets, from Edo, Kyoto, Osaka, Uji-Yamada (near Kyoto), Ōmi, and Sanuki, judged the poems submitted.[9] Poems sent to the small provincial town of Shiozawa were thus judged by accomplished poets from the "three capitals" and other areas. This anthology and the "screen of miscellanies" indicates that at the start of the nineteenth century, Shiozawa culture was held in high regard by both urban and rural inhabitants of Japan.[10]

Other provincial cultural communities of the Kasei period were stimulated by the rise of the silk industry. Large quantities of silk textiles were produced in Kōzuke province, the Chichibu area of Musashi, and the Ueda region of Shinano. The manufacture of indigo was yet another form of commodity production occurring in rural areas. Indigo from the province of Awa on the island of Shikoku was particularly valuable. Awa indigo had been manufactured as a commodity since early times—and from the 1770s until the first decades of the nineteenth century, production increased tremendously. A good example of a family involved in indigo production was the Shima house of Higashi Kakuen village in Myōzai county of Awa. This was a family of farmers that had begun producing indigo in the 1770s. By the turn of the century the Shima house had expanded its sales network to Owari, Ise, and eleven other provinces. In 1806 it acquired the rights of direct sales to the five Kinai provinces. Business then expanded from the Kyoto, Suō, and Nagato area to Kaga, Noto, Echizen, Etchū, Echigo, and Sado. In 1824 a branch store was opened in Matsumoto (Shinano); in 1825 yet another shop began operations in Takada (Echigo), followed in 1826 by still another in Yonezawa (Dewa). Besides selling Awa indigo, these outlets also engaged in dyeing. In 1827 the Shima house succeeded in obtaining a market monopoly from the Akita domain; subsequently its sales net spread still further to cover the Aizu-Wakamatsu, Sendai, Shōnai, Honjō, Yamagata, and other areas.[11]

This type of growth was accompanied by the appearance of a wealthy stratum of indigo dealers, fertilizer merchants, and transporters. Such people tended to show more allegiance to Kyoto culture than to the culture of Edo. The popularity of Kyoto-based leisure pursuits, for example, allowed the Omote Senke school to find many adherents among the Awa area merchant class during the latter half of the eighteenth century. The Omote Senke school had a skilled and powerful backer in Amō Yūshōan from the Awa village of Muya. Amō had made his fortune by shipping herring (used as fertilizer) from Hokkaidō. His influence contributed greatly to the spread of the Omote Senke school in this region.

Traffic, Transportation, and Cultural Diffusion

As commodity production increased during the middle of the Edo period, remarkable progress was made in modes of transportation. This advance contributed much to the development of provincial culture. Sea or river routes and horse trails had of course existed for centuries. From the mid-Edo period, however, the shipment of large quantities of rice, oil, *sake,* soy sauce, and other goods stimulated much expansion and improvement of the transport network. Large merchant houses, themselves the main agents of this change, reaped sizable profits from the shipping business. Amō Yūshōan, the shipper just cited, was from one such family; yet another was the Ōhashi house of Takaoka in Etchū.

The Ōhashi house, which called itself the "Washizuka-ya," was a family of affluent merchants that for generations had served as the Takaoka town elders. The family had made its fortune by transporting goods on the Oyabe River between Fushiki and Takaoka in Etchū province. Ships of the "Washizuka-ya" accounted for some 70 percent of the hundred or so commercial vessels that traversed these waters. In 1808 the Ōhashi house's eighth Hachizaemon began to study the tea ceremony of the Yabunouchi school. By 1816 he was a certified master of the tradition, allowing him to become a regional tea master. With his many students, over one hundred, Hachizaemon organized a cultural community that included members throughout the Hokuriku area. He also maintained close contact with the Yabunouchi school in Kyoto.

Such a phenomenon was typical of Kasei-period provincial culture. Contemporary rural culture owed much to the spread of fashionable trends from the urban centers of Kyoto and Edo. Regional culture tended to pattern itself on authoritative forms from such urban centers. Echigo, Kōzuke, or Shinano textile manufacturers, for example, used traditional Kyoto techniques for weaving and dyeing. Close ties to Kyoto were forged when large amounts of capital from this city flowed into the countryside. From around this time even the *Gion-bayashi*—the music and dance of the Gion Festival of Kyoto—began to be performed at Horinouchi (Echigo), one of the "three markets" of Echigo *chijimi* cited earlier. Close links between the provinces and Kyoto allowed the *Gion-bayashi* to diffuse widely. Eventually this musical genre spread as far as the northernmost areas of Honshū.

Another example of music diffusing along transportation routes is the "Safflower Picking Song" from the province of Dewa. At the very end of the Edo period, a horseload of dyer's saffron from this area cost over one hundred gold pieces *(ryō)*. Impressive profits stood to be made, and safflower, a specialty of the Mogami area of Dewa province, was soon produced in large quantities and transported overland to Ōishida (Dewa). From there it was usually shipped by way of Sakata (Dewa) and Tsuruga (Wakasa) to Kyoto.[12] A "Safflower Picking Song" from the town of Higashine in eastern Murayama county (today Yamagata prefecture) describes a typical scene between Ōishida and Sakata: "I too want to go to the capital, on a black horse, with the safflower." Songs like these were often diffused along such routes. Even today, "Itako bushi," a type of song that was briefly popular in Edo around the Kasei period, can be heard in Ojiya and Takada and in Toyama city. Although "Itako bushi" became extinct in the capital, it survived in the Niigata-Toyama area because it was incorporated into the music accompanying a local festival. Similarly, "Ōtsu-e bushi," another fashionable Edo song, was diffused to Ojiya during the early years of the Kasei period. Such transmission was not, of course, one way. Many rural songs were transmitted to Kyoto along the same routes that brought urban culture to the Mogami area.

Traveling sales agents also played a major role in cultural diffusion. Numerous luxury items made their way into the countryside through the efforts of such vendors, who often transmitted artistic techniques as well. One such vendor was Shirakami Kisaemon Sōgo, an Osaka man originally from the town of Tamashima in Bitchū province. Shirakami became a member of the Yabunouchi school of tea in 1811; by 1819 he had earned a license of high rank. Thereafter he encouraged *chōnin* who lived on his business circuit—in Akashi, Akō, Nishiwaki, Miki, Tamashima, Kurashiki, Osaka, Sakai, Hirano, Ise, Uji, and Yamada—to join this school. Sōgo succeeded in recruiting many students. He was no mere itinerant hawker, but rather a merchant of luxury items, perhaps even tea-ceremony utensils. While making his rounds, he instructed people in the tea ceremony and recruited them as official members of his school. Sōgo's case was by no means an exception: a broad variety of artistic pursuits were diffused in this manner.

Cultural exchange and diffusion did not, of course, rely solely on merchants. Cultured individuals from urban centers made frequent sojourns to remote areas and stimulated the development of provincial culture. Moreover, a number of cheap publications found their way into the countryside. Warriors, too, transmitted culture, for the system of alternate attendance required them to move regularly between Edo and their home provinces. Itinerant performers including blind female musicians *(goze)* also contributed to cultural diffusion, as did people who moved between Edo and the provinces for lawsuits or political negotiations. The provincial gentry and their children came to Edo or Kyoto to become proficient at leisure pursuits; other rural inhabitants went to the city to receive training from an *iemoto* or scholar. All these activities increased the flow of culture from the center to the provinces.

Simultaneously, a specifically provincial culture began to arise, if only on a small scale. Suzuki Bokushi's *Hokuetsu seppu,* noted earlier, and the voluminous travel records of Sugae Masumi (1754?–1829) count as outstanding examples of such culture.[13] The former work, a record of conditions in the "snow country" of Echigo, provides descriptions of theatricals in the snow or the locations and methods used for *chijimi* cloth bleaching.[14] Bokushi even includes many realistic illustrations of contemporary local scenes. Masumi's chronicles cover a still broader geographical range and include

Bleaching *chijimi* cloth in the snow. From *Hokuetsu seppu,* 1835–1836. (In the possession of the Tokyo Metropolitan Central Library.)

descriptions of legends, customs, and scenery of much of northeastern Japan, especially Akita and Shinano. Masumi too includes his own illustrations.

During the nineteenth century, people from the provinces increasingly traveled to other rural areas, thereby prompting further cultural diffusion. In 1816, for example, four members of Bokushi's family took a long journey to Kashiwasaki and Takada (Echigo), the Kōzenji temple in Shinano, Kiso (Shinano), Ise, Wakaura (Kii), the Hyōgo area, the Shikoku Konpira Shrine, Osaka, Yamato, and Kyoto. A member of this party fell sick en route, further lengthening this trip, which lasted some 125 days.[15] Sightseeing proceeded at a leisurely pace; each location was visited for several days. Much new information and many new experiences must have been gained from such an expedition. Similar trips were quite commonly undertaken by rural inhabitants. The popularity of travel led to the publication of the *Miyako meisho zue* (Illustrations of Famous Sites in Kyoto, published in 1780) and more than ten other guides to various cities. Other manuals featured famous sites in the provinces. Examples include the *Saigoku sanjūsan-sho meisho zue* (Illustrations of Thirty-Three Famous Sites in the West-

Merchants at one of the designated inns of the Azuma Association. From the *Azuma-kō akindo kagami* (Mirror of Merchants of the Azuma Association), early 1850s. (In the possession of the Tokyo Metropolitan Central Library.)

ern Provinces, published in 1853); the *Nijūyohai junpai zue* (Illustrations of the Tour of Sites Associated with the Twenty-Four Disciples [of Shinran], published in 1803–1809); and the *Konpira sankei meisho zue* (Illustrations of Famous Sites on the Konpira Pilgrimage Route, published in 1846). Convenient one-page travel guides that could be carried along on trips include the *Nengyoku dōchū-ki* (A New Year's Present of Things on the Road) and the *Shokoku anken dōchū hitori annai-zu* (Illustrated Guide to Sights on the Road Throughout Japan).

In 1804 the Naniwa-kō, an Osaka association of hostlers, introduced a remarkably modern system by which travelers paid for inns by using coupons. Somewhat later a similar organization, the Azuma-kō, was established in Edo. From the Kaei period (1848–1854) this latter association published the *Azuma-kō akindo kagami*[16] (A Mirror of Merchants of the Azuma Association) and its supplement, the *Gokaidōchū saiken-ki*[17] (A Detailed Record of Things on the Five Highways, published in 1853). These were accurate commercial directories as well as superb travel guides, published in cooperation with book dealers from major Japanese cities and sold throughout the land. As travelers everywhere sought to purchase such handbooks, demand increased and their quality improved.

Finally, let us turn to the question of whether provincial culture exerted any significant influence on the center. Cultured men from Edo such as the writer Jippensha Ikku traveled constantly, visiting distant northern regions, Shikoku, and Kyūshū. On his trips Ikku hoped to find a type of robust individual that he could portray in his fiction. Ikku was also on the lookout for anything unusual—for the kind of variety that could not be found in the city. Although the provinces held this type of attraction to urbanites, the direct links maintained by provincial culture to material production allowed little new to develop there. Instead, one usually finds only the passive reception of culture transmitted from the center; or else one finds traditional folk customs that were merely recorded and categorized. In general, provincial culture's influence on the culture of the center was minimal.

An exception to this rule was folk song and dance. These genres were directly coupled to local conditions and modes of production, of course, but they exhibited a healthy development that could help revitalize the culture of the center. Examples of popular songs that originated in the provinces include "Itako bushi," noted earlier, and "Ōtsu-e bushi." The folk song "Niigata jinku" was incorporated into the *kiyomoto* piece *Komori* (The Babysitter).[18] Yet another Niigata folk song, "Shibata goman-goku" (Fifty Thousand Bales of Shibata Rice), was absorbed into the *tokiwazu* piece known as *Kakubee* (Children's Acrobat Troupe).[19] The song "Ise ondo," which had spread to all areas of the land, reappeared in the *kiyomoto* piece entitled *Kisen* (The Priest Kisen) and in the *katō bushi* piece *Sumiyoshi odori* (Sumiyoshi Dance).[20] Such folk songs infused a fresh style into contemporary "art music."

Folk songs were sometimes transmitted over shipping routes to distant harbors. For example, the song "Haiya bushi" of the Kagoshima and Nagasaki area of Kyūshū was transmitted along the "western shipping route" of the Sea of Japan. In Niigata this song subsequently became "Sado okesa." On the "eastern shipping route" the song "Haiya bushi" was brought to Tsugaru and Nanbu in the distant northeast, where it became "Aiya bushi"; a little further south it became "Shiogama jinku."[21]

A similar process can be found at work in *oiwake,* a highly melismatic type of song with no fixed meter. Research has shown that this song originated in the village of Oiwake in Nagano prefecture, from where it was brought to Niigata and then by ship to Matsumae in Hokkaidō. In the process, what was once a Nagano pack-horse driver's song eventually became a boat song. Here too shipping routes transmitted outstanding folk songs to remote harbor towns.

Akita Aiya Bushi

"Haiya bushi" as sung in two areas of northern Japan. "Akita Aiya Bushi" (Kanō Shodai). Recorded in 1941 in Konoura-chō, Yuri county, Akita prefecture. Actual pitch: tritone lower.

The Role of Extant Cultural Communities

Although sacred folk performing arts that function as religious celebrations or prayers tend to resist change when exposed to "high culture," songs and dances of a more entertaining, artistic, and
liberating sort often change historically and are susceptible to outside influence.[22] These latter genres developed remarkably during
the Kasei period: popular songs and the *Gion-bayashi* were incorporated into extant genres; floats and Shinto palanquins *(mikoshi)* were
introduced into festivals; and new *bon* dances were choreographed.
These arts did not, however, replace the fixed annual rites that took
place in traditional village society; instead, they were simply added.
Old cultural communities were usually not supplanted or significantly altered by the new.

Extant cultural communities continued to play an important
role in the provinces. When culture from urban centers was transmitted to rural areas, an established circle of poets might act as a
base for its reception. Or, as in the case of the Yabunouchi school of
tea, religious organizations could help spread cultural forms. As
noted earlier, the Yabunouchi school of the Hokuriku area centered
on Ōhashi Tōsai from Takaoka. The school also flourished in the
cities of the San'yō area along the coast of the Inland Sea, especially
in Akō, Okayama, Kurashiki, Matsuyama, Tamashima, Kasaoka,
Onomichi, Mihara, Hiroshima, and the farming and fishing villages
surrounding these cities. The school's surge in popularity was no
doubt linked to the simultaneous rise in prosperity of the landowning class in farm villages of the San'yō area.[23] Yet there was another
factor as well: the Nishi Honganji, a major Kyoto temple, found
many supporters in both the San'yō and the Hokuriku regions.
Groups associated with this temple formed cultural communities
that played an important role in the spread of the Yabunouchi
school's tea ceremony.

The Sekijima house of Kawaji village in Ina county of Shinano
province provides a good example of how a provincial family was
inserted into an extant Edo cultural community. From the Kasei
period to the end of the Edo period, this house had distinguished
itself as a family of cultured local landowners. For three generations
the heads of the Sekijima house had been doctors. While studying
medicine in Edo, Kyoto, and Nagoya, these men became proficient
in Chinese and Japanese poetry, the tea ceremony, and flower
arranging. The family rated 30 *koku* of official rice and had in its
storeroom one hundred more bales received from tenant farmers.
With a gross annual income of around 150 *ryō* and expenditures

totaling some 120 or 130 *ryō*, the Sekijima ranked among the rural elite both financially and intellectually. Relatives were connected to Gotō San'emon of the Edo gold mint and served as instructors of Chinese classics to the Ogasawara house. Traveling merchants from Nagoya and Kyoto stayed at the Sekijima residence before going to landowning neighbors. From such merchants the family purchased gifts including a glass *sake* pourer costing 1.5 *ryō*, ten *nishiki-e*, Chinese ink from Nagasaki, and fancy high-priced warrior dolls for the Boy's Festival. The family participated in leisure pursuits with other wealthy neighboring houses and even received invitations to banquets held by the Ogasawara house.[24]

The cultural activities of the Sekijima family were made possible by a general rise in village prosperity and the development of the packhorse transport system. The most important factor, however, was the Sekijimas' insertion into existing cultural communities: those associated with the Ogasawara house, the Gotō house of Edo, and warrior-class society in general.

Conclusion

Much more remains to be said about provincial culture during the Kasei period. The cultural level of everyday life—food, clothing, and housing—rose significantly. Even commoners now obtained a family crest; individual grave markers also came into use. Educating one's children became ever more prevalent and "temple schools" proliferated. Annual rituals, marriages, funerals, and the like were increasingly patterned on aristocratic practices from urban centers. To conclude, I should like to reiterate the following six points.

First, the Kasei period was one of peace; no major natural calamities took place. Throughout Japan, cash crops were cultivated and commodities produced. With the improvement of transportation routes, commodities were distributed to all areas of the country.

Second, such conditions allowed provincial culture to flourish. This rise was not limited to small, isolated cultural communities; rather, it took place on a national scale.

Third, while rural towns and villages experienced a rise in the general level of culture, "high culture" in the provinces relied largely on diffusion from the centers (Edo and Kyoto). Provincial culture usually followed the lead of such central locations.

Fourth, "temple schools" *(terakoya)* and village schools operated in rural areas but, in accordance with the official status of the peasant, only the most basic skills were taught. Original, creative thought was not encouraged.

Fifth, provincial cultural communities were without exception staffed by members of the affluent *chōnin* stratum or the landowning class. Although economic activity showed considerable vigor, cultural communities with truly original ideas were rare.

And sixth, folk song and folk performing arts, which remained closely tied to rural life, displayed striking development during this age. Some of these genres even succeeded in revitalizing the musical culture of the center.

CHAPTER 7

ITINERANTS, ACTORS, PILGRIMS

Itinerants

Performers Throughout the Land

During the Edo period over one hundred types of traditional performing artists were active in Japan. Despite their great variety, however, such individuals never constituted more than a small segment of the population. Itinerant performers often settled down in ghettos or flophouses, from which they toured throughout the land for a certain period each year. Tours might take only a month, or they might last for as long as an entire year.

Performers were each associated with a distinctive form of a traditional art. As we shall see in greater detail, some performers, known as *yakuharai, sekizoro, kamabarai,* and *sutasuta bōzu,* performed various forms of exorcism; others, such as the teams known as *manzai,* performed comic dialogues; an even larger variety of performers—*daikagura,* Ebisu and Daikoku dancers, *maimai, kotobure, harugoma, torioi*—presented felicitous music, dancing, or recitation.

Originally almost all performers of such auspicious arts were tied to Shinto or folk religious institutions. Such ancient bonds gradually loosened and gave way to performances in front of doorsteps. For this service itinerant performers received a small donation from the inhabitants. Door-to-door performers were usually received cordially by villagers, for many performances were considered sacred. But the time of year during which villagers welcomed itinerant performers was limited; it centered, in general, on New Year's. For during the summer and fall, villagers themselves sang and danced to celebrate the *bon* festival and the harvest; at such times the arts of itinerant performers were considered superfluous.

The rural population maintained sharp distinctions between arts performed by itinerants and their own dances and performances. In the city, however, the communal bonds associated with rural culture gradually broke down. Differences between the arts began to be blurred and meanings confused. During the Edo period, many sacred performances of itinerants already underwent marked transformation from what they had been during the medieval era. Nevertheless, the lives of villagers and townspeople continued to be greatly enriched by the traditions of traveling performers. The populace always took great pleasure at the arrival of itinerant artists.

Exorcisers

Sekizoro, itinerant exorcisers, usually appeared from about the middle of the twelfth month of the lunar calendar. During medieval times they wore red masks and entered the houses of villagers to perform a dance for exorcising demons. By the Edo period, however, *sekizoro* often wore paper hoods and white paper aprons with a design of the auspicious "pine, bamboo, and plum." They accompanied themselves on *shamisen,* drums, and scrapers. While making their rounds they cried out: "We are *sekizoro*—hey! The lucky *sekizoro!*" This art was originally considered a sacred procession for driving out evil spirits and blessing bystanders with good luck in the coming year.

All year-end itinerant performers to some extent functioned as exorcisers, but exorcism was the sole purpose of the *yakuharai.* While walking about, they shouted: "Out with evil spirits! Evil spirits fall away! Evil spirits fall away!" *Yakuharai* appear in the "Scene on the Bank of the Sumida River" of Kawatake Mokuami's kabuki play *Sannin Kichiza kuruwa no hatsugai.* Ojō Kichiza, disguised as a beautiful young lady, robs the streetwalker Otose of 100 *ryō* and kicks her body into the river. Then, in a series of famous lines, he declaims:

> The moon is covered with clouds on this spring eve; dim are the lights from the fishing boats. A cold wind blows, but it feels warm to a tipsy man. I amble along the riverbank, a solitary crow making its way home by moonlight. Water from the spray of the oars wets my hands. But something else has also splashed into my hands: 100 *ryō!*
>
> [One hears the sound of *yakuharai* making their rounds: "Out with evil spirits! Evil spirits fall away! Evil spirits fall away!" Ojō Kichiza then utters the following lines.]
>
> Tonight must be the eve before the start of spring. The *yakuharai* toss evil into the Western Sea; I've thrown it into the river. That whore dropping into the stream was but an evil spirit falling away. And how much better my bundle of money than the lucky beans and

Yakuharai and a performer of *saimon*. From *Jinrin kinmōzui*, 1690.

one-*mon* coins of the *yakuharai!* Ah yes, it's spring—what an auspicious sign![1]

Mokuami here offers a glimpse of an age when performers who sent off the old year and ushered in the new were still part of the everyday lives of townspeople and villagers.

Kamabarai ("hearth exorcisers") and *sutasuta bōzu* ("shuffling priests") also practiced various kinds of exorcism. The activities of the *sutasuta bōzu* seem to have originated from practices in which merchants rid themselves of the sins that had accumulated during the year from cheating in business transactions. *Sutasuta bōzu* carried a fan and a priest's staff. They tied a rope sweatband around their heads and fastened a straw skirtlike coat around their waists with a sacred rope *(shimenawa)*. While wandering about begging they cried out:

> *Sutasuta sutasuta*
> Here come the *sutasuta bōzu!*
> Around their waists they tie a rope,
>   from which hang nine times seven sacred strands;
> Around their heads they tightly tie a band.[2]

Such performers originally toured rural villages. Later they converged in cities, where they could be seen until the end of the Edo period.

New Year Harbingers of Good Luck

After the old year's demons were exorcised, it was time for the lucky gods to be ushered in. At fishing villages along the ocean these spirits were thought to come from beyond the sea; in farm towns and villages they were believed to arrive from the distant countryside; in mountain villages lucky gods were said to come from the other side of the mountain.

New Year's performances of auspicious and sacred arts brought with them guarantees of good luck and a bountiful harvest. Farming or fishing villages boasted no special facilities or accommodations for such visitors, but the houses at which itinerant artists spent the night generally remained the same year after year. Many performers were officially controlled. In the Kantō area, for example, performers were often placed under the jurisdiction of Danzaemon (the head of outcastes) or the "master of sacred dance" Tamura Hachidayū.

Villagers in remote corners of the countryside greatly looked forward to visits by touring performers. When, for example, dancers of the lucky Ebisu and Daikoku dances (named after two auspicious gods) arrived at an isolated, snowbound village, the inhabitants were sure to rejoice at this symbol of the arrival of spring. But the performers were welcomed for yet another reason: they were cosmopolitan, cultured individuals. They had circulated in faraway places and had a broad knowledge of the world.

Of all the auspicious performing arts, *kotobure*, *manzai*, and *daikagura* exhibited perhaps the most unique development. Kashima diviners *(Kashima no kotobure)* roamed the country announcing the oracle of the deity enshrined at the Kashima Shrine (Hitachi). These performers traveled farther than most itinerants. In the fourth chapter ("The Fellow Who Left the Mailbag Behind at an Inn") of the first story ("The Story of Seijurō in Himeji") of Ihara Saikaku's *Kōshoku gonin onna* (*Five Women Who Loved Love*, published in 1686), a passage describes travelers who are waiting for a ferryboat at Shikama Harbor in the province of Harima:

> There were some pilgrims bound for the Great Shrine at Ise, a hardware merchant from Osaka, a dealer in lacquer from Nara, a Bud-

Kashima diviner. From *Morisada mankō,* 1830s–1860s.

dhist priest from the monastery at Daigo, a tea-set seller from
Takayama, a mosquito-net peddler from Tanba, a clothing merchant
from Kyoto, and a diviner from the shrine at Kashima. What makes
travel on a ferry so interesting is the fact that all the passengers come
from different places.[3]

At the start of the Edo period, Kashima diviners were evidently active
in the Himeji area, riding ferryboats with other travelers.

A performance of Kashima diviners in Kyūshū is vividly described in the fourth act of Chikamatsu Monzaemon's *Yōmei tennō shokunin kagami* (The Mirror of Craftsmen of the Emperor Yōmei, first performed in 1705). Chikamatsu's plot runs as follows. The Shinto priest Ikoma has disguised himself as Katsufune, the regent and judicial chief of the Imperial Prince Kajin (later to become Emperor Yōmei). Ikoma goes to Katsufune's province of Bungo (in Kyūshū), where he settles down at the house of a wealthy man named Mano. Ikoma professes to have come to woo Mano's daughter Tamayo. At exactly the same time, however, the real Katsufune, who is concerned about the well-being of Prince Kajin, secretly goes to Kyūshū. He hears of Ikoma's evil plot and hurries to Bungo province. To gain entry to Mano's residence he disguises himself as a Kashima diviner and delivers an "oracle" supposedly from the Kashima Shrine. He predicts that disaster is about to befall the house. This ruse succeeds: the wealthy Mano is alerted, Ikoma's stratagem is unveiled, and the perpetrator is driven away.

Chikamatsu's Kashima diviner is modeled on contemporary performers who traveled as far as Kyūshū. The description of this diviner's appearance and performance is instructive. Katsufune, who has secretly watched Ikoma being wined and dined in grand style at the home of the wealthy Mano, takes out a small pocket mirror and fastens it to his cane. He shreds a handkerchief and attaches these "sacred" strips to the end of the cane. Next he empties a tobacco pouch and folds it to give it the appearance of a formal lacquered hat. In this disguise he enters Mano's premises and delivers his "oracle." Although this speech is of some length, it deserves to be quoted in full:

> I beg the indulgence of all ye assembled: I bring thee an oracle delivered by the gods enshrined at Kashima and Kandori. Not one phrase, not one word, I utter is false. I have prophesied while passing throughout the land; I can give expression to the silences, fill in the gaps.
>
> At the Kashima Shrine dwell ninety-nine priests: thirty-three priests of high rank, thirty-three priests of middle rank, and thirty-three priests of a low rank. On the seventh day of the new year, all priests solemnly sign before the god a promise of grave import. They forswear the telling of all untruths. They forswear the coveting of all worldly things. They forswear the taking of any possession not given to them. In turn, they solemnly pledge not to refuse offerings, no matter how trifling. Thus no falsehood is told as they travel through the sixty-six provinces of the land.

This year a great luminous body burst forth at the Kashima Shrine and disappeared in the direction of Tsukushi (Kyūshū). The doors before the venerable god flew open; the white sand before the god parted; the sacred horse stamped the ground with its four hoofs and broke into a profuse sweat. The priests, high and low, were in an uproar. They fed the horse twenty-one bushels of beans; they beat the *kagura* drum; they offered hot water and partook in a seven-day abstinence at seven shrines.

Out of compassion for parishioners of the holy Kashima divinity, permit me to deliver its revelation: This year is a *kinoto* year of the cock. Since the springtime, the parishioners of the Kashima Shrine have fared well, like a thousand cocks roosting on their branches. All is well in the world, but for one thing of grave concern: ye with daughters, beware! Savage spirits and demons have appeared; they gather strength! On occasion they deceive by masquerading as hand-some young men; or they disguise themselves as high-ranking nobles, regents, or messengers. They may promise, by monstrous deception, to turn thy daughter into a noble dame or princess. Beguiled by such treachery, parents are robbed of their daughters and possessions by these evil barbarous demons. Ah, how cruel!

Thus reveals the oracle, which without fail speaks the simple, candid truth. Thus resounds the adamantine judgment of the myr-iad gods and spirits. To the supreme Shinto gods and spirits I offer this as a prayer![4]

Kashima diviners always began their litany with the words "I beg the indulgence of all ye assembled" before proceeding to an impro-vised, plausible-sounding oracle appropriately contrived to suit the occasion. Such oracles were the diviners' main source of income, and performers were not above offering stinging political criticism reflecting the views of the local populace. An example of such senti-ments can be found in the *Hōei rakusho* (Hōei-Period Scribblings) of 1710.[5] This "Kashima oracle" condemns the avarice and selfishness of town officials and the citizenry, denounces the dog kennels and the bad policies of the "Dog Shogun" (Tokugawa Tsunayoshi [1646–1709]), and lashes out at the devaluation of currency. Similar senti-ments can be found in the plays of Chikamatsu Monzaemon. For example, the plot of his *Sagami nyūdō senbiki no inu* (The Sagami Lay Monk and the Thousand Dogs, first performed in 1714) recounts an incident in which the ferocious dog Shiraishi bites to death Godaii—an allusion to the eccentric priest Ryūkō (1649–1724), who was the motivating force behind Tsunayoshi's issuance of the order forbid-ding the killing of any beast. The spirit of the urban commoner, struggling against governmental oppression, was at this time on the rise; Kashima diviners walked the streets proclaiming oracles that reflected these nascent trends.

The auspicious and often comic dialogues known as *manzai* also had a long history. By the Edo period this art was performed especially in the Yamato and Mikawa areas. *Manzai* performers also resided in Kawachi, Mino, Owari, Iyo, Echizen, Kaga, Aizu, Sendai, and Akita.[6] The outstanding representatives of the art of *manzai* were the *Mikawa manzai* of Bessho (today in Anjō city), a village near Okazaki in Mikawa province. Mikawa was the home area of the Tokugawa family, and Ieyasu quickly seized the opportunity of using these itinerants as spies. The *Mikawa manzai* possessed a dubious license supposedly bestowed on them by Lord Ieyasu. With this license they could claim a special connection to the shogunal house. *Mikawa manzai* also headed the government bureau of the Tsuchimikado family's Mikawa office. By using this position, they obtained passes allowing them to freely cross all barriers throughout the land. *Mikawa manzai* wore a *suō* robe and long, divided *hakama* trousers. Dressed in this costume, these performers of "my lord's *manzai*" *(goten manzai)* toured the domiciles of various daimyo and other high-ranking families. Their performances might even take place in the inner quarters of daimyo residences, an area normally off limits to men. *Mikawa manzai* were always warmly welcomed, for the women of the nobility had little other opportunity to experience the humane worldliness these itinerants represented.

Mikawa manzai worked in pairs. One member was the "master" *(tayū)*, who was outfitted with two swords, a dyed blue cotton *suō* robe with a fivefold hollyhock-pattern crest, long trousers, and a tall *eboshi* hat. His accomplice, the *saizō*, wore a *suō* robe and a folded formal hat *(ori-eboshi)* and carried a drum. While dancing and singing, this team called out: "May everlasting youth and good fortune prevail! May the land remain under prosperous rule!" Then the two might smile at each other in a strange, mysterious manner. Next the *saizō* put on a humorous, auspicious display—racing around the room, lifting up the skirts of good-looking servant girls, or slapping the mistress of the house on the back. This display of feigned lower-class affection caused the inhabitants of such august residences to burst out in inopportune laughter. But such a reaction served only to heighten the mood of vernal good fortune.

In addition to Bessho, *manzai* villages were found in several other locations throughout Mikawa province. The *tayū* from these villages gathered in Edo toward the end of the year. On the last days of the year, a *"saizō* market" was held in the vicinity of Edobashi.

Here *tayū* selected a *saizō* partner with whom they would tour the following spring. *Senryū* verses record that "At Edobashi each hires a clown," or "They come to Edobashi from Mikawa to buy a partner," or "Renting themselves out at the year-end street market, all the *saizō* broaden their smiles."[7] *Manzai* who toured rural villages should not, however, be confused with those who performed in the residences of the aristocracy.

Daikagura performers, who specialized in the "lion dance" *(shishimai)*, were based at the Ise and Atsuta shrines.[8] A *daikagura* group was usually headed by a leader who humorously brandished a sacred Shinto staff with attached strips of paper. This leader wore a robe *(hitatare)*, white skirtlike trousers *(hakama)*, and a mask with a pointed nose. Following the leader were the operators of the lion head and body. Then came bearers of a large chest *(nagamochi)*, then musicians playing flutes, drums, and various percussion instruments. Such performers toured towns and villages with much commotion.

Daikagura received rice and coins from the inhabitants of the houses before which they performed. Occasionally a resident of a grand palatial dwelling might offer only a meager, stingy reward. At such times the performers resorted to speaking a unique *daikagura* jargon incomprehensible to "outsiders." Several hundred words existed, some of which remained in use until quite recently:

mokoi ("good")
gomui ("bad")
fukareru ("to be turned down")
hitotsubo ("1 *shō*," or 1.8 liters)
mochi ("police")
gosha ("5 yen")

Daikagura. From *Jinrin kinmōzui,* 1690.

gendai ("10 yen")
suba ("cooked rice")
sukesa ("*miso* soup")

The custom of using such code words was to some extent shared with other sorts of performers.

Yet another type of performance seen in the springtime was the *kakubee-jishi* of Echigo province. This genre featured children who performed acrobatics. Spectators enjoyed watching such a show, but they also felt a sense of pity at the sight of children set to work touring the land.

Itinerant Priests and Monks

Travelers of a quite different sort included various types of monks: the *Kōya hijiri* ("monks of Mount Kōya"); the *rokujūroku-bu* ("sixty-six areas," also commonly known as *rokubu*, "six areas"); the *shakuhachi*-playing monks called *komosō* (later *komusō*); and the *gannin bōzu* ("petitioned monks"), who claimed to originate from the northern peak of Mount Tiantai (Tendai) in China.

The *Kōya hijiri* of the Edo period evolved from ascetics who concentrated all their religious efforts on chanting an invocation to Amida Buddha. One type of *Kōya hijiri*, known as the Renge-dani monks, came from a line of priests that started with Myōhen (1142–1224); others, such as the Senjuin-dani monks, traced their roots to the tradition of the renowned priests Ippen (1239–1289) and Shinkyō (Ta'a, 1237–1319). These monks often sold a variety of wares while traveling throughout the land.

The *rokubu* of the Edo period deposited copies of the Lotus Sutra at sixty-six designated holy sites. For some participants known as *nakama rokubu* ("*rokubu* associates"), such travels merely served as a pretense for begging. In any case, both male and female *rokubu* were clad in a gray cotton outfit, breeches, leggings, spats, and hand coverings. From the front of their sash they suspended a small gong. While making their way from door to door, *rokubu* shook a short staff with jingle bells *(suzu)*. Many also carried a small portable shrine housing an image of the Buddha. The figure on the next page shows the approximate route of the *rokubu* as they toured the sixty-six holy sites around 1707.[9] For depositing a copy of the Lotus Sutra at each of the designated sixty-six sites, the *rokubu* were awarded a certificate and a small donation of money by temple and shrine officials.

Gannin bōzu were yet another type of monklike itinerant. Toward the end of the Edo period, *gannin bōzu* performed genres such as the

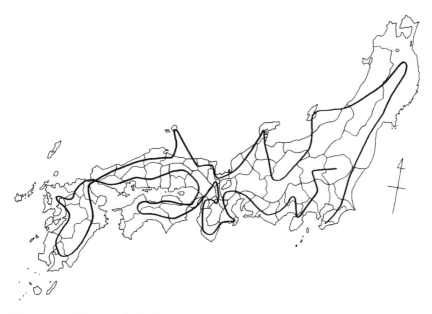

The route of sixty-six holy sites.

Shimotsuke: Takio-san
Kōzuke: Ichinomiya
Musashi: Rokusho
  Myōjin
Sagami: Hachiman
Izu: Mishima
Kai: Shikkaku-san
Suruga: Fuji
Tōtōmi: Kokubunji
Mikawa: Hōraiji
Owari: Ichinomiya
Mino: Ichinomiya
Ōmi: Taga
Iga: Enjuji
Ise: Asamagatake
Shima: Jōanji
Kii: Kumano Hongū
Izumi: Matsuodera
Kawachi: Kami no
  taishi
Yamato: Hasedera
Yamashiro: Kamo-sha
Tanba: Anaōji
Settsu: Tennōji

Awa: Ōgamedera
Tosa: Godai-san
Iyo: Ichinomiya
Sanuki: Shiromine
Awaji: Senkōji
Harima: Shosha-zan
Mimasaka: Ichi-
  nomiya
Bizen: Kibitsu no miya
Bitchū: Kibitsu no
  miya
Bingo: Jōdoji
Aki: Itsukushima
Suō: Niidera
Nagato: Ichinomiya
Chikuzen: Dazaifu
  Tenjin
Chikugo: Kōra Tama-
  dare
Hizen: Chiriku
Higo: Asogū
Satsuma: Shinden
Ōsumi: Hachiman
Hyūga: Hokedake

Bungo: Tawara
Buzen: Usa
Iwami: Hachiman
Izumo: Taisha
Hōki: Daisenji
Oki: Takuhi
Inaba: Ichinomiya
Tajima: Yabu
Tango: Narioi
Wakasa: Ichinomiya
Echizen: Heisenji
Kaga: Haku-san
Noto: Sekidō-san
Etchū: Tateyama
Hida: Kokubunji
Shinano: Kami-Suwa
Echigo: Zaō Gongen
Sado: Kobie-san
Dewa: Yudono-san
Mutsu: Shiogama
Hitachi: Kashima-sha
Shimōsa: Kandori-sha
Kazusa: Ichinomiya
Awa: Kiyosumidera

"*Sumiyoshi* dance" and the comic "*ahodara* sutra." Some worked in pairs: an old and a young man might perform in dialogue. When *gannin bōzu* became beggar-performers they tended not to tour. Instead, they limited their activities to the city of Edo.

The *komusō* of the Edo period maintained the art of playing the *shakuhachi* as transmitted by the Fuke sect of Zen Buddhism. These monks formed an association that functioned as a kind of relief organization for masterless samurai. The way of the *komusō* was an honorable calling. As a member of the warrior class, a *komusō* might theoretically be summoned to rout an enemy. *Komusō* were thus granted freedom to travel anywhere they pleased. They were given the right to use ferries free of charge and even attended the theater without paying admission. *Komusō* often misused their privileges, however, and were known to wreak havoc on the road or in the villages through which they passed. The bakufu responded to such behavior by repeatedly issuing various prohibitions.

Komusō were required to tour either alone or in pairs; no large groups of *komusō* roamed the land during the Edo period. Moreover, *komusō* were not allowed to stay at a location for longer than a day; nor did they have the right to use horses or palanquins. The *komusō* were, however, never required to remove their basketlike hat. No matter how exalted a presence they might encounter on the road or at an inn, they were not obliged to show their faces. Hence both on the road and at inns, *komusō* were highly conspicuous.

Over one hundred *komusō* temples existed throughout Japan. At the end of the Edo period, the Myōanji in Kyoto functioned as a major Kansai-area *komusō* temple. As a result, many Myōan *komusō* appeared. After the fall of the Tokugawa bakufu, however, the Fuke sect was abolished by law. The Myōan school made a comeback during the middle of the Meiji period, reestablishing itself as an important school of *shakuhachi* performers. Thus even today Myōan-school *komusō* can occasionally be seen traveling on foot in the Kyoto vicinity.

Touring Actors

Touring Theater Troupes

From the early Edo period, Japanese cities developed rapidly. Urban centers functioned as a magnet for troupes of performers from throughout the land. Kyoto, Osaka, and Edo were sites of fierce competition, for the winners would obtain the rights to a theater

A duo of *komusō* perform on the *shakuhachi*. From *Jinrin kinmōzui,* 1690.

monopoly. Armed with an official license and housed in a permanent structure, the victors then set about further developing new
theatrical genres. By contrast, theater troupes that failed to secure a
place on the stages of the "three capitals" were condemned to tour
the provinces. Little is known of such troupes during the early Edo
period. Laws restricting or prohibiting their activities, however, attest
to their existence.

After the middle of the Edo period, kabuki theaters of the "three
capitals" changed little; but rural towns and rural culture still developed rapidly. For example, a village might regularly hire traveling
troupes to perform the play *Sugawara denju tenarai kagami* at rain-
making festivals. Such demand fostered the appearance of small-
scale kabuki and puppet theater troupes throughout the land.
Iizuka Tomoichirō and others have shown that throughout western
Honshū, Shikoku, and Kyūshū, certain villages functioned as home
bases for rural theater troupes. My own research also demonstrates
that rural kabuki existed from Hyōgo prefecture all the way to the
Kantō area.

Details of the activities of one rural theater troupe are recorded in the *Wakashima-za ikkan,* a late-eighteenth-century document discovered in Yamaguchi prefecture by Iizuka Tomoichirō. Together with oral transmissions from Harima province and Shikoku this document can aid us in understanding the activities and social context of rural touring theater troupes.

Troupe Organization

During the Edo period, entertainment was subject to strict control. Local small-scale theater troupes negotiated with fief officials to secure monopolies on performance rights and to ban unauthorized performances. Each troupe based itself in a village—a "theater village"—from whence it organized its membership and its tours. In the case of the Wakashima-za, the leader *(zamoto)* Wakashima Umesaburō based his troupe of some thirty actors and accessories in the village of Kawatana in Nagato province. This troupe included a manager *(tōdori),* a leading female impersonator *(tate oyama),* a juvenile male lead *(nimaime),* a juvenile female role *(musume yaku),* a comic role *(sanmaime),* a "central man" *(chūjiku),* a "popular young star" *(kakidashi),* a "lower role" *(shitamawari),* and a child's part *(koyaku).* These members were supplemented by a number of people required for staging a show on the road: two costume specialists; a wig dresser; an actor's assistant *(kōken);* a stage assistant and playwright *(kyōgen kata)* who doubled as a performer of the wooden clappers to mark the drawing of the curtain; three musicians *(hayashi kata),* two of whom played the *shamisen;* and a chanter with his *shamisen* accompanist. The actors of this troupe might also serve as stage assistants; or the temporary playwright might function as a choreographer. In any case, the Wakashima-za was unable to fill all its positions with its own members. When the troupe gave performances in villages in Buzen and Bungo, it was augmented by two or three local people. At other times, actors from the Osaka area were hired.

The troupe's negotiator was responsible for contracting performances. Many types of contracts and performances existed. In drawing up the yearly itinerary, local modes and schedules of production were taken into account; annual local festivities were also considered. With the itinerary set, the troupe then took to the road, traveling from village to village.

Bonten *and Theater Tower Licenses*

Domanial authorities granted the Wakashima-za a special permit, valid even outside the domain. This permit allowed the troupe to erect a theater tower *(yagura)* and display *bonten,* ceremonial poles with ornamental paper ribbons attached to the ends. The Wakashima-za raised such a tower on permanent theater houses and also temporary village playhouses. A curtain emblazoned with the troupe's crest was drawn around the top of this tower; from within this assembly protruded the *bonten.* In addition, the tower was surrounded by some eighty poles with streamers.[10]

Less fortunate theater troupes were allowed to build a tower and display *bonten* only after paying money to the holder of these rights. If this procedure was ignored, a protest was sure to ensue. An itinerant theater troupe had to be constantly on the alert: a lapse in attention could have disastrous consequences. With business as usual, the Wakashima-za toured the Chūgoku area, Shikoku, and Kyūshū, giving "local theater" or "wish-fulfilling" performances at village festivals. Sometimes the troupe even gave command performances for the lord himself.

The Itinerary

Troupes from Harima province visited the Izumo Shrine, Shirosaki, Toyooka, Deishi, Fukuchiyama, Ayabe, Maizuru, Kyoto, Osaka, Hikone, Ishiyama, Ōtsu, Akashi, Kakogawa, Himeji, Tatsuno, Akō, Seidaiji, Okayama, Itosaki, and Omichi. Troupes crossed the Inland Sea to the island of Awaji, and from there they proceeded to various areas in Shikoku, perhaps even including performances at the Kanamaru theater at the Konpira Shrine.

From September until the end of December, the time of the "autumn festivals," rural troupes from Harima were on the road giving "wish-fulfilling" performances in Okayama, Hiroshima, Yamaguchi, and Hyōgo prefectures. From December to February, actors often appeared as extras at major Osaka theaters, where they added new pieces to their repertory. The Wakashima-za apparently expanded its regular cast of actors exclusively with actors from Osaka theaters. From March until the end of spring, troupes from Harima targeted various smaller cities. The Wakashima-za seems to have done the same. During the fourth month of the year 1800, the troupe traveled to Ōmishima in Iyo and to Mitarai in Suō; in the fifth month everyone was back to Iyo, giving performances in Kuwamura. During the sixth month, plays were staged in Miyajima (Aki).

When performances were staged on islands, separate boats were used to transport actors, and props, wigs, and costumes.[11] Foul weather or choppy seas could result in long delays, causing substantial financial losses and much anguish for the local producer. When, for example, the Wakashima-za was on its way home from performances in Hirado (Hizen), a major winter storm ruled out travel by sea. For some fifteen days troupe members idled at the harbor and lamented their miserable fate.[12]

Leaders of Provincial Culture

On occasion, a handful of Wakashima-za actors might be contracted to perform at a remote mountain or fishing village. As is recorded in the volume *Hokuetsu seppu,* members of itinerant theater troupes were sometimes hired to serve as teachers for villagers who wished to stage a charity performance.[13] Traveling theater troupes provided more than mere passive entertainment; they also served as a vehicle for transmitting the latest urban culture to outlying rural areas.

Rural audiences were often extremely naive. Spectators might climb onto the stage and injure actors playing villains such as Sadakurō in *Kanadehon chūshingura* or Iwafuji in *Kagamiyama kokyō no nishiki-e.* Conversely, a handsome actor of young lover roles was lionized by rural girls. Their squeals of delight were sure to accompany him wherever he went.

Events on the Road

While traveling from village to village throughout the land, actors often encountered situations for which they were ill prepared. On the road a troupe might be surprised by a group of hunters pursuing a wild boar; or actors might receive some type of odd reward for their efforts. During a performance in Kawamoto in Iwami province on the eleventh day of the eleventh month of 1764, a giant salmon over six feet long was presented to the Wakashima-za with the explanation that at the moment many such fish were swimming upstream in a river nearby. For a full two days the entire entourage of twenty-five members feasted on this catch, after which everybody seems to have had enough.[14]

The biggest calamity for a troupe was to play to empty houses and lose money. During lean times, troupe members often turned their back on the leader and absconded. Misfortunes never came singly: fires, illness, injuries, and blackmail could turn the troupe into living hell. When, for example, a group of eighteen members from the Wakashima-za went to perform in Ōwasa (Aki), they found themselves in the midst of a measles epidemic. Eight members soon took ill, forcing the remaining ten to play two or three roles at a time.[15] But this was still a relatively minor annoyance. Worse things were in store when the troupe played at Hamanoichi in the province of Bungo. Here the local entrepreneur sponsoring the event was Mizuhara Shin'emon, a sumo wrestler from Hikoichi in Beppu (Bungo), who, unbeknownst to the troupe, was a notorious swindler. This man promptly put the group through a harrowing ordeal.[16]

Fires were yet another scourge. In 1787, at a performance at Yatama in Nagato province, the only articles rescued from a blaze were the *Okina-sama* (the sacred image of the Wakashima-za) and the troupe's genealogical records. All props, costumes, wigs, and everything else went up in smoke.[17]

Command Performances

Although the Wakashima-za was merely an itinerant rural troupe, it possessed an official permit from the Chōshū (Nagato) domanial authorities. The troupe was thus frequently summoned to perform for the lord of the domain. At such times, shows on the road were immediately canceled and the troupe raced back to play at Hagi castle. A request from the lord could never be turned down, even if the troupe was in the midst of contracted prepaid performances.

Official performances were gala events. Ten horses and ten porters were supplied for traveling to and from Kawatana, and all expenses were paid by the lord. When performances took place at more distant locations, twenty horses and up to thirty-five porters were provided. The financial reward for these performances was slight, but it was always paid. Plays staged at Hagi castle included *Ōmi Genji senjin yakata* (The Genji in Ōmi at the Battlefront Lodge),[18] *Seigen Sakura hime* (The Priest Seigen and the Cherry Princess),[19] *Yoshitsune senbon-zakura* (Yoshitsune and the Thousand Cherry Trees),[20] and *Ashiya Dōman ōuchi kagami* (Ashiya Dōman: A Mirror of the Imperial Court).[21] "Local plays" such as *Kasuke mukoiri* (Kasuke Becomes a Son-in-Law) and *Ukare mumakata* (The Libertine Packhorse Driver) were also staged.[22]

Thousand-Ryō Actors on Tour

When fires forced the largest Edo theaters to shut down, the top stars—whose fees in Edo earned them the nickname "thousand-*ryō* actors"—often went on tour. As these tours did not include the Edo theater managers, actors could thus give free rein to their theatrical skills. Programs were arranged in an original manner, and experimental plays were staged. If such plays proved to be a success, they were sure to be produced in Edo somewhat later. Performances of "thousand-*ryō* actors" in provincial towns never failed to cause a great stir. The price of admission varied, but the shows, which were advertised in published playbills, were invariably attended by capacity crowds.

A tour of top-ranking "thousand-*ryō* actors" from the major urban areas was a severe blow to local theater troupes. But since many of the actors in local troupes were students of the big stars, the stars frequently gave benefit performances for rural troupes.

The High Quality of Traveling Theater

Rural theater seems to have maintained a surprisingly high standard. In 1796 the entire Kawatana troupe of thirty members arrived to perform at the Ōnishi theater at Dōtonbori in Osaka. At the time, Osaka theaters boasted a lineup of stars: the chanter Toyotake Echizen no Shōjō (1681–1764) was performing at the Toyotake puppet theater; Arashi Hinasuke (1741–1796) and Ichikawa Danzō IV (1745–1808) were appearing at the Kado and Naka kabuki theaters, respectively. For a small itinerant rural theater troupe such as the Wakashima-za, the situation must have seemed hopeless. Surprisingly, however, the opening performance of the Kawatana troupe was received favorably; successful performances continued until the twenty-ninth day of the third month.[23] During this year the Wakashima-za was entangled with the swindler mentioned earlier, Mizuhara Shin'emon. Although the troupe had come to the Ōnishi theater expecting to perform until the sixth month, Mizuhara's fraudulent schemes were exposed and the show was discontinued during the fourth month. But the troupe soon received offers to perform in Kyoto and Kii province. Here again one sees that even though the Wakashima-za was merely a group of provincial actors, its performances must have been quite good by contemporary standards. Mediocre small-scale troupes (which often staged genres other than kabuki) existed as well, but provincial theater was not necessarily inferior to contemporary urban theater.

Pilgrimages

Since ancient times, the Japanese people have participated in an almost infinite variety of pilgrimages. Pilgrims usually wore a sedge hat, a kimono tucked up behind, leggings, and straw sandals. On their backs they carried a few belongings wrapped in a cloth. Some used a walking stick, others did not. Quite a few went on horseback. Let us examine a few representative examples from the Edo period.

Kumano Pilgrimages

Two of the most popular Edo-period religions were associated with the shrines at Mount Kumano (Wakayama prefecture) and Ise. Priests from these shrines traveled throughout the country, paying visits to village religious groups and acting as intermediaries between local associations and the holy shrines at Kumano and Ise. Conversely, since time immemorial the populace itself had made pilgrimages to Kumano and Ise.

A medieval *enkyoku* (banquet song) entitled "Kumano mōde" (Kumano Pilgrimage) describes such a journey. This song is in five sections, the first four of which end with the intonation, "Holy is the pilgrim's dance for the Heavenly Prince; holy are the tones of the sutra. Ah! The pilgrimage to Kumano, Japan's supreme sacred miracle!" In the fifth section the three Kumano avatars (Sanjo Gongen, that is, the avatars at the Hongū, Shingū, and Nachi shrines) and the sight of the holy mountain of Nachi are expressed in song:

> Ah! What a joyful appearance!
> This indeed is the gate to religious awakening!
> Passing through it removes all impurities.
> Only the pure water of the soul remains,
> Distilled to its depth, cleansed and clarified.
> All sins are absolved before the shrine,
> Quiet is the river of the gods,
> Soundless the flow of the waves . . .[24]

The Kumano religion thrived from ancient times until the middle ages, but declined thereafter. Nuns *(bikuni)* of the three Kumano shrines took to begging throughout the land. In return for donations they transmitted the oracles of the gods, explained pictures of heaven and hell, or distributed so-called Goō amulets to ward off evil spirits. During the Edo period these nuns sang songs and accompanied themselves on clappers *(binzasara)*. They also earned a reputation for prostitution. According to the *Seiritsuen zuihitsu,* Mount Kumano flourished as the headquarters for the *bikuni.*[25] These "singing nuns," whose population numbered in the thousands, could be seen throughout Japan until the mid-Edo period.

Pilgrimages to Mount Kumano continued throughout the Edo period; innumerable pious visitors from Osaka, Kyoto, and elsewhere streamed to this mountain. Pilgrims first hiked around the mountain, visiting its holy sites. After completing this tour they emerged at the town of Tanabe. Here, once again in contact with the outside world, they partook in a special "mountain celebration." At local inns pilgrims eagerly consumed glutinous rice cakes made especially for them.

Ise Pilgrimages

The origin and historical function of the sudden mass pilgrimages known as *okagemairi* and *nukemairi* have been the subject of much scholarly inquiry. Here I would simply like to discuss the conditions and customs of the pilgrimages themselves. Trips to the great shrine at Ise became common during the Edo period. Votive pictures and votive lanterns commemorating visits to Ise can be found throughout Japan. Village heads and officials were confronted with the vexing problems of obtaining permission for such pilgrimages or dealing with abscondences.

When a wife was forced to sleep alone for many months while her husband was visiting Ise, she might well begin to think fondly of her spouse. Superstition had it that if a wife engaged in adultery while her husband was on a pilgrimage to Ise, she would be unable to separate herself physically from her lover. *Senryū* verses from the *Sue tsumu hana* (Safflower Buds, published in 1776–1801) testify to this belief:

> Threatened with "You'll be stuck!"
> she doesn't dare
> while he's away at Ise. [No. 1438, vol. 4]

> "You'll be stuck!"
> he threatens his wife,
> and heads for Ise. [No. 189, vol. 1]

> First he puts it in quickly,
> then checks to see if it comes out—
> while her husband is at Ise. [No. 74, vol. 1]

Adultery accompanied by any form of piety—not simply trips to Ise—supposedly made it impossible to break away from a lover. Umesaburō, the author of the *Wakashima-za ikkan*, records that while traveling to Kyūshū to hire actors, he made a pilgrimage to Mount Hiko.

Here too he found an example of illicit love. A lady-in-waiting from Hizen had gone on a "proxy pilgrimage" and had fallen in love with a young samurai. The two, locked together in their amorous embrace, were put on display at Mount Hiko. Such unfortunate couples could supposedly extricate themselves only after being viewed by one thousand bystanders.[26]

Mass abscondences—in which hundreds of thousands of seemingly possessed individuals suddenly left for trips to Ise—were common during the Edo period. These pilgrimages were quasi-pathological phenomena in which travelers visited brothels on the way, took to pickpocketing, and engaged in wild gambling. Examples of such behavior are even described in kabuki plays. The play *Saruwaka,* for example, a "house play" of the Edo Nakamura-za, contains a plot in which the character Saruwaka talks to a daimyo about buying a whore while on a pilgrimage to Ise. Another example can be found in "The Mustering Scene at the Inase River" of Kawatake Mokuami's play *Shiranami gonin otoko* (The Story of Five Notorious Thieves). Tadanobu Rihei, one of the five hero-bandits, declaims:

> Then comes me, a son of Edo, brought up under the moon of Musashi. I was light-fingered even as a brat and turned criminal while on a pilgrimage. I earned much while wandering through the western provinces, and finally wound up at Mount Yoshino. In the Ōmine Mountains I met with great success. Then I spent some time in Nara. . . .[27]

If secret pilgrimages could provide opportunities for evil deeds, they might also lead to love affairs. In feudal society traveling provided a tremendous sense of liberation. The play *Katsuragawa renri no shigarami* (The Unbreachable Vow at Katsuragawa)[28] contains a plot in which the protagonists Ohan and Chōemon fall desperately in love at an inn at Ishibe, one of the fifty-three stations of the Tōkaidō highway. Their journey is expressed in the famous *kiyomoto* piece known as *Michiyuki shian no hoka* (Unexpected Events on the Road),[29] commonly known as *Ohan.* One section of this work describes a scene on the way to Ise:

> Ah! A wonderful horse, and passengers donning sedge hats made in Edo! They ride in baskets on both sides, their bedding packed behind. "Hey! Mr. Stripes! Miss Blue! You in the middle! Give me something! Throw me something!" On the unfamiliar Ise highway . . .[30]

Three pilgrims on horseback near Ise. From Jippensha Ikku, *Kane no waraji*, vol. 3, ca. 1814. (In the possession of the translator.)

The beginning of this piece includes a phrase from "Komoro bushi," a packhorse driver's song. The "you in the middle" refers to the middle passenger on a horse saddled for three riders. Only one or two travelers might ride a horse, but all horses were outfitted with a saddle meant for three. Pleasure trips were not undertaken by solitary individuals, but rather by small parties. While riding together, such a group could relish the feeling of freedom on the road. Far away from home, bad behavior was unlikely to have serious consequences.

At times when Ise pilgrimages exploded in popularity, many beggars would station themselves on the way to the shrine. These indigents, who depended on donations solicited from pilgrims, called out to the passersby—the "Mr. Stripes, Miss Blue, you in the middle" of the song. The sight of these beggars on the road impressed travelers and eventually found its way into song. The *tokiwazu* piece known as *Utsubo-zaru* (The Monkey-Skin Quiver)[31] contains the following lines, which clearly repeat the cries of such beggars:

> Make the rounds, make the rounds, Ise pilgrims! "Once there were carts, now there are coins—throw me some, throw me some! Mr. Stripes, Miss Dark Blue, Miss Light Blue. Hey! Hey! Hey! Hey you, in the fine-patterned kimono! Give me some!" That's what one hears returning on the footpath between rice fields.[32]

In the mouth of a great *tokiwazu* performer these words recreate the sounds of Edo-period Ise beggars. These ubiquitous mendicants were often disliked by travelers. As a result, the popular phrase "Kamigata good-for-nothings and Ise beggars" ended up branding all natives of Ise as indigent.

By far the most famous beggars in Ise were Osugi and Otama. These two women sat on a bench and played the *shamisen* at Aino-yama, between the inner and outer shrines. An Ise folk song goes as follows:

> If you look far to the south
> You'll see the Outer Shrine and the Inner Shrine.
> At Ainoyama you'll find Osugi and Otama.
> While playing the *shamisen* they sing:
> "Mr. Stripes, Miss Blue, you in the middle!
> Give us one *mon!* Throw us one *mon!*
> Over here! Right over here!"

The scene of these two women playing the *shamisen,* singing the Ainoyama song, and simultaneously picking up the coins thrown by travelers was not to be missed. A *senryū* recounts that "if it weren't for Edo pilgrims, Otama wouldn't suffer." In other words: only high-spirited *Edokko* threw so many coins that Otama was unable to retrieve them without interrupting her *shamisen* performance. Only the *Edokko* were generous enough to allow themselves the pleasure of causing such suffering. Here as elsewhere, *senryū* show favoritism to Edo natives. In any case, this comic poem suggestively captures a scene sure to be witnessed by Ise pilgrims.

Konpira Pilgrimages

Pilgrimages to temples and shrines around Edo—to Narita, Eno-shima, Ōyama, Ontake, and the like—could be made in a few days. Such visits barely qualified as a true journey. By contrast, a trip to the Konpira Shrine in Shikoku required several weeks. Such a visit was made even more enjoyable by stopping off at picturesque sites in Harima, Hizen, and the Inland Sea around Shikoku.

After sightseeing activities at Suma (today in Kōbe city) and Akashi (Harima), the trip might proceed to the pleasure quarters at Murotsu (Harima). This area featured a coastline with countless inlets, the result of a large-scale land subsidence. Scenic bays could be viewed at Sakagoe, Akō, Katakami, and Ushimado. From Shimo-tsui a boat took travelers across the Inland Sea to Marugame

Osugi and Otama play the *shamisen* and sing while passersby throw coins. From *Saigoku sanjūsan-sho meisho zue*, 1853. (In the possession of the Tokyo Metropolitan Central Library.)

(Sanuki). Here travelers were greeted by rows of stores selling local specialties such as woven baskets, fans painted with persimmon tannin, or round straw mats. Pilgrims bought these articles as souvenirs. Peasants who had never left the environs of their home village took in all the unfamiliar sights along the way with wide-eyed enthusiasm.

Inns for the night were not reserved. When evening fell, each traveler searched for an appropriately priced, convenient hostel. Although peasants undoubtedly knew that things on the road were unpredictable, in Sanuki province they might be in for a special surprise. Here the maid at the inn might enter the room and ask, "Shall I kill you? Or shall I beat you half to death?" Unaccustomed to such a query, travelers put their heads together for a quick consultation. If violence were inevitable, it was probably best to get it over with quickly. Thus decided, they replied, "Go ahead and kill us." But soon an entirely harmless servant girl was seen standing in the doorway holding a large number of steamed yams. Only then did the travelers realize that in the Sanuki dialect "killing" *(marugoroshi)* meant sweet potatoes and "half-killing" *(hangoroshi)* meant *ohagi*—rice dumplings covered with bean paste. Such an incident on the road then became the memory of a lifetime. Once back home in their local village, travelers recalled such a tale over and over, telling it to anyone who would lend an ear. Even now such stories of unforgettable moments on the road are recounted by residents of rural farm villages.

The Konpira Shrine in Shikoku was a highly popular destination for pilgrimages, but accurate statistics of the kind one finds for mass abscondences to Ise do not appear to exist. A rough idea of the number of visitors can be obtained from the fact that the theater troupe mentioned earlier, the Kanamaru-za, could build a grand theater house with the 3- or 5-*mon* commission that it obtained from the earnings of the town's geisha. Such a minuscule fee brought in an enormous sum of money. During the Bunsei period (1818–1830), for example, it totaled some 70,000 *ryō*.

After finishing their visit to the Konpira Shrine, travelers had several choices. Some went on to tour the eighty-eight famous temples of Shikoku; others preferred to see the historical sites at Yashima. When the season was right, yet others might take pleasure in viewing the unique net-fishing methods used on the Inland Sea.

The "Thirty-Three Sites of the Western Land"

Travel fever heightened after the middle of the Edo period. Throughout Japan, tourists and pilgrims made the rounds to famous scenic locations, historical spots, well-known temples, or holy sites. The popularity of such journeys led to the publication of numerous travel guides directing travelers to the desired destination. Illustrated guides existed for the Tōkaidō highway, the Kiso highway, the Ise highway and Grand Shrine, the pilgrimage routes to the Konpira Shrine in Shikoku and the shrine at Narita, as well as to spots in Kyoto, Settsu, Yamato, Kawachi, Izumi, Harima, Sumiyoshi, Suma, Akashi, Kii, Owari, Ōmi, and Kumano.

One of the most common pilgrimages, surpassed in popularity only by the Kumano and Ise circuits, was that of the thirty-three holy sites of western Japan. This ancient route had deep religious significance. In addition to its religious function, it also provided a way for rural Japanese to assimilate unfamiliar forms of culture and have a good time. As this tour increased in popularity, circuits of thirty some holy sites were established throughout Japan: the thirty-three sites of the Bandō circuit; the thirty-four sites on the Chichibu circuit; and circuits of the thirty-three Kannon in Kyoto and Osaka. A scene featuring the thirty-three Kannon of Osaka can be found in the first section of Chikamatsu Monzaemon's *Sonezaki shinjū (The Love Suicides at Sonezaki)*,[33] documenting a tour of the heroine Ohatsu.

Many groups that toured the thirty-three sites of the western land came from eastern or northeastern Japan. Outfitted with a light jacket, a sedge hat, leggings, and a tag that carried the words "pilgrims of the thirty-three sites of the western land," husbands and wives, or groups of two or three relatives, journeyed around the Kinki region examining holy sites and famous historic or scenic spots. After stopping at Ise, pilgrims entered the Kumano area. From here the real pilgrimage began. The first stop was the Kannon at Nachi:

> At the waterfall at Mount Nachi,
> At the Kumano Shrine—
> Echoes of Mount Potalaka in India,
> And waves pounding against the shore.[34]

Then, heading west on the Kumano highway, travelers soon arrived at the Kimii Temple:

> Ah, the Kimii Temple! How far from home—
> But how near the splendid capital . . .

While touring, pilgrims clearly looked forward to visiting the old capital of Kyoto. The Kokawa Temple was the third stop on the route. In Chikamatsu Hanji's masterpiece *Keisei Awa no Naruto* (Courtesans and the Straits of Naruto, first performed in 1768), the child Otsuru is on a pilgrimage. She sings a pilgrim's song:

> Our parents gave us profound blessings;
> At the Kokawa Temple
> Might we not also trust the Buddha?[35]

While singing this ancient song, pilgrims proceeded to Kawachi, Izumi, Yamato, and Yamashiro before arriving at the "splendid capital" of Kyoto. Here they again toured holy sites, familiarizing themselves with many outstanding examples of Japanese culture. After a short rest in the city, pilgrims headed for Yamashiro, Tanba, Settsu, and Harima. At Mount Shosha (Harima) they visited the holy site where Saint Shōkū (910–1007) founded his temple. This was the twenty-seventh and westernmost stop of the circuit and it presented a splendid panorama. From the great southern gate near the peak of Mount Shosha, pilgrims could gaze at the beautiful mountains of Tajima, Hōki, and the Chūgoku area to the north; the Inland Sea lay below to the south. Far in the distance, where the travelers themselves had hiked only a few days earlier, stretched the purple mountain ranges of Kii and Yamato; from the distant sea rose the island of Awaji. Immediately below were the Iejima Islands; to the right one could see four-cornered Shōdo Island; even farther away one could just barely make out the mountains of Shikoku with their holy sites related to the great priest Kūkai.

To those from the eastern provinces, everything here seemed splendid and fresh, everything had a long history: the mountain paths of white granite sand, the cedar and pine forests, the marker with a poem by Izumi Shikibu at the Shosha Enkyōji. Having reached the westernmost tip of the circuit, the travelers then retraced their steps, making their way through Tango and Wakasa. After enjoying a superb view of the Japan Sea, they trekked down the ancient highway from Tsuruga through the mountains to Kaizu and then crossed Lake Biwa by boat to worship at Chikubushima. Here they found stone markers engraved with the command "No taking of life on this 8-chō [950-yard] area along the water." After hearing the legends surrounding this rocky island they moved eastward to the Miidera (Yamato) and Ishiyamadera (Ōmi) temples. The thirty-third and final stop was the Tanigumidera in Mino. From here each party returned to its home province.

The Shikoku Circuit

The Shikoku circuit of eighty-eight sites associated with Kūkai began in the province of Awa and took the traveler to Tosa, Iyo, and Sanuki. Like the pilgrims just mentioned, pious travelers on this circuit too sang a special song supposedly written by Kūkai himself. The Shikoku route was also populated by many professional beggars.

This circuit is described in Chikamatsu Monzaemon's play *Saga tennō kanro no ame* (The Shower of Nectar During the Reign of the Saga Emperor, first performed in 1714).[36] During the Edo period, a leisurely trip to holy sites and famous spots in Shikoku required much careful preparation and money. Not everyone could afford such a luxury. As a result, abbreviated versions of the eighty-eight sites appeared. At many Shingon sect temples, parishioners could take in the entire tour of eighty-eight sites by simply hiking on the hill on which their temple was built. Even today such arrangements survive in many parts of Japan.

Shinran's Twenty-Four Holy Sites

This circuit—the twenty-four holy sites associated with the priest Shinran—is not very well known, but along with the Pure Land sect's circuit of twenty-five holy sites of the priest Hōnen (1133–1212), it was of major significance to the believers of Nenbutsu sects of Buddhism. To such believers only the Honganji Temple in Kyoto was of greater consequence.

Innumerable legends of the auspicious events surrounding the priest Kūkai have been transmitted: stories of the "shrine where no greens are eaten,"[37] of a "waterless river,"[38] and the like. Though probably developing independently, similar tales surrounded the twenty-four holy sites of Shinran (1173–1262). When Shinran stuck his old boxwood or bamboo cane into the ground, it took root and grew; when he did the same with a bamboo pole, it sprouted leaves that all faced downwards. Shinran's miraculous powers were also responsible for an incident in which an evil mother-in-law who donned a demon mask to frighten her son's young wife was unable to remove it. Countless similar tales testified to Shinran's miraculous powers. The Zenkōji Temple (in Nagano) also boasts a pine supposedly planted by Shinran. Such a tree may well have taken root if stuck into the ground here. In any case, a solitary pine grows at this holy spot within the temple grounds. A similar story claims that the city of Ōme (Musashi) derives its name (written with the characters for "green" and "plum") from the fact that the divination stick of Hachiman Tarō (Minamoto no Yoshiie, 1039–1106) sprouted a green plum tree. This story was later associated with tales about Shinran and gave rise to all kinds of miraculous tales.

Each of the twenty-four sites related to Shinran refers to an event in the life of Shinran himself. The circuit begins in Kyoto and includes various sites in Echigo (where he was exiled), as well as Shinano and Hitachi (where he proselytized). From Kyoto the tour passed through Ōmi, Echizen, Kaga, Etchū, Echigo, and Shinano before arriving in the Kantō area.

Unlike pilgrims on other routes, pilgrims on the Shinran circuit did not sound bells, sing songs, or even intone the formula *Namu Amida Butsu*. Consequently, this tour was quite monotonous and unsuited for professional beggars or itinerant performers. At the temples they visited, pilgrims obtained amulets that ensured their safety in crossing streams or shallows or guaranteed their personal welfare. Pilgrims were deeply impressed and grateful for the mysterious powers of the Amida Buddha as embodied in these amulets.

After spending many days on the road with its numerous inconveniences, pilgrims arrived at the city of Niigata in the northern province of Echigo. Just as the Kumano pilgrims held a celebration at inns at Tanabe, the pilgrims of the Shinran circuit often threw a wild party in Niigata. Complete with *shamisen*, drums, and other musical instruments, austerities were lifted; with luck, pilgrims might even hear a few passages of *gidayū* chanted behind a screen by Takemoto

Kadayū, who had come here from Osaka. While listening to such a performance, pilgrims drank and made merry.

Hiking from village to village, pilgrims sometimes encountered unusual local customs or perhaps festivals at which unique performing arts could be observed. Young women in distinctive garb might be seen in several dozen villages on both sides of the Ogami River in the Gokayama area (Toyama prefecture). Here too the unique "woodcutter's dance" (*kikori odori*) caught the eye of pilgrims and afforded them an unforgettable experience. In this dance, old men and women held fans in their hands and performed a frenzied dance accompanied by drums and hand gongs:

> Worries and love, loaded into a boat of bamboo grass:
>   worries burden it, but love is light.
> My heart melted at the first words of love;
>   unbeknownst to mother and father
> I gave myself to my lover—
>   and became a "virgin" wearing an Iwata obi.[39]

After their long trip through steep mountain passes, travelers could relax and view the dragnets used in Oshiage village or examine the unusual fish caught in the Japan Sea. They might even hear a performance of itinerant performers at a house of a wholesale merchant of Echigo *chijimi* cloth. (In the countryside, performers went where the money was.) When heading back to their home provinces, travelers might encounter itinerant medicine vendors from Toyama. These hawkers wrapped their medicine box with a large light green or navy blue cloth on which were stained ideographs spelling their place of origin—"Etchū Toyama"—and the name of their best-known product—a digestive aid called "Hangontan." Vendors carried this bundle on their backs as they wandered the countryside in small groups.

Translator's Summary

As we have seen, the roads of Japan were populated with many types of travelers and itinerant performers. Some of these, including *seki-zoro, sutasuta bōzu,* and *kamabarai,* functioned mainly as exorcisers. Such quasi-religious performers tended to make their rounds at the end of the year. A few days later, at the start of the new year, other types of itinerants appeared and provided an eager public with auspicious arts including divination, comic dialogue, and the "lion

Two itinerant musicians stop off at a wholesaler of Echigo *chijimi* cloth. From *Nijūyohai junpai zue,* 1803–1809. (In the possession of the Tokyo Metropolitan Central Library.)

dance," as well as dances associated with the lucky gods Ebisu and Daikoku.

Travelers closely tied to religious functions included itinerant monks such as the *Kōya hijiri, rokubu,* and *gannin bōzu,* many of whom were little more than beggars. The *shakuhachi*-playing *komusō,* too, were linked to a religious institution, the Fuke sect of Zen Buddhism. This group of performers was unusual in that it was officially limited to members of the warrior class.

Other travelers of the Edo period were actors. Small theater troupes provided rural towns and villages with kabuki performances whose level was often quite high by contemporary standards. Some troupes were granted an official monopoly by a regional daimyo and might even be asked to perform for the lord himself. Touring troupes contributed greatly to the diffusion of urban theatrical culture to the rural areas.

The general public, too, traveled frequently during the Edo period. Pilgrimages by the common populace to famous holy sites were particularly popular. Two of the most common destinations were the shrines at Mount Kumano and Ise. Pleasure trips to these shrines were described in musical works of the day. Yet another pop-

Medicine vendors from Toyama on the road. From *Nijūyohai junpai zue,* 1803–1809. (In the possession of the Tokyo Metropolitan Central Library.)

ular target for pilgrimages was the Konpira Shrine on the island of Shikoku. This area of Japan featured a famous pilgrimage route of eighty-eight holy sites associated with the great priest Kūkai. There was a route of thirty-three holy sites of western Japan, and many other circuits existed throughout Japan.

Pilgrimages often served as a pretense for pleasure travel. The Edo-period populace greatly enjoyed tourism. Besides savoring the food and sights that differed from those of the local village, commoners delighted in the feeling of liberation provided by trips away from home.

CHAPTER 8

EDO-PERIOD CUISINE

The *Iemoto* of Cooking

Food of the Warriors During the Civil Wars

In a memo in the possession of the Ikarugadera, a temple near Himeji, Toyotomi Hideyoshi (1536–1598) outlines troop mobilizations in the advance on Himeji, part of a campaign that climaxed in the Battle of Takamatsu (1582). Hideyoshi, who personally led the Himeji attack, was still merely a general in Oda Nobunaga's forces. He had risen to this position from his origins in rural Owari, and his rustic, unrefined exuberance was still evident at every turn. The memo at the temple was written in wartime, of course, but its scrawled script can hardly fail to surprise the reader. Such scribbling stands in sharp contrast to Hideyoshi's later calligraphy. During the Korean campaign, he would send beautifully penned letters to his wife from his camp in Kyūshū. One can only wonder when he found the time to acquire such calligraphic skills.

From fine brushwork to the luxury of a gorgeous castle compound, Hideyoshi's tastes, like those of other daimyo, gradually turned aristocratic. But though Hideyoshi and the daimyo imitated aristocratic ways, they still valued the rural home town and exhibited much democratic goodwill. In the tenth month of 1587, for example, Hideyoshi held a grand tea ceremony at Kitano, to which he invited even ordinary commoners. This lavish party included both high and low, rich and poor.

A tale recorded in the *Jōzan kidan* (Memoirs of [Yuasa] Jōzan), published in 1738, suggests that the cuisine of the high-ranking warriors was at first not at all aristocratic.[1] Here we read that one Tsubouchi, a retainer and renowned chef of the Miyoshi family, was taken captive around the time of the Miyoshi house's fall in the 1560s. Several years later, a vassal named Ichihara Goemon reported to Oda Nobunaga (1534–1582) that "Tsubouchi is skilled in the cutting of

144

crane and carp, and an expert preparer of banquets and 'seven-five-three' meals.[2] With due permission, I should like to recommend him as a chef." Nobunaga answered that he would make a decision after sampling the following day's breakfast. Tsubouchi was immediately ordered to prepare this meal. The next morning, when Nobunaga tasted the fare, he was outraged: "This watery slop is disgusting! The cook should promptly be put to death!" Tsubouchi was terrified and pleaded, "I am entirely to blame, and beg for your forgiveness. Please allow me to serve Your Highness just one more time. If the food again displeases thee, I shall disembowel myself on the spot." Nobunaga agreed. The following day he found Tsubouchi's meal indescribably delicious, exactly to his liking. Tsubouchi was promptly awarded an official post and stipend.

After this incident, Tsubouchi told Nobunaga that the first meal had been in the style of the Miyoshi house. "But this morning's fare," Tsubouchi explained, "was of third-rate cooking. The Miyoshi house controlled Japanese politics for many years, and everything about this family was highly refined. Although your anger was aroused, the food that I served yesterday was of premium quality. Today's meal, however, was of an unrefined, rural sort, and thus may have pleased you." Bystanders felt this explanation to be an inexcusable affront; Tsubouchi had gone far beyond the bounds of propriety. Nevertheless, this story shows that in matters of cuisine, Nobunaga embodied the spirit of the day: the low had usurped the position of the high. The likelihood of such a story is confirmed by other accounts concerning Nobunaga. When, for example, he led his army in the surprise attack on Imagawa Yoshimoto (1519–1560) at the Battle of Oke Hazama (1560), Nobunaga is said to have personally prepared the rice to feed the troops.

Both Hideyoshi and Nobunaga considered polished rice a luxury and discouraged its consumption. They did not exclude themselves from this ban. Tokugawa Ieyasu, too, was famous not just for advocating a mix of barley and rice as a staple food, but for actually following this recommendation himself. The second shogun Hidetada (1579–1632) continued this practice and went to great lengths to enforce simple warrior manners. When, for example, Hidetada threw a banquet for Lord Ikeda Mitsumasa (1609–1682), he presented only a meager treat of white turnips in soup and roasted dried fish. Daimyo of the day often followed the shogun's example. Lord Mōri was delighted at a mere piece of salted salmon. Even the lord of the great hereditary-vassalage house of Abe ate only rice balls for lunch. Such food was taken along on boar hunting or falconing expeditions. Thus with the exception of the cuisine prepared for special ceremonial occasions or Buddhist memorial services, the food of the warrior class did not differ significantly from that of the commoners. Thanks to this coarse diet, no stratum of the Japanese population yet suffered from beriberi.

The Importation of Culinary Arts

During the early years of the Edo period, Japan engaged in much trade with East Asian countries. As a result, a remarkable amount of foreign cuisine was imported. Unusual ingredients, previously seen but rarely in Japan, were introduced. Their use was at first limited to social or ceremonial events and special banquets, but in time they were consumed by a broad range of the population.

A number of new foods are recorded in contemporary writings: red-and-white *hanpen* (a cake of pounded fish); *yaki-dōfu* (broiled bean curd); *sarasa-jiru* (a soup made with fresh chrysanthemums); a Javanese dish called *gōren* ("goreng") made with fried fish; and *furu-gasuteru* ("frikadel"), a dish apparently of Dutch provenance in which beef and cabbage were finely minced, combined with egg, seasoned with wine, covered with bread crumbs, and fried.

The spread of such cuisine brings to mind my own experiences as a child. My hometown was in the Kansai area, in a rural area around the city of Akō in Harima. Things may have changed now, but in my childhood we called a dining table a *shippoku-dai*. Usually everyone ate from individual boxlike trays, but local tradition required the use of a *shippoku-dai* when guests arrived. The word *shippoku,* which originates from the Chinese word *zhuofu* (tablecloth), denotes a Chinese-style dining table. But what we called *shippoku-dai* was a purely Japanese-style table with no hint of Chinese influence. *Shippoku* cuisine, a Japanese version of Chinese food, is today a specialty of Nagasaki; this cuisine and the *shippoku-dai* were probably transmitted to Japan in much the same manner. Although *shippoku* cuisine did not spread to the rural areas, the *shippoku-dai,* by contrast, spread to every nook and cranny of the Japanese countryside. Many people of the Kansai area must have fond recollections of this kind of table.

The Establishment of Iemoto of Cuisine

From the sixteenth century to the start of the seventeenth, Japan still lacked a truly hegemonic social or cultural force. Ambition and optimistic vigor were found on all levels of society. The quality of everyday necessities and the level of cultivation of rulers and ruled was not yet clearly differentiated. With some exaggeration one might

claim that Japanese culture was still uniform and unstratified. Hideyoshi, however, instigated policies that were to differentiate nearly
everything according to social rank. These policies were continued by
the Tokugawa bakufu. As the shogunate went into its second and third
generations, an aristocratic ruling-class culture began to emerge.

Warriors, who had once delighted in rice balls, tofu, and *manjū*
(buns with bean-jam stuffing), were now accorded high social rank
that set them apart from the commoners. In all cultural pursuits the
ruling warrior and courtier nobility granted itself a monopoly of
privileges. The music of the nō drama of the Kanze, Hōshō, and
three other schools was designated as the official bakufu ceremonial
music; Kanō school painters became the official house artists. Newly
established *iemoto* monopolized techniques for martial arts, calligraphy, music, the tea ceremony, sword appraising, historical knowledge, scholarship, textile design and production, and poetry writing
based on court transmissions of interpretations of the *Kokin wakashū*
(Collection of Poems Ancient and Modern).[3] Techniques for cutting
and preparing food were no exception. They too became an art or
"Way" controlled by an *iemoto*.

The first Japanese schools *(ryū)* of cuisine did not appear until
the Muromachi period (1333–1573). Such schools were established
mainly on the basis of techniques used in ceremonies and banquets
held at the home of the host, for until the 1680s restaurants did not
exist in Japan. The oldest schools of cuisine included the Shijō-ryū,
Sonobe-ryū, Ōgusa-ryū, and Shinji-ryū. The latter two schools had
been in charge of cuisine for the Ashikaga shogunal house. Schools
of cuisine declined markedly during the turbulent period of the civil
wars; but with the start of the Edo period, a resurgence occurred.
Venerable old schools were revived and reorganized. In addition,
new schools such as the Ikuma-ryū were founded. From all of these
schools, the Shijō-ryū eventually emerged as the leader.

Secret Transmissions Concerning Food Preparation

The Shijō school still exists today; indeed, Shijō Butoku is the for-
tieth *iemoto*. Written "secret transmissions" recording the school's
teachings are extant as well. One such book, the *Shijō-ke hōchō shoroku*
(Records of the Cuisine of the Shijō House), is a gorgeous treasure
whose use is strictly limited to school members.

Records of Japanese secret transmissions usually confine their
discussion to the technical elements of an art or skill. Theoretical
background may be provided by citing Chinese and Indian scholarship and philosophy. As a result, one is often left wondering what

teachings and techniques were developed by the school's founder. This is to some extent true of the *Shijō-ke hōchō shoroku,* as well. But this book also contains much fascinating information concerning the details of the aristocratic banquet tradition.

The *Shijō-ke hōchō shoroku* comprises three volumes compiled in 1642, 1649, and 1774, respectively. A preface notes that since individual writings are easily scattered and lost, these records have been collated as one book. The first volume provides explanations and detailed, richly colored illustrations of menus used on ceremonial occasions. For such events three courses (with trays of seven-five-three dishes or five-five-three dishes, respectively) were offered. The order in which dishes are to be presented is explained as well, as is etiquette. This portion of the book appears to have been the school's main secret teaching since Muromachi times.

The second volume, from 1649, attempts to marshal scholarly evidence, including the *Hōchō shoroku* (Written Records on Cuisine) of Hayashi Razan (1583–1657). Razan's treatise records historical precedent from Japan and abroad. In the four or five parts entitled "Correct Form," one finds minutely detailed descriptions of the origin and content of appropriate cuisine for such events as the five annual festivals, the ceremony of assuming manhood, weddings, and a baby's first meal after birth.

The most interesting sections of the second volume of the *Shijō-ke hōchō shoroku* are those devoted to the cutting and display of carp. Styles of preparing and presenting carp are shown here in beautiful, delicately colored illustrations. Some fifty-five versions are included: "formal carp," "left carp," "five cuts," "the isle of eternal youth," "snowy morning," "flower viewing," "fisher lord," "Yasoshima pilgrimage," "upright tail," "raft," "carp in a boat," and many others. This section also includes some ten versions each of sea bass *(suzuki),* sea bream *(tai),* pomfret *(managatsuo),* and trout *(amenouo),* as well as wild goose, crane, and pheasant. Each example of cutting and presentation is displayed as a work of art superbly arranged on a large unvarnished cypress *(hinoki)* cutting board used for the cutting ritual.

Carp and sea bass seem to have been the most commonly consumed foods. Preparation of these fish boasted a long tradition. Carp and sea bass cutting rituals can even be seen in *kyōgen,* which faithfully transmit such procedures and attest to their age. One such scene occurs in the *kyōgen* entitled *Suzuki-bōchō* (How to Cut Sea Bass). In this tale a chef lies to his nephew, telling him that a fish ordered for a celebration has been eaten by an otter. The nephew has been looking forward to this treat, and the chef tries to send him away satisfied by demonstrating the way carp and sea bass are pre-

"Flower-viewing sea-bass." From *Shijō Sonobe-ryū hōchō kiri-zoroe no kan* (A Volume of Shijō Sonobe School Cutting and Presentation), vol. 2, by Funagi Dennai, published in 1811. (In the possession of the Tokyo Metropolitan Central Library.)

pared. At a particularly humorous moment, one can witness the beautiful ritual for cutting the fish.

> Now take this fish and wash it well. Then arrange a fine cutting board, plain wooden fish-handling chopsticks, a high-quality Bizen cooking knife, and a piece of folded paper. . . . Set yourself firmly before the board, take the chopsticks and the knife, cut the paper in three; set aside two pieces, and place the remaining one at the top of the cutting board. Wet the board with ceremonial water. Then make three cuts: first pierce the head of the fish, and then slice off the flesh from the front. Next, place the fish with its head at the top of the cutting board, turn the fish over, and slice the flesh off the back. The remaining flesh can be cut in three and used for stew.[4]

The *kyōgen* actor performs this scene with nothing but a fan. He acts out a highly realistic pantomime, making the spectators feel that they too have been invited to a banquet.

Food preparation can also be seen in the *kyōgen* known as *Hōchō muko* (The Cook Son-in-Law) and *Sōhachi* (A Priest and a Cook). In *Fuzumō* (Wrestling by the Book), a man is asked what skills he possesses. He responds: "I am skilled at archery, ball games, *go*, backgammon *(sugoroku);* I can wield a cooking knife, make horses stand and lie down, and wrestle."[5] In the Muromachi-period *Shuhanron* (Treatise on Food and Wine) or in illustrations of contemporary scenes, one also often finds depictions of food being prepared. These styles quickly diffused to the countryside around Kyoto and reached a broad sector of the population.

By the Edo period, such styles of food preparation were formalized into secret transmissions that became ever more complex, developing to a point of truly unnecessary intricacy. In the "written secret transmission" of the Shijō school, passed on by Takahashi Gosaemon to Nakamura Jūemon in 1642, and in the *Shikishō hōchō ryōri kirikata hiden shō* (Digest of Secret Transmissions on Correct Food Preparation and Cutting) published somewhat later, thirty-six styles for preparing carp are listed. In cookbooks of the Ōgusa-ryū, or in books of secret transmissions of the Ogasawara-ryū and Shinji-ryū, over thirty techniques are described. A legend was even invented claiming that thirty-six versions of Shijō-ryū carp existed because all carp, regardless of size, have thirty-six scales running down the middle; Shijō minor counselor Fujiwara Ason Yamakage had thus devised thirty-six ways of cutting this fish.

Such appeals to spurious traditions were the order of the day. The same phenomenon can be witnessed when guns were transmitted to Japan during the second half of the sixteenth century. Schools of gunnery soon split into several dozen independent factions, leading to the formation of schools such as the Inatomi-ryū, the Tsuda-ryū, and the Nanban-ryū ("southern barbarian school"). The Nanban-ryū claimed one "Haburasu" as its founder and produced licenses embossed with a seal in roman letters. The Ōtsubo school of horsemanship even boasted the mythical hero Yamato Takeru as its founder. The Shijō school's claim that Lord Yamakage invented its carp preparation techniques was thus by no means unusual.

The *Shijō-ke hōchō shoroku* carefully prescribes what a cook is to do: for flower viewing he must present "flower-viewing carp"; for festive occasions, there was "congratulatory carp." A parlor surrounded by a beautiful garden in which the sound of a waterfall might be heard called for "dragon gate carp"; for times when a plum branch was displayed in the alcove *(tokonoma),* "snowy morning carp" was right. The display of a white chrysanthemum required the presentation of "the isle of eternal youth carp"; "misty morning carp" was deemed proper for maple leaf viewing. These formalized schemes were the product of much experimentation. Lord Yamakage was probably invoked only later to lend these secret transmissions the voice of authority.

Different schools and cooking masters developed different cutting styles and different procedures for food preparation. For example, the elegantly named "Yasoshima pilgrimage carp" that appears in the *Shijō-ke hōchō shoroku* and the identically named dish listed as one of twenty-seven styles in the *Hōchō shiki hō* (Ways of Cutting Food) are completely different. Each school of cuisine apparently developed its own style independently, leading to such variation.

Forms of cutting were undoubtedly first devised in response to the needs of specific occasions. By the time these styles were linked to Lord Yamakage or the thirty-six scales of a carp, the original meaning of the forms may already have been forgotten. Today, of course, both the traditional techniques and the original meanings of many of these styles of cutting have been lost.

The "Way of the Cooking Knife"

Nevertheless, many traditional cutting rituals and the chef's archaic costume—a wide-sleeved ceremonial court robe and a tall black lacquered hat—have been passed down to today's *iemoto*. In the past, the "Way of the cooking knife" was highly esteemed. Guests at banquets derived great pleasure from watching a chef give a brilliant, virtuoso performance with the cutting knife. The *Kaka gunbuzu byōbu* (A Screen of Groups of Dancers Under the Cherry Blossoms)[6] provides a glimpse of the way in which guests were treated during the early Edo period. This screen depicts a chef preparing some large fish and fowl for a banquet in honor of "southern barbarians" (that is, the Portuguese).

Carp and river bass *(kawasuzuki)* were highly prized by the Kyoto aristocracy and eventually by the public at large. The Yodo River yielded carp that were a renowned local specialty. River bass was considered more authentic than the ocean variety, and the cutting ritual differed accordingly.

As mentioned earlier, the *Shijō-ke hōchō shoroku* gives not only cutting rituals for fish, but also for crane, wild goose, duck, pheasant, and other fowl. Until recently duck and thrush *(tsugumi)* could still occasionally be seen hanging on display in poultry stores in the wintertime. Similar scenes, in which wild geese, storks, and cranes are exhibited, are portrayed on "southern barbarian" screens from the early Edo period. Cranes are today a protected species, but during the Edo period they were found throughout the land. Although crane is today only rarely eaten in Japan, in the past this bird was considered a high-class delicacy. During the Edo period, wealthy individuals offered guests cranes purchased at poultry shops. In the tenth month of 1699 the fifth shogun Tsunayoshi (1646–1709) sent a relay of high-speed couriers to Kyoto to present a crane as a gift to the emperor and the retired emperor. In falconing expeditions bagging a crane was always the source of great joy. One such expedition, in which the eleventh shogun Ienari (1773–1841) participated, netted three of these birds. On the way home, Ienari stopped to rest at the Hashiba branch of the "Yaozen," the best restaurant in Edo. The three cranes were bound with green bamboo and strung from the branches of a pine tree in the garden of the restaurant. Sakai Hōitsu (1761–1828), a Kasei-period connoisseur, happened to be present and promptly sketched this scene. His picture is still in the possession of the "Yaozen."

Crane was often consumed by courtiers as well. On the nineteenth day of the first month of each year a demonstration of *bugaku* (traditional court dance) was given at the imperial court. The day's banquet always included crane soup, so the *bugaku* performance was preceded by the cutting ritual for crane. This ritual was performed on stage for the emperor, the court, and attendant military dignitaries. Dressed in full court attire, all of these guests watched this splendid ritual. When the performance came to an end, a beautifully prepared "thousand-year crane" or "dancing crane" was presented on the cutting board. Starting with the prime minister, the spectators then partook of this highly prized delicacy.

The systematic organization and formalized techniques of the Shijō school as codified in the *Shijō-ke hōchō shoroku* indicate that these secret teachings and oral transmissions were largely fixed by around the Keian period (1648–1652). By this time the pretentious but plausible-sounding argument linking the cutting board, chopsticks, and cutting knife to Buddhist doctrine had appeared; and oral traditions, such as the one involving crane soup, had been established as well. Eventually, the person who stood before the cutting board and wielded the knife came to be known as the *itamae* ("before the board"); later the words *itamae san* referred to anyone who engaged in the cutting and preparation of food.

The third volume of the *Shijō-ke hōchō shoroku*, from 1774, was a response to the plebeian counteroffensive in cookbook publishing. As I shall argue later, the cuisine of the commoners developed rapidly during the first half of the eighteenth century. From the late seventeenth to the early eighteenth centuries restaurants appeared in

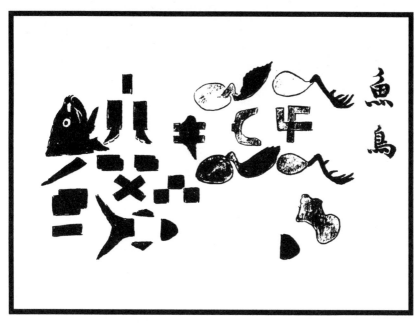

"Fish and fowl." From *Shijō-ryū hōchō kiri-zoroe no kan* (A Volume of Shijō School Cutting and Presentation), vol. 2, by Tomisaka Tasuke, published in 1805. (In the possession of the Tokyo Metropolitan Central Library.)

Edo and Osaka, and many treatises on cuisine were published by and for the citizenry.

From the Genroku period (1688–1704) cookbooks such as the previously mentioned *Shikishō hōchō ryōri kirikata hiden shō* (a secret transmission of the Shijō school) were being published quite openly. After the Kyōhō period (1716–1736), many such books were issued in rapid succession and sold well. Examples include the *Banpō ryōri himitsu-bako* (Secret Chest of a Myriad Cooking Treasures), the *Tai hyakuchin ryōri himitsu-bako* (Secret Chest of One Hundred Sea Bream Delicacies, 1785), the *Fucha ryōri shō* (Digest of Chinese-Style Meager Fare, 1772), and the *Daikon ryōri hiden shō* (Digest of Secret Ways for Preparing Giant White Radish, 1785).

No solid evidence exists to prove that a member of the aristocratic Kyoto Shijō house had ever acted as a true *iemoto*, regulating this school's practice, transmitting its secrets, and granting licenses. Records do show, however, that from the middle of the eighteenth century the Shijō family issued licenses and certificates to its pupils. The school's disciples now demanded licenses, records of secret transmissions, and the Shijō seal. This required the establishment of

Women cutting and roasting tofu. From *Tōfu hyakuchin* (One Hundred Tofu Delicacies), published in Osaka, 1782. (In the possession of the Tokyo Metropolitan Central Library.)

a Shijō family office that oversaw such matters. In a late-Edo-period register, one finds a list of Osaka *chōnin* licensed by the Shijō school. The licenses read as follows:

> As a disciple who has shown great devotion to this house and this school, the person listed below is hereby granted the right to wear a broad-sleeved upper garment *(suō)* and a ceremonial underrobe *(noshime)* when making offerings to the gods or preparing food for ceremonial occasions. His assistant shall be granted the right to wear a ceremonial underrobe and formal attire *(kamishimo)*.

These licenses, which carry the signature and seal of an official of the Shijō family office, seem to have been granted to the listed individuals during the 1860s.

Recipients of such a license, with its large seal from the office of Lord Shijō, were probably very proud of their privilege. Poulterer Genpachirō from the third block of Awaji-chō, for example, had not yet been granted a full license, but he was allowed to display a paper lantern hanging from his shop front. Such a lantern was probably decorated with the words "Genpachirō, poulterer, disciple of the Shijō *iemoto*," written in bold brushstrokes for all to see.

Tea Ceremony Cuisine *(Kaiseki)*

During my childhood in the province of Harima, the arrival of an honored guest required the removal of inside sliding doors to create a large temporary space for a lively party with much food and drink. On such gala occasions, a chef always came to our house. Everything, down to the sweet bean jelly dessert *(yōkan)*, was prepared under this chef's direction. The invitation of a guest was always accompanied by several days of commotion both before and after the event. For me this tumult was a source of great enjoyment. Trays, bowls, and large plates were brought up from the storeroom and carefully wiped clean by the many women who had come to help. These dishes were treated with great respect; in fact, many of the lacquerware containers were given individual names. I heard words such as *oyawan* (teapot), which were otherwise never used. Although I was entirely ignorant of the meaning of many of these words, they aroused my curiosity and left a deep impression.

One term that puzzled me completely was *kwaisekizen* (*kaiseki* tray). In the Harima countryside the food served to guests had little relation to the *kaiseki* cuisine of the traditional tea ceremony. Nevertheless, food offered to guests may well have been a simplified version of such cuisine. Kyoto culture had filtered deep into rural areas, reaching even remote farm villages of the Kamigata area.

The unique tea-ceremony style of cuisine known as *kaiseki* is not yet found in the tea parties popular among the Kamakura and Muromachi-period upper classes—the aristocracy and the clergy. The *Kissa ōrai* (Manual of Tea Drinking), for example, written by the priest Gen'e (1269–1350) during the period of northern and southern courts, describes a party in which first three rounds of three cups of *sake* and refreshments were followed by noodles and tea. Then came a meal of delicacies from the land and sea, which was succeeded by fruit. Tea drinking, tea discrimination games, and conversation over the merits of the country versus the city then ensued on the second floor of the teahouse. Next, beautifully prepared fish was consumed and generous amounts of *sake* imbibed. All this was accompanied by so much dance, song, and music that bystanders were astonished.[7] Such a lavish event, complete with competitions and games, in which the utmost in luxury was flaunted for a day and a night, contains no hint of the spirit of *kaiseki*.

The banquet style of the aristocracy of this time was, however, quite unlike this kind of tea party. This style had developed stiff ritualistic forms such as the "seven-five-three" format noted earlier. Members of the Ashikaga shogunal house, for example, partook of meals in which a dance from the nō was performed between each of the dozen or more courses. This general format was maintained by the Tokugawa bakufu. In seventeen-course meals of the Muromachi period, trays with food were presented after the third course. This change shifted the focus of the meal from drink to food. The ensuing courses were then presented in a fixed format. *Kaiseki* cuisine arose from the combination of such old-style banquet styles and the subdued-style tea ceremony known as *wabicha*. Clearly, the old-style banquets were extravagant; but so too was the *kaiseki* cuisine of the age of Hideyoshi. By this time, however, the effects of the *wabicha* tea ceremony were already clearly felt.

According to a highly persuasive theory of Tada Yūshi, the head of the Tokyo Ura Senke Association of tea, a strong sign that *kaiseki* cuisine developed from the old-style banquet format is that *kaiseki* cuisine does not simply function as a stimulus for *sake* drinking. Instead, *kaiseki* places food itself in a position of central importance. An Edo-period *kaiseki* meal was usually characterized by an opening course of rice and soup, followed by a tray with the so-called *mukō-zuke* (raw fish or vinegared fish or vegetables). This was succeeded by a course in which a *sake*-warming pan and a saucer with a *sake* cup were presented. Only a small amount of *sake* was drunk. Next, something boiled and something broiled was served, followed by rice and soup. A small tray was then presented and *sake* sweets were consumed. In a normal *kaiseki* meal, *sake* drinking thus played only a minor role. Since old-style banquets began and ended with some ten rounds of drinking, here too the consumption of alcohol was necessarily relegated to secondary importance during the main courses.

The format of *kaiseki* cuisine was taken from the portion of the banquet in which food was consumed. When this occurred—or who was responsible for its development—remains a mystery. During the time that Sen no Rikyū (1522–1591) was active, a fixed scheme did not yet exist. A set format may perhaps be derived from records found in the *Rikyū hyakkai-ki* (Records of One Hundred Gatherings of Rikyū), but a comparison with the *Imai Sōkyū chanoyu kakinuki* (Excerpts [1534–1588] from the Tea Ceremonies of Imai Sōkyū, compiled in 1820) and the *Kamiya Sōtan nikki* (Diary of Kamiya Sōtan [1551–1635]) shows that no general practice yet existed. The *Imai Sōkyō chanoyu kakinuki* records, for example, the menu and the circumstances surrounding a tea party at Osaka castle on the seventh day of the seventh month of 1583, with Hideyoshi, Sen no Rikyū, Imai Sōkyū (1520–1593), Yamanoue Sōji (1544–1590), and other tea connoisseurs in attendance.[8] The *Kamiya Sōtan nikki* gives a detailed description of a menu presented during the sixth month of 1587 when Hideyoshi, encamped in Kyūshū, was invited to a tea gathering by the wealthy Hakata merchant Kamiya Sōtan.[9] Also described is the menu from a tea gathering that took place on the twenty-first day of the first month of 1593. This event, to which Sōtan was invited, was hosted by Tokugawa Ieyasu, then encamped at Nagoya (in Kyūshū) for the Korean expedition.[10] In none of these tea gatherings does one see any *kaiseki*-style courses.

The *Nanbōroku* (Records of Tea Master Nanbō, 1593) gives the following description:

> Cuisine for a small parlor *(ko-zashiki):* one soup, two or three other dishes, and small amounts of *sake*. The menu for a *wabi-zashiki* is inappropriate. It goes without saying that the extreme lightness of the assortment of food is to be understood in the spirit of the tea ceremony.[11]

Here one finds an indication of the spirit of *kaiseki* but nothing about the form or the content. The stress on unqualified simplicity in the *Nanbōroku* was a form of protest against contemporary attempts by members of the ruling elite to revive the old-style ban-

quet style. Hideyoshi was especially fond of extreme luxury. According to a record in the *Gunsho ruijū* (Collected Writings, Classified),[12]
when Hideyoshi went to a banquet at the residence of Maeda Toshiie
(1538–1599) on the eighth day of the fourth month of 1594, a meal
of thirteen courses was presented. After the first course, the head of
the Konparu school of nō danced the dance *Takasago;* the usual
fourth course was expanded into three rounds of food and drink. It
was this kind of extravagance that the *Nanbōroku* countered with its
emphasis on simplicity, eloquence, and evocativeness. Although
Hideyoshi did at times engage in pompous displays of luxury, he also
appreciated the beauty of a single morning glory in Rikyū's tearoom.
The spirit described in the *Nanbōroku* no doubt also permeated the
kaiseki cuisine of Hideyoshi's tea ceremonies.

Tea masters of the day designed their practices with great freedom and imagination. The Nagoya tea ceremony held by Ieyasu
took place at New Year's, for example, but only *udo* shoots with
dressing were served. Or, as is recorded in the *Edo ryōri-tsū taizen,*
when certain high-placed personages paid a visit to the Buddhist lay-
man Sen no Rikyū, this great man presented only tea and a heap of
washed rice in an earthenware bowl. The legend that Rikyū considered this a model of tea ceremony cuisine is in itself instructive. It
shows a lack of concern over constraints and formalities regarding
the procedures of the tea ceremony. This age placed a high value on
creative activity. True freedom in form and behavior was possible;
formality and custom were not yet valued higher than the people
who participated.

With the arrival of the Edo period, however, all aspects of life
began to be formalized. Society itself was rigidly divided into the
four status groups of warrior, peasant, artisan, and merchant, and
the Ogasawara house devised many troublesome, inflexible rules of
etiquette. Within this context, schools such as the Enshū-ryū and
Sekishū-ryū formalized the tea ceremony. These schemes then
spread to all the feudal domains, each of which wished not to lag
behind the bakufu.

Such trends encouraged the formalization of the techniques of
kaiseki cuisine. By the Kyōhō period (1716–1736), the "three Senke
schools" (the Ura Senke, Omote Senke, and Mushanokoji) and the
Yabunouchi school were codifying a "Way of tea" that differed greatly
from earlier practices of tea masters who had served the daimyo. Tea
masters now became specialists and the "Way of tea" turned into a
profession. After the middle of the Edo period, *iemoto* organizations
of tea appeared and found many adherents. Thus the "Way of tea"
extended its reach even to provincial *chōnin* and remote farm villages.

It would have been impossible to control the practices of the tea ceremony if *kaiseki* gatherings had been ruled only by free fantasy. Instead, detailed procedures for brewing tea were codified and a *kaiseki* format stressing simplicity was fixed. This formalization allowed a huge number of people thoughout the land to learn and appreciate the forms and techniques of *kaiseki* cuisine and the tea ceremony as taught by many different *iemoto*.

Rural Cuisine

The Masses: Making Do with Coarse Fare

A pitiful story recounts that at the deathbed of the provincial poor, a bamboo tube filled with a few grains of white rice was shaken. The dying person was then told, "Listen! This is white rice." Unable to consume such a treat while alive, the poor were at least to be granted the pleasure of hearing its sound in extremis.

This tale is no doubt an exaggeration. But a look at conditions of the peasantry during the Edo period will show that the peasant diet was no laughing matter. Bakufu policy dictated that peasants be deprived of everything but the absolute minimum necessary to continue production. Contemporary wisdom had it that "peasants are best ruled by giving them neither too much nor too little." Peasants were likened to falcons: too much freedom made them fat and lazy; but starving them, too, induced lethargy. A lesson on treating peasants could be learned by observing how oil was derived from sesame seeds: the more you squeezed, the more you got.

The bakufu promulgated numerous laws governing consumption. In 1642, brewing or selling *sake* in farm villages was forbidden. The production of tofu and the overconsumption of rice was proscribed. Buckwheat noodles *(soba)*, wheat noodles *(udon)*, vermicelli *(sōmen)*, rice-flour buns *(manjū)*, or anything else that required the use of the "five grains"—wheat, rice, barley, and two kinds of millet *(awa* and *kibi)*—was neither to be made nor sold. The *Gōyū hatto* (Ordinance Concerning Villages), the legal basis for the control of the peasantry, was issued in 1649.[13] According to this edict, neither *sake* nor tea was to be drunk; rice consumption was to be held to a minimum. The peasant was ordered to feed on wheat *(mugi)* and Deccan grass *(hie)*. Potatoes, giant white radishes *(daikon),* and the like were to be treated as staples, not as dietary supplements.

To what extent this law was effective remains unclear, but the diet of the average peasant appears to have been coarse indeed. In the latter half of the seventeenth century Kumazawa Banzan (1619–1691) described the conditions of the peasantry in the Kansai area:

> Peasants toil and suffer all year long; everything they produce is taken away as annual tribute. Those who cannot provide enough are forced to sell their wives, daughters, fields, forestland, or livestock. Peasants thus leave home, becoming vagrants and beggars; those who remain in the village die of starvation in years of bad harvests.[14]

The conditions of the peasantry in the Musashino area (now part of Tokyo) during the first half of the eighteenth century are described by Tanaka Kyūgu (1663–1729) in his *Minkan seiyō* (Reflections on Civil Society, 1721):

> Peasants who reside in areas with rice paddies may sometimes eat rice, but only in combination with other edibles. Many of those who live in the mountains or areas with dry fields cannot even eat rice for the three festive days of the new year. Even when cooking millet, Deccan grass, or wheat, they mix in so many greens, turnips, potato leaves, bean leaves, or other leaves that one can hardly see the grain. Moreover, they eat such food only once a day—not twice—and supplement their meal with watery gruel. They do not even sit for their meal. . . . Despite this horrible diet, they must work [in the fields] from four in the morning until midnight, after which they twine rope or make shoes and straw sandals.[15]

The diet of all except the wealthiest peasants was obviously miserable.

Tanaka Kyūgu notes that city dwellers probably will not believe what he writes, leading us to assume that those living in castle towns had it somewhat better. But not everyone. A young warrior student of the Shōheikō, the official school of the bakufu, recorded that he usually ate only pickles for breakfast, soup for lunch, and leftover rice for supper. A warrior-class student of the official school of the Saga domain noted that here too breakfast meant pickles, lunch was one vegetarian dish, and supper meant nothing more than a few parched sesame seeds mixed with salt. Schooling of course implied ascetic spiritual training and austerities, but a large portion of the Edo-period population, whether warrior, peasant, artisan, or merchant, lived on a diet much worse than one might imagine.

Ceremonial occasions, however, were often the scene of lavish festive parties with mountains of food and endless drinking. Here, too, the contemporary reader is left puzzled. Yet overconsumption at marriages, funerals, and other ceremonies was a deeply rooted practice. Grandiose feasts at New Year's, the five annual festivals, *bon*, and other special public ceremonial occasions provided dietary supplements to the masses. At these festivals participants regaled on foods such as sushi or *kamaboko* (boiled fish paste). Such fare contained protein that was otherwise lacking in the diet. For the peasantry, festivals were thus recreation in the true, physiological sense of the word.

Food Offered to Guests

Though peasants ordinarily survived on a very meager diet, the arrival of a special guest required a feast fit for a king. This was all the more true when the guest was a government official. Let us consider an example.[16]

On the thirteenth day of the ninth month of 1727, the night of moon-viewing festivities, Chōbee, the village headman *(shōya)* of Kusaka village in the province of Kawachi, recorded in detail the circumstances surrounding inspections of rice plants by Osaka officials. These officials had come to gather evidence, based on which the amount of the annual tribute was to be calculated. The eleven inspectors and other officials who were feted on this occasion were divided into two groups differentiated by rank: a higher-ranking group of two top officials, two lower officials, and two men-in-waiting, for a total of six men; and a lower group consisting of two porters, two sandal carriers, and one servant, for a total of five members. Room and board for each group differed, but for the village both groups were important guests indeed.

A professional chef from Yabeemachi in Osaka was hired to prepare the meals. Rice and three types of soup were offered to both groups: loach soup, soup with burdock cut in thin strips to look like bamboo grass, and stone-leek soup. Octopus and *kamaboko* were offered to the high-ranking group, but the lower group was only given octopus. The latter group was also offered a vinegared dish *(namasu)* consisting of something called *meshiro,* giant white radish, chestnuts, ginger, and *kikurage* mushrooms; as a "take-home present" members received a broiled carp *(funa).* The high-ranking group feasted on a deluxe combination of raw sliced carp and sea bream with a *choku* of mustard *(karashi)* and vinegared miso, a *tsubo* of tofu and yam *(nagaimo),* and a "take-home present" of a broiled young sea bream.[17] Also served were *kokushō* (the flesh of carp boiled in a thick *miso* soup) and dried Japanese peppers. The loach for this meal was ordered five days in advance. Tobacco for the guests was specially cut for the occasion. Three people were sent to Osaka to purchase various necessities; ten more servants were set to cleaning the vicinity of the house and the well. The food served on this day was clearly the best cuisine that contemporary farm villages could muster for important warriors and officials.

Substitute Foods in Times of Famine

Major famines—striking over thirty times in two and a half centuries—were one of the hallmarks of the Edo period. Responsibility for dealing with such crises was borne by the domains, each of which was in effect an independent feudal state. During times of famine, neighboring domains regarded each other as little more than enemies. Such sectionalism made effective intervention difficult. Northeastern farm villages were dealt a particularly severe blow by the great famines of the Tenmei period (1781–1789). Conditions of those disastrous times are described in the *Tenmei nendo kyōsai nikki* (Diary of the Terrible Years of the Tenmei Period), which makes for almost unbearable reading.

To combat famine, little-known substitute foods were studied and recommended. The *Minkan bikō-roku* (Records for Civil Preparedness, 1755) and the *Kyūkō mago no tsue* (A Prop for Relieving Hardship, 1836) list a number of edible substances, some of which were again used as substitute foods during World War II: rice bran, partly ripened unhulled rice, a type of bindweed *(hirugao)*, the tuberous roots of a snake gourd, and bitter acorns. Acorns were consumed after being steeped in lye to remove the bitterness and then soaked in water to remove the taste of the lye. The young leaves of a greater plantain *(ōbako)*, plantain lily *(giboshi)*, dandelion, garden balsam *(hōsenka)*, amaranth *(hageito)*, the blossoms of forget-me-nots, honeysuckle, gardenia, wisteria, and chrysanthemum were scalded, dressed with *miso,* or cooked with rice.

The *Gōyū hatto,* cited earlier, admonishes: "It is wasteful to discard the leaves of soybeans, *azuki* beans, cowpeas, potatoes, and the like. Just consider times of famine!" Times in which the leaves of beans and potatoes could be eaten were still relatively good; frost and snow rendered even such food unavailable. As a last resort even rice straw and pine bark were consumed. Since such substances could not simply be ingested as found, they were first processed or mixed with rice or wheat flour to make dumplings. Cattle, horses, dogs, and monkeys were of course consumed, as were all kinds of wild animals. A book from the second decade of the nineteenth century, the *Kyūki seishoku-hō shūsho* (Collected Writings on Famine Relief and Preparing Food), even explains how to prepare clay for consumption.[18]

During the German army's siege of Leningrad in World War II, Russian troops are reported to have resorted to devouring mice whole; then, as a last resort, they licked the glue used to hold together furniture. No such reports exist from the Edo period. And, strangely, one finds no instructions on preparing snakes, lizards, or earthworms.

Delicacies for Travelers

After so much talk of famine, we too need some relief. Let us turn next to the food that travelers ate at the fifty-three stops of the Tōkaidō highway. In 1817 Yamagata Heiemon Shigeyoshi, the master of the scholar Yamagata Bantō (1748–1821), was summoned by the lord of Sendai.[19] Yamagata left Osaka by boat on the eighteenth day of the first month and then traveled on highways to arrive in Sendai on the twelfth day of the second month. In his detailed travel diary, he recorded exactly what he ate at each of the inns at which he lodged.

For lunch on the nineteenth, while looking out over Lake Biwa near Atsuta, Yamagata ate corbicula soup; a dish of carrots, burdock, and kelp; and a dish of trefoil dressed with white sesame sauce. Toward evening he arrived at Kusatsu in snowy weather; here it was so cold that even the lamp oil froze. Supper consisted of a vinegared dish *(namasu)* of giant white radish *(daikon)*, persimmon, and greens; a soup of greens and dried bean curds; a *hira* of *kamaboko*, gourd shavings *(kanpyō)*, and burdock; and a broiled salted mackerel. The next morning he ate white beet soup; a *hira* of Japanese cabbage *(mizuna)*, *shiitake* mushroom, and dried bean curd; a *choku* of pickled salted plums; and a roasted dried fish. Yamagata crossed Suzuka Pass in heavy snow and spent the night at the bottom of the opposite slope: the twenty-first found him in Kuwana; the twenty-second, in Miya. Although the surroundings changed considerably, food on the Tōkaidō highway stayed basically the same at every inn. As soups, *hira*, *tsubo*, or broiled fish were not varied by introducing locally available specialties, the cuisine was quite monotonous.

This was an official trip. Travel expenses for Yamagata and his attendant, a doctor, five porters, three packhorse drivers, and three horses were probably paid by the lord of Sendai. Thus meals at each post town must have been of a high quality. Although one must take into account that Yamagata's journey took place in the middle of winter, the lack of variety in the cuisine is surprising. Soups always included giant white radish, either fresh or dried; the *hira* always featured combinations of dried gourd shavings *(kanpyō)*, tofu, burdock, carrot, potato, kelp, *shiitake* mushrooms, and, as recorded on a few occasions, dried laver *(nori)* and *kamaboko*. The *tsubo* consisted of *kokushō;* of tofu boiled in water, soy sauce, and *sake;* of burdock; or of light wheat gluten cakes. Broiled fish usually meant mackerel, young sea bream, sole, or yellowtail. Exceptional meals included the eel served for supper at an inn at Arai and the "fluffy eggs" eaten for breakfast at Fukuroi. Today Japanese travelers would tire of such fare in two or three days. Such cuisine gives us yet another insight into conditions on the Tōkaidō during an age in which the pace of life was much slower than it is today.

Once Yamagata had passed Edo and headed for the northeast, some local color appears in his meals. At Kasukabe broiled carp *(funa)* was served; at Odawara he ate a wild duck. Broiled fish was almost invariably salmon or gurnard *(kanagashira)*, but at Koshigawa he received dried cod flavored with *sake*. Nevertheless, both soups and *hira* featured nothing out of the ordinary. Even the fact that *udo* (probably *yamaudo*) was eaten at the stay at Kasukabe on the fifth day of the second month seems remarkable in this context. If high-class inns on the Tōkaidō and Ōshū-kaidō served this kind of fare during the late Edo period, one may assume that both the quality and preparation of food at townsmen's homes must have been quite mediocre by today's standards.

Emergence of the Restaurant *(Ryōrijaya)*

Restaurants and the Pleasure Quarters

Imagine the lively *shamisen* sounds of "Tsukuda no aikata." From a rowboat you hear someone singing:

Blow, river winds! Up with the bamboo blind!
Let me see the countenance of my songstress within![20]

This was the atmosphere of the San'ya-bori quarters (commonly known as the *"hori,"* the canal) leading from Edo to the Yoshiwara pleasure district. Also located at San'ya was the "Yaozen," a renowned and highly popular restaurant.

According to a story in the *Kanten kenbunki* (Eyewitness Accounts from the Kansei to the Tenpō Periods [1789–1844]),[21] one day at the start of the nineteenth century several men entered the "Yaozen" after a bout of drinking. Making their way through the blue and white curtain at the entrance, they sat down and ordered rice with extra-fine green tea and pickles. But wait as they would, no food

Tsukuda no aikata

Tsukuda no aikata. From *Ō-Edo mangekyō.*

appeared. Finally, after nearly half a day's wait, the desired pickles, rice, and an earthenware teapot of green tea arrived. The pickles were of a very rare variety: an assortment of melon and eggplant pickled in *sake* lees. After such a long delay, the three men eagerly wolfed down the food. But when the bill was presented they were taken aback: 1 *ryō* and 2 *bu* for rice and tea—today the equivalent of several hundred dollars. Dumbfounded, they asked for an explanation. According to Zenshirō, the head of "Yaozen," the pickles were indeed expensive, as was the tea. The steep price of the meal, however, was a result of the lack of suitable water for brewing high-grade tea. Since no such water was available locally, a runner had been sent to the Tama River. The exorbitant price of hiring this runner had been the main expense of the meal.

True or not, this story indicates that by the start of the nineteenth century such restaurants were present in Edo. Let us examine the emergence of these businesses. At the start of the Edo period no specialty shops offered cuisine for sale as a commodity. Confectioners or buckwheat noodle (soba) shops can be found from an early time, but in the "three capitals"—Edo, Osaka, and Kyoto—true restaurants seem not to have appeared until after the middle of the seventeenth century. In the volume Saikaku oki miyage (A Present Left by Saikaku), published in 1693, Ihara Saikaku notes that "recently a teahouse at the Kinryūzan, a temple at Asakusa, has begun to sell 'Nara tea'. One serving costs 5 bu in silver. Many kinds of beautiful dishes are used. . . . Such a convenient arrangement cannot be found in the Kansai area."[22] From this we may gather that not long before this book's publication, restaurants selling something known as "Nara tea" had appeared in Edo. "Nara tea" is described in greater detail in the Kinsei kiseki-kō (Miracles of Recent Years), published in 1804.[23] The author, Santō Kyōden, comments that after the great Meireki fire of 1657 a shop opened up at Asakusa, where under the

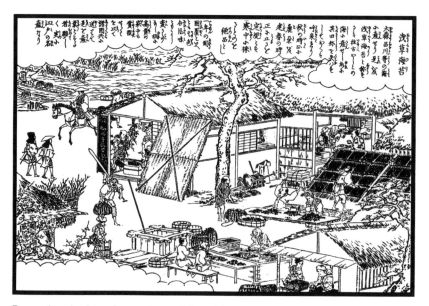

Preparing Asakusa laver. From Edo meisho zue.

name of "Nara tea" a combination of tea over rice, soup with tofu, fish and vegetables boiled in soy sauce, and boiled beans was served. This dish aroused the curiosity of the citizenry, which eagerly came to sample the fare. Such a restaurant must have been established during the 1660s, in the restoration that followed the Meireki conflagration.

Cookbooks were frequently published from around the time Asai Ryōi issued the gazetteer *Tōkaidō meisho-ki* (Record of Famous Spots on the Tōkaidō, published ca. 1658–1661) and a collection of fantastic stories entitled *Otogi bōko* (published in 1666). The *Ryōri monogatari* (Tales of Cooking), which came out in 1643, is one of the earliest examples of a published cookbook in Japan. This book is completely different from the secret transmissions of the Shijō school. Here one finds no descriptions of stiff, formal rituals for food preparation. Instead, the *Ryōri monogatari* treats food actually consumed by the citizenry. Instructions are given on preparing some twenty types of soups, vinegared dishes, broiled fish, and much else. A similar book, the *Edo ryōri-shū* (Collection of Edo Cuisine), was published in six volumes in 1674, shortly after the appearance of "Nara tea."[24] In the sixth volume one finds, for example, some forty-three detailed descriptions of such dishes as clear soup with sea bream or clear soup with whitebait *(shirauo).*

Shops specializing in cuisine first appeared in Edo, but they did not develop rapidly. For the gourmet, both *chōnin* and warrior, the center of social life continued to be the licensed quarters at Yoshiwara. Until the Hōreki period (1751–1764) one hears nothing of Edo restaurants other than the plebeian ones serving "Nara tea." During the tranquil Tanuma period (1767–1786), however, two teahouses suddenly changed the world of Edo cuisine. One of these houses, the "Surugaya," was located at Asakusa Komagata-chō; the other, the "Masuya," stood at Suzaki. In the 1770s and 1780s the "Surugaya" became the site of the annual general meeting of Asakusa *fudasashi.* This gathering always featured a lavish feast. Hence the "Surugaya," though not offering any noted specialty, must have been a large-scale restaurant. The "Masuya" was patronized by rich merchants, "connoisseurs," and Edo representatives of the various daimyo. Meetings for entertaining bakufu or domanial officials were held here so often that the "Masuya" became known as the "Orusui-jaya"—the "teahouse of daimyo representatives stationed in Edo." From the *Kumo no itomaki* (The Spider's Reel, 1846) one learns that this restaurant's architecture was extremely sumptuous and that the "Masuya" was frequented by Lord Nankai (Matsudaira Munenobu, 1729–1782), the father of the famous daimyo and tea master Matsudaira Fumai (or Harusato, 1751–1818), as well as Fumai's younger brother Matsudaira Sessen (1753–1803).[25]

After the heyday of the "Surugaya" and "Masuya," other Edo restaurants begin to appear. One reads of the "Niken-jaya" at Fukagawa, of the forerunner of the "Yaozen," and of the "Momokawa" (later in charge of the food offered to Admiral Perry). *Shippoku* cuisine also became available at Ukiyokōji in Nihonbashi. Other well-known establishments included the "Yamafuji" at Saeki-chō, the "Kasai Tarō" at Mukōjima (famous for chilled carp), and the "Daikokuya Magoshirō."

After the oppressive Kansei era (1789–1801), Edo witnessed an upsurge in vitality and popular restaurants entered their golden age. It was said that in Edo "every five paces, one finds a large building; every ten paces, one finds a stately one—each serving food and drink." Famous older restaurants were joined by countless new establishments. The former included the "Yaozen" at San'ya and the "Hirasei" at Fukagawa Ōhashi. These were considered the best two restaurants in the city from the end of Edo period until well into Meiji times. Other notable restaurants of the time included the "Kōshiya" at Massaki, the "Shikian" at Nakasu, the "Yanagiya" at Hashiba, the "Kinparō" at Imado, the "Daishichi," "Musashiya," and "Ogura-an" at Mukōjima, the "Sakuragawa" and "Manpachi" at Yanagibashi, and the "Tagawa" at Ryūsenji.

Almost all these restaurants lay along the boat route of the Sumida River. On the banks of this river, fresh ocean and river fish were available in abundance and at a reasonable price. Indeed, this geographical advantage was a major reason why the pleasure quarters were constructed there. The presence of the *Tatsumi geisha*—the unlicensed but fashionable "town geisha" of the Fukagawa area—contributed greatly to the success of these teahouses and restaurants. Much of the culture of the city of Edo, with its standards of *iki* and *tsū*, arose here. Fine cuisine, the manners of the "town geisha," and the efforts of prosperous *chōnin* and "men of taste" *(tsūkaku)* provided the ingredients for the creation of many new cultural forms. Restaurants such as the "Yaozen" and "Hirasei" gained their reputations within this historical context.

The atmosphere of gatherings of *tsūkaku* at such first-rate Edo restaurants was something truly special. One can sense this, for example, in a scroll entitled "Tamagiku" (1826) painted by Watanabe Kazan (1793–1841) and today still in the possession of the "Yaozen." This scroll depicts a meeting of renowned literati at the anniversary commemorating the death of the famous courtesan Tamagiku. Ōta Nanpo, Tani Bunchō, and Sakai Hōitsu are present, as are the fourth and fifth generations of "Yaozen" chefs, who are depicted preparing food. At a similar gathering Ōta Nanpo composed the following verse:

Chinese poetry means Shibutsu; calligraphy, Hōsai; *kyōka*, me.
The best geisha, Kokatsu; the best food, "Yaozen."

The Shibutsu mentioned here is Ōkubo Shibutsu (1767–1837), who included many references to contemporary restaurants and sushi shops in his Chinese poems. Hōsai is Kameda Hōsai (1752–1826), who, together with the priest Ryōkan, ranked as one of the best calligraphers of the day. Both Shibutsu and Hōsai often patronized the "Yaozen," as did Hōitsu, Bunchō, and others. Kokatsu seems to have been a famous geisha from the San'ya-bori area immediately behind the "Yaozen."

Such gatherings of literati were characteristic of Edo. Meetings took place at the five annual festivals, on moon-viewing occasions and other festive days, or even at times when nothing in particular was being celebrated. A look at the detailed programs of *nagauta* performed by the eleventh Kineya Rokuzaemon (1815–1877) allows one to imagine how such gatherings must have felt. Rokuzaemon was a master singer and *iemoto* active from the Kasei period to the late 1850s. He was often invited to perform by daimyo, bannermen, nō masters, and powerful merchants. Quite often town geisha, or *tokiwazu* and *gidayū* musicians, were also in attendance. On such occasions elegant parties were staged at the inner parlors of warrior mansions or at restaurants; strangely, large restaurants such as the "Yaozen" and "Hirasei" are not mentioned in Rokuzaemon's programs.

Although Edo boasted many notable restaurants, the most fashionable site for social gatherings continued to be the "Yaozen." This establishment set the tone of Edo style in general. At the "Yaozen" *daikon* were supposedly washed with sweet *sake;* the ingredients of both *kamaboko* and *kinton* (mashed sweet potato with sweetened chestnuts) were subject to incredibly stringent inspections; and much labor was invested in all kinds of food preparation. Such practices gave rise to stories such as the one about the expensive tea.

Appearance of the Sushi Shop

With the opening of Japanese harbors, the collapse of the bakufu, and the arrival of the Meiji period, large-scale social changes occurred throughout the city. Many famous Edo restaurants moved

from the Yanagibashi area to Tsukiji, Shinbashi, Akasaka, and elsewhere. By the early years of the twentieth century, political parties
often supported specific restaurants. The "Shinkiraku" at Tsukiji, for
example, was backed by the Seiyūkai; its star rival, the "Kagetsu" at
Shinbashi, was supported by the Kenseikai. Such high-class restaurants were an important presence in the city during this era.

Other restaurants were patronized chiefly by the citizenry. One
such establishment, famous for its wild boar meat, was the "Momon-
jiya" at Ryōgoku. And no discussion of the city's cuisine at the time is
complete without a mention of split and broiled eel, known as *oka-
bayaki*. An early illustration of a plebeian eel shop—with rattan
screens propped against the walls and a large paper lantern emblazoned with the words "Fresh from Edo: Broiled Eel on Rice"—can be
found in Jippensha Ikku's *kibyōshi* entitled *Bunbuku chagama* (The
Magic Teakettle, published in 1799). From the end of Edo until
Meiji the "Ōnoya" at Fukiya-chō in Edo, or the "Chikuyō" at Shimabara in Kyoto, found great favor for such fare.

At the end of the Edo period the charming sight of sushi vendors
selling *kohada-zushi* (sushi topped with a small gizzard shad) could be
seen in the streets of Edo. *Nigiri-zushi*—bite-sized sushi made by
squeezing a small amount of rice in the hand—was an Edo specialty

A shop specializing in broiled eel. From *Bunbuku chagama*, 1799. (In the
possession of the Tokyo Metropolitan Central Library.)

that appeared during the Bunsei period (1818–1830). This sushi soon became all the rage. The most conspicuous *nigiri-zushi* vendors sold *kohada-zushi*. These hawkers covered their heads with a hand towel in Yoshiwara fashion; they wore narrow-striped kimono tucked up behind, short coats with broad stripes and black silk collars, sashes known as a Hakata obi, cotton leggings with white socks, and sandals made of straw and linen. Such a unique outfit made *kohada-zushi* vendors quite striking in appearance. From the start of spring until early summer, sushi peddlers sauntered through the streets and called out in a mellifluous voice, "Sushi! Hey! *Kohada-zushi!*" One can even find an Ansei-period (1854–1860) popular song that went: "I tricked a priest and returned him to secular life—how I'd like to see him sell *kohada-zushi!*"

Nigiri-zushi was also sold by "Atakematsu" of Atakegura in Honjo; eventually this sushi came to be known simply as "Matsu's sushi." Similar sushi shops were located throughout the capital. The *Morisada mankō* reports that one or two could be found on each city block.[26] Most were mere street stalls, but true restaurants existed as well. At any rate, sushi was highly popular. From Edo the sushi fashion spread to the Kamigata area. In the late 1820s a restaurant called "Matsu no sushi" appeared south of Ebisubashi in Osaka. This was the first Osaka outlet of Edo sushi; but before long this specialty was sold at shops throughout Osaka.

Edo *nigiri-zushi* included versions topped with egg, whole shrimp, steamed shrimp that was crushed and parched, whitebait, tuna, sea eel, *kohada*, and sushi wrapped in laver. *Nigiri-zushi* with octopus, squid, or shellfish may also have been consumed, but no records seem to substantiate this practice. During the Kaei period (1848–1854), around the time of Perry's arrival, such sushi was commonly called "8-*mon* sushi" in reference to its price. Sushi with egg, however, was twice as expensive. These figures are of course mere approximations: prices varied according to the restaurant and the quality of the ingredients.

The "Kenuki," another famous old sushi shop, is still in business in Tokyo today. It produced *sasa-zushi*, a special kind of sushi sold at Hettsui-gashi. Each piece was individually wrapped in bamboo grass (*sasa*), stacked in a wooden tub, and pressed using a rock as a weight. This was high-grade sushi selling for 16 *mon*, double the usual price. The name "Kenuki" ("tweezers") is said to originate from this restaurant's practice of removing fish bones with tweezers, but the word *kenuki* may have also implied, in pun form, "delicious."[27] Perhaps this name was also an oblique reference to the tweezers that appear in the well-known kabuki play *Kenuki* (one of

A sushi vendor's booth of the late nineteenth century. From *Morisada mankō*, 1830s–1860s.

the "eighteen favorites"). Although the "Kenuki" was the first restaurant to market *sasa-zushi,* it was not its inventor. One can find *sasamaki-zushi* listed in the book *Fukijizai* (1777),[28] where it appears as a specialty of Shinagawa-chō. This type of sushi must have been popular in Edo from an early date.

Types of sushi known as *chirashi-zushi* and *gomoku-zushi* (or *okoshi-zushi*)—in which vinegared rice is placed in a small bowl rather than squeezed into small bite-sized pieces—were made almost the same way they are today. This sushi cost between 100 and 150 *mon*. When *chirashi-zushi* was put in a large dish for a group of guests, each person took out a small amount and placed it on a small saucer from which it was eaten.

Today sushi shops operate year-round, but in the past the

demand for sushi fell drastically in the winter. During the winter, all but the most famous sushi restaurants are said to have sold carp wrapped in kelp.

Many Edo restaurants specialized in tofu dishes. During the Bunsei period (1818–1830), tofu dishes were known as *sasa no yuki* ("snowy bamboo grass"). The section on food in the preface of the *Fukijizai* lists *awayuki* (tofu dressed with liquid starch) from the "Hinoya" and "Akashiya" at Ryōgoku and the "Tsuboya" at Fukiya-chō.[29] Other tofu dishes cited include *Gion-dōfu* from restaurants in Yushima and *yudōfu* (tofu boiled in water) from restaurants at Nezu-monzen. Many tofu restaurants existed; famous ones included the "Hamadaya" at Ueno-Yamashita and the "Kameya" at Asakusa. One such restaurant, the "Niken-jaya" at Negishi-Shinden, was renowned for catering to customers on their way to Yoshiwara. As a result, *sasa no yuki* became something of a proper noun identifying this restaurant.

The Success of Soba Shops

As noted earlier, the first Edo restaurant was the one at Asakusa that served "Nara tea." Famous *shitamachi* restaurants were usually located at popular spots in the city. Business flourished because such restaurants allowed people to fill their bellies quickly and cheaply. Even more convenient were shops serving buckwheat noodles *(soba)* with soup. Many shops selling noodles made of wheat flour *(udon)* operated in the Kamigata area, but in Edo *soba* shops prevailed. Even today, few Tokyo restaurants display signs announcing only *udon* for sale.

Soba was once called *soba kiri* (buckwheat cuttings). The *Ryōri monogatari,* cited earlier, gives instructions on how these are made:

Good results may be obtained by kneading [the buckwheat flour] with water from boiling rice. For kneading one may also use [plain] warm water or water obtained by grinding tofu. The dough should be cut into small bits. These should be boiled with sufficient water. After cooking, excess water should be drained using a bamboo colander. Quickly rinse in warm water, put in a bamboo colander, and pour on hot water. Then cover with a lid to prevent cooling. Drain excess water before serving.

The soup is the same as used for *udon,* but *daikon* juice may be added. Shavings of dried bonito, *karashi* [a kind of mustard], *wasabi* [a kind of horseradish], or things such as grated *asatsuki* [a kind of chive] may also be added.[30]

Roasting tofu and making noodles. From *Jinrin kinmōzui.*

Shops specializing in *soba kiri* did not appear until long after this recipe was published. The *Morisada mankō,* however, records that by the nineteenth century *soba* shops existed on nearly every block of Edo. By this time both *morisoba* (*soba* served on a screen-bottomed vessel) and *kakesoba* (*soba* served in a bowl with soup) differed little from today. During the days when one piece of *nigiri-zushi* cost 8 *mon,* a serving of *soba* or *udon* was priced at 16 *mon.* Contemporary signboards and lanterns placed outside such restaurants were often marked with the words "*ni-hachi* (twice 8) *soba/udon.*"

A good description of Edo *soba* shops can be found in Asada Denkyō's "Soba no mukashi-banashi" (Tales of *Soba*). Asada was a wholesaler of *soba* ingredients. Indeed, he distributed between three thousand and five thousand 72-liter sacks of buckwheat annually and could judge the place of origin, quality of soil, and even the type of fertilizer used simply by sampling a few kernels of the grain. Even local farmers were reportedly impressed with his skill at judging buckwheat. In the "Soba no mukashi-banashi," one finds the following excerpt:

Just as the *soba* shops of the old days had cooks and delivery boys, they also had millers who worked a mortar found at each shop. The millers were controlled by bosses, each of whom had his own jealously guarded territory. Each miller normally ground an eighty-one liter sack of flour a day.

In the kabuki a few years ago, the *soba* delivery boy in the play *Sukeroku* mentioned something about whose employee he was, that he was good looking, and that he was from Rokkenbori. But the boss mentioned was not from the correct territory. This provoked a great scandal; peace was restored only after the lines were changed. If I

Morisoba and *kakesoba*. From *Morisada mankō*, 1830s–1860s.

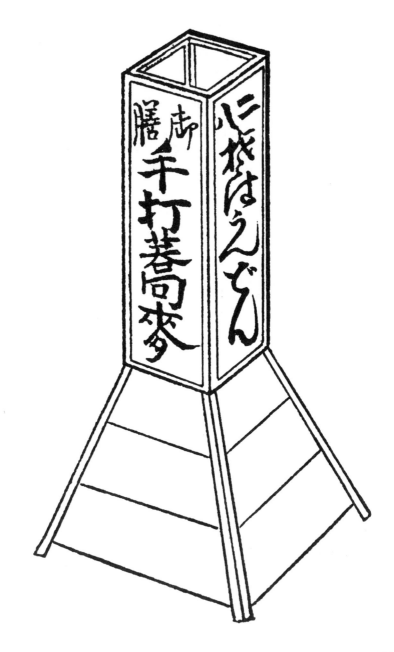

A sign for "two times eight" *soba* and *udon*. From *Morisada mankō*, 1830s–1860s.

remember correctly, the actor who played the delivery boy was named Matsusuke; but he has since passed away.[31]

The delivery boy in *Sukeroku* could only have been a reference to a famous *udon* shop at Sakai-chō. If Matsusuke (Onoe Matsusuke IV, 1843–1928) did indeed play this role, the story must be referring to Meiji times. Today one can no longer witness the sight of flour being ground by hand before being kneaded into *soba*. During the Meiji era, however, such scenes were still common. Social relations among the merchant and artisan classes remained almost unchanged from the Edo period. Similarly, strong ties continued to exist between bosses and underlings, even for delivery boys and millers.

In another interesting tale, Asada describes a special kind of *soba:*

> There was a type of high-class *soba* known as *goshiki soba* [five-color *soba*]. A red color was derived by peeling a prawn, grinding and straining the flesh, and then kneading this into the *soba* flour; green was obtained by mixing in ground green tea; kneading in egg yolks yielded a yellow color; including the egg white made it white; black *soba* resulted from mixing in roasted powdered kelp. In other words, "five-color *soba*" included what was otherwise called "tea *soba*" or "egg *soba*" and the like. The five types of noodles were carefully placed in a stack of lacquered boxes. In the old days housekeepers of daimyo often ordered *soba*. This made *soba* a profitable business.[32]

This story, told by an old-time professional, clearly dates from the end of the Edo period.

Translator's Summary

Throughout the Edo period, much cuisine was shared by both the warrior nobility and the common people. At the start of the period some types of food were introduced from China and other foreign countries. Shortly thereafter, the warrior class set about refining its cuisine by borrowing elements of the culinary arts developed by the imperial court in Kyoto. Warrior cuisine had hitherto been somewhat coarse, for only a short time earlier many warriors had been unsophisticated rural inhabitants. Indeed, well into the Edo period some daimyo and shogun continued to consume only coarse fare.

As Japanese society became more sharply divided into social classes, types of cuisine began to symbolize distinctions of rank. Methods of food preparation were also increasingly codified, and *iemoto* often controlled the transmission of a family's traditional culinary techniques. The most powerful *iemoto* of cuisine was the Shijō family, which still exists today. This school's secret teachings are carefully recorded in manuscript form.

Yet another style of Japanese cuisine that developed rapidly during the Edo period was *kaiseki*. This style probably resulted when elements of the elegant, subdued *wabicha* tea ceremony were combined with parts of the banquet style of the medieval aristocracy. At the start of the Edo period, *kaiseki* allowed for great freedom and imagination. During the next few centuries, however, the *kaiseki* style became increasingly rigid. Tea ceremony *iemoto* now spread this style to the commoner classes.

Most of the Edo-period populace, however, lived on coarse fare. In fact, many expensive delicacies were prohibited by law. Travelers, too, even the wealthiest, had little to choose from on the road. During times of famine, which occurred with alarming frequency, the masses made do with whatever was available. During good times, however, festive occasions such as weddings or the arrival of high-ranking guests meant lavish feasts and overconsumption.

During the latter half of the Edo period, Japanese commoner cuisine, especially that of the urban areas, developed rapidly. By the eighteenth century many cookbooks explaining "secret teachings" of various *iemoto* were being published for the citizenry. Already at the end of the seventeenth century restaurants had sprung up in large cities such as Osaka and Edo. Many eating establishments were associated with the pleasure quarters and were patronized by both the common folk and wealthy merchants or warriors. Other small shops or vendors offered buckwheat noodles, broiled eel, or various types of sushi.

Today many of the traditions associated with the court and various *iemoto* of cuisine have been lost. Nevertheless, many types of food described in Edo-period sources continue to be consumed by the Japanese public.

PART III

THEATER AND MUSIC:

FROM THE BAKUFU TO THE BEGGAR

CHAPTER 9

THE SOCIAL CONTEXT OF NŌ

Support for nō during the Edo period came from members of three social groups: the bakufu; the daimyo and other high-ranking members of the warrior class; and the general public. Nō masters employed by the bakufu were granted rice stipends. These salaries were in effect supplied by various domains, but the nō masters' privileges were guaranteed by the bakufu itself.

Peace prevailed throughout the land after the Genna period (1615–1624), allowing the population of nō devotees to increase rapidly. Bakufu officials such as bannermen and household retainers, as well as daimyo and their high-ranking retainers, were in fact allowed to stage performances of the nō. For them, dancing the nō and playing the instrumental accompaniment on the flute (*fue* or nōkan) and drums *(kotsuzumi, ōkawa,* and *taiko)* were cultural accomplishments and an important part of social life. Although few men were sufficiently proficient to give authentic performances of the dances, a large warrior-class population learned the chants and the instrumental accompaniments. In fact, nō chant *(utai)* became highly fashionable. As a result, nō troupes began to change their conservative methods for transmitting their "house arts" *(iegei).* To meet the demands of a large population of amateurs, both warrior and commoner, an *iemoto* system began to arise.

Nō at the Date House in Sendai

An example of a daimyo house that practiced nō is provided by the Date family of the Sendai domain in Mutsu province. Throughout his life, Date Masamune (1567–1636), the founder of this domain, sponsored nō performances. Indeed, he was so fond of nō that he learned to play the *taiko.* Daimyo and sometimes even the shogun were invited to these performances.[1] Masamune's personal nō master was Sakurai Hachiemon; but Hachiemon's abilities did not fully satisfy Masamune. Masters *(tayū)* of the Ōkura school, as well as the *iemoto* of the Kanze, Hōshō, and Kita schools of nō, were therefore invited to Sendai. Sakurai Hachiemon, in turn, was sent to the main Konparu school in Nara to master this school's style.[2] From around this time, Konparu-style nō was taught and performed at the Date house. One finds, for example, that in 1691 Tsunamura, the fourth head of the Sendai domain, learned *Okina* from Ōkura Shōzaemon,[3] a master from a branch house of the Konparu school.[4]

Of the long line of Sendai daimyo, Tsunamura and his son Yoshimura showed the greatest interest in nō. From the end of the seventeenth to the first half of the eighteenth centuries, these two men learned much of the tradition from Ōkura Shōzaemon. Records documenting the transmission of the repertory are preserved at the nō research center (Nōgaku kenkyū-jo) at Hōsei University in Tokyo. Here one finds numerous books of the Ōkura house copied by Yoshimura, the fifth Sendai daimyo. One such volume is a 1726 copy of the 1688 manuscript *Rokurin ichiro nukigaki* (Extracts from the *Rokurin ichiro* [a volume on the theory of nō of Konparu Zenchiku]). Other works copied include the following:

Okina no narai katatsuke (The Secret Play *Okina* and Its Dance Steps)
Dōjōji narai no kudensho (Oral Transmissions of the Secret Play *Dōjōji*)
Sekidera Komachi sōden (The Tradition of the Play *Sekidera Komachi*)
Konparu-ryū sōden kikigaki (Records of Oral Transmissions of the
    Konparu School)
Konparu-ryū migamae ashi no suriyō no jōjō (Items on Stances and Steps
    of the Konparu School)
Tsue no tsukiyō sono ta (How to Use a Cane, etc.)
Sarugaku-den kuketsu no bensho (Explanatory Writings on the Oral
    Tradition of *Sarugaku*)
Hashi, Mimosuso, Fujisan, Takuren (Bridges, Clothing, Mount Fuji,
    Takuren)[5]

In works such as *Senju kusemai no koto* (On the *Senju kusemai*), *Tadanori no hantome no koto* (The Half-Close of the Play *Tadanori*), or *Nonomiya kuruma no koto* (On the Carriage in the Play "The Shrine in the Fields") one finds detailed descriptions and instructions concerning the performance of Konparu-school versions of *naraigoto*— works whose performance rights were granted only to certain licensed individuals. Yoshimura was granted licenses for performing even the secret plays *Dōjōji, Sekidera Komachi,* and *Okina.* The transmission of *Okina,* in particular, seems to have been accorded extraordinary significance. The record of this secret transmission, entitled *Sarugaku-den kuketsu no bensho,* was tightly sealed and secured. On the recto of the outermost wrapping of this volume one finds the words:

> Enclosed is a copy of the secret oral transmission of the play *Okina* as handed down by the Konparu house. This transmission is to be handed down only to the eldest son of the house; even a second son is not to be granted permission. Even after the transmission has been fully mastered, these writings are to be viewed only after the proper religious observances. This teaching is the highest secret among all the transmissions granted exclusively to the eldest son.

On the verso one finds the words: "The ninth month of the fourteenth year of Kyōhō [1729], resealed by Ōkura Shōzaemon."[6] This covering also carries Yoshimura's seal. Beneath this outside wrapper, two more covers of Japanese paper are sealed and marked with the words: "secret writings on the transmission of the play *Okina* to an eldest son." Finally, a sealed inner wrapper bears the words: "copy of a divinely mystical oral tradition." Only after removing these four layers of wrapping, each carrying words written by Yoshimura, does one come to the secret writings themselves.

Yoshimura also learned such top-secret transmissions when the Ōkura *tayū* came to Sendai in 1732. Inside Yoshimura's copy of *Hashi, Mimosuso, Fujisan, Takuren* one finds the following words in Yoshimura's hand:

> This was copied in its entirety from a volume graciously lent to me by the Ōkura *tayū* during his recent stay in Sendai. The original was returned to him on his departure for Edo in the tenth month, the day before the text was to be set to a melody.
> The middle of the tenth month, 1732.
> Yoshimura

By such means Yoshimura learned the entire nō tradition from Ōkura Shōzaemon.

In the bakufu bureaucracy's arrangement of nō schools and performers, the Ōkura school was considered a branch of the Konparu school; Ōkura Shōzaemon was thus under the jurisdiction of the Konparu school's head family. Yet judging from the fact that top-secret works such as *Okina* and *Sekidera Komachi* were transmitted by the Ōkura house with no visible interference by the Konparu school's head family, the Ōkura house's transmission of the repertory seems to have occurred independent of the Konparu school. As far as transmitting the techniques of nō was concerned, Ōkura Shōzaemon was invested with the highest authority. He thus functioned as an independent *iemoto*. Similar conditions probably prevailed in other large domains.

The relation of Ōkura Shōzaemon to other nō masters stationed in Sendai is not clear, but a 1904 conversation of the nō flutist Morita Hatsutarō recorded in Ikenouchi Nobuyoshi's *Nōgaku seisuiki* (Records of the Vicissitudes of Nō) is suggestive:

> I had many disciples, over ten direct pupils in Edo alone. Pupils of my disciples taught at many daimyo residences. If one included all their students down to the most distantly related, the number would have been enormous. For this reason, during the days of the bakufu, my disciples taught almost all the lessons, and I personally gave lessons to only a very few daimyo.[7]

This statement refers to the end of the Edo period, but conditions in seventeenth-century Sendai may have been similar. No relation between the Konparu head family and the Date house can be detected at the time that Ōkura Shōzaemon came to Sendai for two or three months at a time. Thus Ōkura Shōzaemon may have functioned like Morita Hatsutarō, that is, giving lessons to Yoshimura, the Hakugoku family, and members of the house of Sakurai Hachiemon.

In summary, then, the history of nō at the Date house falls into two periods. At first, during the age of Date Masamune, Sakurai Hachiemon, a nō master of the Konparu school, was hired as an official nō instructor. Later, however, Sendai daimyo were instructed not by members of the head family of the Konparu school but by Ōkura Shōzaemon, who was from a branch family. It remains unclear how the shift from Sakurai Hachiemon to Ōkura Shōzaemon occurred, but evidently the Konparu head family did not have complete control over all of its branches. Thus the Ōkura family was able to control all nō performed within the Date domain. The Ōkura school eventually succeeded in earning the support of a large number of warrior-class nō performers. In effect, the *iemoto* system of the Konparu school was established by the Ōkura branch family, rather than the head family.

This discussion constitutes only a preliminary attempt to analyze the Date family's activities. More research is needed on nō in other domains and the economic power of the head families of other schools of nō.

Nō as portrayed in the *Jinrin kinmōzui*, 1690.

The World of Nō Chant

Although staged performances of nō were officially limited to warrior society, unaccompanied chant *(su-utai)* was very popular within civil society at large. *Su-utai* has been carefully studied by Nonomura Kaizō in his book *Nōgaku kokonki* (Records of Nō Past and Present). Nonomura makes use of historical sources such as Hokumonshi Bokkai Mohee's *Shinkyoku shōmyō higen* (Profound Words on the Secrets of Nō 1756) and Sasaki Haruyuki's *Su-utai yoyo no ato* (Traces of Unaccompanied Nō Chant Through the Ages, 1818).[8] From these documents Nonomura concludes that *su-utai* was created by the Fukuō school's Hattori Sōha (1609–1673) during the Kanbun period (1661–1673); later *su-utai* increased even further in popularity.[9] In 1957, however, Omote Akira published an article in which this theory is challenged.[10] According to Omote, *su-utai* had already appeared at the end of the Muromachi period. At this early date, gatherings for both unaccompanied chant and accompanied musical performances of complete pieces had already taken place in aristocratic circles. By the Keichō period (1596–1615) even professionals performed the plays *Ohara gokō (The Imperial Visit to Ohara)*, *Kinuta* (The Cloth-Beating Board), and *Semimaru* exclusively as unaccompanied chant. This trend then spread to Edo, where *su-utai* was performed by a broader sector of the populace. *Su-utai* teachers such as Hattori Sōha emerged from within this historical context.

Here I want to examine this kind of chant in the Kamigata area, for it was there that *su-utai* found the greatest popular support. According to Omote, *su-utai* can be traced to the Muromachi period, but it was not until the late seventeenth century that it spread to the general public and could no longer be ignored by schools of nō. Highly valuable documentation of activities within commoner society during the Genroku era (1688–1704) can be found in the *Kawachiya Yoshimasa kyūki*, a diary kept by Kawachiya Gohee Yoshimasa, a headman from Daigatsuka village (today in Osaka-fu).[11] The renowned nō master Kongō Ukyō-dayū, popularly known as "Hana Kongō," had lived in Daigatsuka during his youth and his influence led many people in the vicinity to learn Kongō school chant. One man even left his native village to chant in the nō chorus *(ji-utai)* of the Kongō company. The diary also records the existence of someone named Seiemon, who was fond of *waki* (supporting) roles and had received instruction from a teacher of the Fukuō school. Seiemon, who is noted as having had his differences with the Kongō school, had also learned to chant. Chūbee, another man mentioned in the diary, struggled to become a leading actor *(tayū)*. The diary also lists the names of several villagers who played the nō flute, the *kotsuzumi* drum, and the *ōkawa* drum. Then one reads that

> besides those listed above, since the old days, everyone living in this area plays an instrument, sings in the chorus, or acts the parts of subordinate to the *waki* or the *tayū*. The populace especially devotes itself to *utai*.[12]

Or one hears that at Higashi-machi (in present-day Yao city, Osaka-fu), Kan'emon, the town elder and owner of a flourishing *sake* brewing business, had a son named Tarōemon who

> followed the footsteps of his father and became the town elder; but he had many sick children and resigned his post. He was quite good at chanting *utai*, so he accepted *utai* students to make a living.[13]

Nearby Kasuga village also had its *sake* brewer, a man named Kasugaya Kyūzaemon, who had bought a share of the *sake* business of

Sakuemon from the same village. Together with Kawachiya Yoshi-masa, Kyūzaemon learned to play the *tsuzumi* and to chant the nō during his youth. Later, as his family's fortunes waned, he too supported himself by teaching nō chant and calligraphy to beginners. Such remarks show that during the Genroku period *utai* was sufficiently popular to allow a professional *utai* teacher to make a living in such villages. This popular demand indicates that learning *utai* must have had a long and flourishing tradition in this area.

Kawachiya Yoshimasa was a *tayū* who actually performed the dances of the nō. According to his diary, the presence of a *tayū* in this village had been a tradition since the Kan'ei period (1624–1644). Some eighty years later, at the time the diary was written, Chūbee had become a *tayū* and Seiemon a *waki*. To ensure the survival of the village tradition, Yoshimasa had his son Kosaburō become a nō *tayū*. Since both Chūbee and Seiemon were of the Fukuō school, Kosaburō probably received his training from this school also. When Kosaburō performed as a *tayū,* Yoshimasa himself played the role of the *waki*. This father-son team of leading and supporting roles toured Nara, Osaka, and Sakai. During the third month of 1696, both men even performed a five-day "subscription nō" *(kanjin nō)* in the castle town of Yodo (today Kyoto). For this performance the head of the domain and members of his household showered Yoshimasa and Kosaburō with a number of gifts. On the way home, as an expression of joy and gratitude, father and son gave a performance for headmen invited from all over the county.

Excuses for performing at private homes or at temples were always easy to find. On the twenty-sixth day of the third month of 1697, for example, at the celebration of the eighty-eighth birthday of the nun Myōju (the mother of the sixth head of the Fukuō school's Asano house), Yoshimasa and others performed *Kantan, Sakuragawa, Tōboku, Chōryō, Kumasaka,* and other plays. Comic plays *(kyōgen)* such as *Shūku-garakasa* (The Riddle Umbrella), *Kaki yama-bushi* (The Persimmon Thief), *Kikazu zatō* (The Deaf Man and the Blind Man), and *Akutarō* (Akutarō Reforms) were also staged. A small number of participants from Nara joined in, but all the other performers stemmed from Daigatsuka. On this occasion Yoshimasa played the part of the *waki* in *Chōryō;* all the lead *(shite)* roles were played by Kosaburō.

When the site of a hall of the Kenshōji, a temple in the town of Kyūhōji (today Osaka-fu), was granted tax-exempt status, a performance of "Felicitous Nō" *(yorokobi no nō)* was staged. At Daigatsuka, Nara Gon'emon often performed celebratory New Year's Nō *(matsu-bayashi)*. Nō was also frequently staged at nearby Tondabayashi by

Sugiyama Hachiemon, whom Wakita Osamu has identified as a rich merchant.[14] Performances by someone named Riemon and others also took place at the village of Shindō. Among the plays presented between 1703 and 1706 were *Okina, Takasago, Shunnei, Kashiwazaki, Matsukaze, Kantan, Raiden, Utaura, Aoi no ue, Fujito, Koi no hi, Ryūzenji, Ama, Kumasaka, Kōya monogurui, Nonomiya, Sumidagawa, Tōru, Kamo, Tadanori, Funa Benkei, Nue, Tamura, Miwa, Shōjō, Miidera, Kasuga ryūjin, Hagoromo, Hachinoki,* and *Uneme.*[15]

Comments in the *Kawachiya Yoshimasa kyūki* suggest that even when the artistic lineage of students was not indicated, the nō and *utai* recorded there were all learned from a master. Yoshimasa notes:

> Teachings *(denju)*, oral traditions, and secret teachings exist in all the arts. The nō, in particular, has many secret transmissions. Such things often appear to be useless, but this is not so. These transmissions impart a great respect for the Way and strengthen one's resolve to practice. Thus these secrets are in fact the supreme teaching. Secret pieces *(naraigoto)* and transmissions *(denjugoto)* are highly principled. One must learn them from one's teacher with reverence. Just as the Way of poetry has many teachings that cannot be fathomed by those who have not entered this Way, other Ways, too, require that one must learn what the master teaches before making it one's own. "First learning, then making one's own"—this phrase even appears in poetry.[16]

Villagers appearing in the diary were not listed in the Fukuō school's official register, but they were nevertheless part of this school's tradition. By the Genroku period, the *iemoto* organization of the Fukuō school had made great inroads into this area, transmitting even secret pieces and teachings. We know the details of nō as practiced by wealthy villagers in Daigatsuka, Shindō, and Tondabayashi only because Kawachiya Yoshimasa kept a diary of current events. In fact, nō was probably supported by a large sector of the public in and around Osaka. The spread of nō among the affluent *chōnin* stratum was a result of rapid growth in the Osaka area economy. During the Genroku period, a newly established system of main and branch stores—and the influx of a large quantity of capital from Osaka—stimulated the economy. As Osaka developed and the nationwide distribution system improved, villages such as Daigatsuka, Tondabayashi, and Shindō succeeded in marketing large quantities of locally produced cotton and other commodities. As a result, many *chōnin* from the area around Osaka prospered. It was such *chōnin* who often supported nō.[17]

Nō Text Publication

Another sign of the broad support accorded to nō is the great number of nō texts published during the seventeenth and eighteenth centuries. According to Ejima Ihee's *Kurumaya-hon no kenkyū* (A Study of the Kurumaya [Nō] Books), more than a thousand different *utai* texts were published during the Edo period.[18] Most of these were texts of the Kanze school, written in Konoe-style calligraphy. Next in number were books written in the "house calligraphy" of the Konparu, Kongō, Hōshō, and Kita schools. Early Edo-period texts start with the Nishimura book of 1640 and include some thirty books of the Shindō school (a house of *waki* actors and a subsidiary of the Kanze school). In a 1670 book catalog, some thirteen titles appear to be *utai*. Twenty-two years later, in 1692, a catalog known as the *Genroku shojaku mokuroku* (Catalog of Genroku Books) gives sixty-four nō-related books of which forty-four are *utai*. Some *utai* books present excerpts; others are small annotated editions for travelers or books used at banquets. One also finds new pieces such as *Bonsama utai* (The Priest), *Goshaku tenugui utai* (The Five-Foot Hand Towel), and *Kenkō hōshi utai* (The Priest [Yoshida] Kenkō).

In the *Genroku taiheiki* (Record of the Great Genroku Peace), writ-

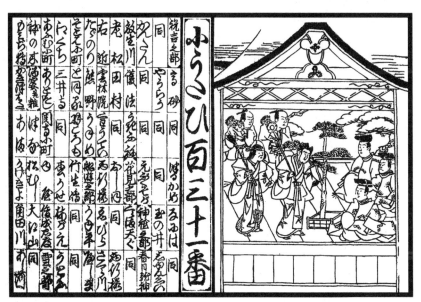

Opening pages of a cheap booklet of Nō excerpts from the late Edo period *(Ko-utai hyakusanjūichi-ban)*. (In the possession of the translator.)

ten in 1702, Miyako no Nishiki (Shishido Kōfū, b. 1675) makes the following remarks:

> I was fond of *utai* since the days of my childhood. I memorized all
> the *utai* books published in Japan, even *Goshaku tenugui* and *Kenkō-
> zuka*. There exists, however, no tradition of calling a top-ranking
> courtesan a "pine" *(matsu)*. This notion must have been taken from
> Chinese song books.[19]

This quotation suggests that many *utai* books, including new works such as *Goshaku tenugui* and *Kenkō-zuka*, were highly popular. These books appear to have functioned as sources of historical allusions.

According to Sasaki Haruyuki's *Su-utai yoyo no ato,* around 1701 Ogawa Shōemon Tokuyuki, a member of the Kyoto Fukuō school, planned the publication of a book of one hundred *kusemai* dances.[20] Before doing so, Tokuyuki asked for permission from the *iemoto* of the Fukuō school, Hattori Sōseki (1660–1721), but this request was denied. One reason for the refusal may have been that Hattori had himself published the book *Shichijū-ni ban kusemai* (Seventy-Two *Kusemai*) the previous year. In any case, Hattori argued that out of deference to the Kanze school—of which the Fukuō school was a subsidiary—publication should not occur. Ignoring Hattori's advice, Tokuyuki published the book anyway. Hattori responded by excommunicating Tokuyuki from the Fukuō school.

Omote Akira has shown that of the roughly five hundred Kanze-school *utai* books included in the Kōzan collection, the majority were published independently of the Kanze school's head family. The independent publication of a number of *utai* books suggests that many "town teachers" were transmitting Kanze-school *utai* to students who did not officially belong to any organization and did not fit into any *iemoto*-type student/teacher lineage. Indeed, with no system of copyright, nō texts could theoretically be published freely. Hattori Sōseki, however, maintained strong feelings of deference toward the Kanze school's head family. As a result, the Fukuō school did not publish *utai* books without the authorization of the Kanze school. During the early years of the Edo period the Shindō school had published many of its own texts, but by this time most schools probably followed the example of the Fukuō school. In other words, even if a head family did not expressly state its wishes, branch families or schools of *waki* actors or musicians deferred to the head family, which retained de facto control over *utai* book publication. This state of affairs may explain why the convenient and sensibly revised "corrected editions" that appeared from the Genroku period were never widely accepted, and why these books were never published by Yamamoto Chōbee, who maintained strong links to the Kanze head family. In any case, the Fukuō school must have used Kanze-school *utai* texts.

Nō, Ihara Saikaku, and *Haikai* Poetry

Other indications of the rise of the *utai* population can be found in the works of Ihara Saikaku (1642–1693). Saikaku's stories are, of course, largely fiction, but they present a realistic picture of the contemporary world.

In the *Saikaku oridome* (Saikaku's Bolt End), Saikaku tells a tale of a couple that operated a sandal shop in Osaka. Forced to close their business, the pair flees to the Sumiyoshi area of the city. Then, as an emergency moneymaking measure, the husband becomes a calligraphy teacher and an overnight nō master.[21] In another tale, from the volume *Saikaku nagori no tomo* (A Friend Saikaku Left Behind, published in 1699), one reads of Rakugetsuan Saigin (who died in 1709 aged over seventy), a *haikai* poetry teacher from the village of Sakurazuka in Settsu, who had learned all there was to learn from a non-Kanze school.[22]

Murata Atsushi has argued that Saikaku's ability to compose thousands of verses a day depended largely on his intimate knowledge of countless allusions to the classics found in nō.[23] Even Saikaku's literary rival Miyako no Nishiki admits in the *Genroku taiheiki* that Saikaku was well versed in nō. *Haikai* poetry and nō seem to have been closely related. Nō texts functioned as a valuable and convenient source for classical references used in composing *haikai* poetry.[24] Nō texts thus served both as a form of music and as a foundation for general cultivation. This double nature allowed nō to become a popular form of leisure culture for the new affluent stratum of Edo-period commoners. Both Rakugetsuan Saigin and Kawachiya Yoshimasa were members of such a stratum. Indeed, the latter was a skilled *haikai* poet who took lessons from teachers in Tenma (Osaka), Sakai, and Kyoto. Moreover, Yoshimasa taught poetry to many advanced students who had artists' names. Such students usually came from the nearby villages of Taishi, Kasuga, and Yamada.[25]

A list of *haikai* poets of the Kyoto-Osaka area can be found in the *Kawachi no kuni meisho kagami* (Mirror of Famous Spots in Kawachi Province) written by Mita Jōkyū (1608–1688) in 1679.[26] Jōkyū, a wealthy merchant and shipowner, lived in Kashiwara village (Kawachi province) and was a student of the poet Kitamura Kigin (1624–1705). The *Kawachi no kuni meisho kagami* includes *haikai* by many poets and records the contributors' names and addresses. One finds that 64 poets resided in thirty towns and villages in Yamato province; another 118 lived in fifty-nine towns and villages of Kawachi province. Kawachiya Yoshimasa is represented with nine poems.

The *haikai* craze in this region took place around the end of the Genroku period. According to the *Kawachiya Yoshimasa kyūki,* not a single *haikai* poet could be found within the county before the Enpō period (1673–1681).[27] Yoshimasa reports, however, that during the previous ten years, *haikai* composition had become all the rage. Women, children, and even mountain bandits found pleasure in writing such verses. This sudden increase in the population of *haikai* poets extended well beyond Kawachi. Judging from Yoshimasa's correspondences, the *haikai* wave spread throughout the entire Kyoto-Osaka area. In the Genroku book catalog cited earlier one finds some 669 *haikai* books published during the year 1692. Such a figure would have been unthinkable without an enormous population interested in this genre.

Rise and Fall of the Fukuō School

Members of the Kyoto-Osaka *su-utai* community were usually linked to the Fukuō school. From the late seventeenth century this school—also known as the Kyoto Kanze school—saw a dramatic increase in its population of disciples. This increase led, in turn, to a rapid expansion of the Fukuō school's *iemoto* system.

The surge in popularity of *su-utai* presented a new challenge to the Fukuō school. Never before had a school of nō commanded such a large *utai*-performing following. The Fukuō school, however, lacked the organizational skills to control and unify its disciples. Unable to respond adequately, the school's *iemoto* system began to disintegrate internally. In 1694, Hattori Sōseki, the seventh *iemoto* of the Fukuō school, retired to Kyoto. Before doing so, he relegated the Edo branch of the school to the eighth *iemoto* Moemon Moriari (1677–1746). Sōseki then devoted himself solely to *su-utai.* From records such as the *Shinkyoku shōmyō higen,* the *Su-utai yoyo no ato,* and the *Itazura uta jujuden* (Transmissions on Solo Chant),[28] one learns that Sōseki functioned as an *iemoto* of *su-utai.* Although this situation has already been described in detail by Nonomura Kaizō in 1931,[29] I would like to subject parts of Nonomura's work to reinterpretation.

During the first year of his Kyoto retirement, Sōseki excommunicated Takemura Jinzaemon (Sadakatsu) for disobedient activity. In the tenth month of 1707, fifty-eight of Takemura's students were forced to become direct disciples of Sōseki's school.[30] A passionate, temperamental man, Sōseki subsequently expelled Ogawa Shōemon Tokuyuki (in 1699), Andō Ichiyū, Ichiyū's student Yamamoto Tazaemon (1709), and Hiraoka Hachiemon (1718).[31] According to the *Su-utai yoyo no ato,* such expulsions were to a large extent the result of Sōseki's character. Yet another reason, however, was that the contemporary *su-utai* community was in the midst of a period of rapid expansion and development. Constant crises led to frequent expulsions. Takemura, for example, was in charge of a flourishing *su-utai* group and wished for independence. This desire led to clashes with Sōseki and, finally, to Takemura's expulsion. Similarly, as noted earlier, Ogawa Shōemon Tokuyuki was discharged for unauthorized publication of *kusemai* books. These incidents show that the Fukuō school's *iemoto* organization of *su-utai* was unable to resolve the predicaments it faced during this age of rapid transformation.

Perhaps the most vexing problem for the Fukuō *iemoto* was the tendency for students to abandon the school and become direct disciples of the head Kanze family. At the time of Takemura's expulsion (1694), Nakamura Rokuemon, Iwai Shichirōemon, and four others of the fifty-eight students who were later made direct disciples of Sōseki's school had already become students of Kanze Oribe Shigenori (1666–1716), the Kanze school's thirteenth *iemoto.* This transfer in allegiance was mediated by the Kanze school's twelfth head, Shigetoshi (1657–1746).[32] Later, immediately before his death, Takemura Jinzaemon succeeded in having his excommunication annulled (in the first month of 1698) by offering three conditions for peace. One of these was that his grandson Koreyuki be officially permitted to fulfill a long-standing wish to become a student of Kanze Oribe Shigenori.[33]

Students who became direct disciples of the Kanze head family's school did not, however, simply cut their relations with the Fukuō school. Although Koreyuki did become a student of Kanze Oribe Shigenori, another of the three conditions for Takemura Jinzaemon's reentry into the Fukuō school included the clause that Takemura would "not neglect the Kanze head family or the Hattori house, nor disobey any orders."[34] Similarly, the six students for whom the twelfth head of the Kanze school interceded jointly sealed a document by which they became direct disciples of the Kanze school; but they also sealed an affidavit stating that "though [placing our seals here] we do not [make this promise] with the spirit in the depths of our hearts. This must be kept in mind."[35] This document was then presented to Sōseki. It seems that at this time it was still impossible to make a clean break with the Fukuō school and become a direct disciple of the Kanze head family. Although the details remain unclear, students leaving the Fukuō school were apparently affiliated with both the Fukuō and Kanze schools. In other words: students were not powerful enough to disassociate themselves fully from the Fukuō school. This led to a transitional form of double affiliation.

Troublemaker Sōseki died in 1721. He was succeeded by his widow (and now Buddhist nun) Chisei, who managed the business affairs of the Fukuō school. In her old age Chisei turned over all the Fukuō school's business matters to the Katayama house, which was a direct descendant of the main Kanze family. After Chisei's death in 1759, the Fukuō school evacuated its premises and returned the land to the main Kanze school. How the Katayama house, originally a house of amateurs studying under the direction of the Iwai house, could rise to the position of the most influential Kyoto subsidiary of the Kanze school remains a puzzle. Nor is it clear why, after the death of Sōseki and his wife, the Fukuō school could no longer directly govern its own affairs. What is certain is that during this time the Fukuō school—which had been headed by its own *iemoto* and controlled *su-utai* students throughout the Kyoto-Osaka area—now found itself under the control of the Kanze school's head family.

Despite these changes, the *iemoto* system of the Fukuō school was not thereby weakened. During the Hōreki period (1751–1764), the activities of Suzuki Ichiyū (a direct disciple of the Fukuō school's *iemoto*), Suzuki's student Hokumonshi Bokkai Mohee, and Hokumonshi's student Kida Tamekuni show that the Fukuō school's *iemoto* organization was still powerful. After Chisei's death, Hokumonshi wrote a treatise entitled *Shinkyoku shōmyō higen*. In 1764 a version of this volume, retitled *Yōkyoku higen kai* (Explanation of the Secrets of Nō), was issued in Japanese (the original had been in Chinese) by Hokumonshi's student Kida Tamekuni. As Hokumonshi was a highly influential Kyoto *chōnin*, it is unlikely that the power of the Fukuō school had declined. In any case, the Fukuō school remained linked to a large public throughout the Kyoto-Osaka area. According to Nonomura Kaizō's *Nōgaku kokonki:*

In Mino county [today Hyōgo prefecture] there were several Fukuō shrines—seven or eight, some say twelve—all of which had nō stages. At these shrines the Fukuō school performed nō as offerings to the gods. Clearly there existed an intimate relation between the Fukuō school and [the people of] this area.[36]

With this base of support, the power and authority of the Fukuō school were unlikely simply to be absorbed by the Kanze school's head family.

By the Meiwa period (1764–1772) the Edo branch of the Kanze school had increased its power vis-à-vis the Kyoto branch (that is, the Fukuō school). This is shown by an incident in which Sono Kyūbee, once a student of Sōseki, went to Edo to become a direct disciple of Kanze Motoakira, the fifteenth head of the Kanze school. After becoming a disciple, Kyūbee returned to Kyoto, where he staged an unofficial nō performance. For this performance, however, three men who had promised to be present failed to appear—an act of disobedience that constituted the crime of "nō obstruction." The three culprits—Iwai, Inoue, and Hayashi—were all members of the Takemura faction that had once rebelled against Sōseki. When this incident was reported to the head Kanze family, the three delinquents were expelled from the school. Undaunted, Inoue and Hayashi went directly to Edo and received a pardon from the Kanze head family. Later, in 1772, at the occasion of Kanze Motoakira's coming to Kyoto, Iwai too finally succeeded in obtaining a pardon.[37]

Because the Fukuō school's Asano family had a large number of faithful followers, the Fukuō school could not simply be absorbed by the Edo Kanze head family. But when Sono Kyūbee, a powerful figure and student of Sōseki, became a direct disciple of the Kanze head family, high-ranking disciples of the Asano house also had an incentive to join the Kanze head family. A good opportunity for such a switch came when Kanze Motoakira came to Kyoto in 1772. Strong opposition by the nun Myōju, the mother of Asano Eijū (the sixth head of the Asano house), caused this first attempt to end in failure. In 1796 Hiroaki, the seventh head of the Asano house, went to Edo and negotiated unsuccessfully for the Fukuō school's *iemoto* to become a disciple of the Kanze head family. Finally, in the spring of 1808, when Hiyoshi Ichijūrō, a messenger from the Kanze head family, came to Kyoto, fifteen members of the Asano house could at last join the Kanze head family's school—though without the permission of the Fukuō school's *iemoto* and only after the intercession of the Katayama house. In 1811 the long-standing issue of incorporation into the Kanze school's head family was taken up again. This time the *iemoto* of the Fukuō school allowed the fifteen members to enter the Kanze school formally. The long-pending problem of the Asano house's desire to join the Kanze school was thereby finally resolved.

The motive behind the Fukuō *iemoto*'s prohibition of students' entry into the head Kanze school is explained at the end of *Su-utai yoyo no ato: iemoto* simply desired to demonstrate that they still wielded authority.

In summary, then, there is little doubt that the Fukuō school's *iemoto* system was created in response to the appearance of a large population of *utai* students in the Kyoto-Osaka area. From the Genroku period onward, fissures began to appear in the Fukuō school's organization. Gradually this school was absorbed into the main Kanze school. The pace of this assimilation remained slow during the first half of the eighteenth century, a time when the Fukuō *iemoto* was strong enough to exercise real control over his school. By the second half of the eighteenth century, however, the affairs of the Fukuō school were no longer under the control of the school's *iemoto*. The reins of real power were now in the hands of the Katayama house. The pace with which the Fukuō school was assimilated by the Edo Kanze school gradually accelerated; by the beginning of the nineteenth century, the Fukuō school was largely dominated by the main family in Edo.

Translator's Summary

Interest in nō among all levels of society increased rapidly during the Edo period. The warrior class, including the shogun and daimyo, supported entire nō troupes or hired teachers of nō dance and chant to serve at their domains. Nō was also highly popular among the merchant and wealthy peasant strata. Records from the Kamigata area show that rural inhabitants not only chanted nō texts but actually formed troupes that toured and performed for an appreciative commoner public. Literary works by Ihara Saikaku also demonstrate that urban commoners both learned and taught various types of nō chant. Nō texts, which served as a basis for general cultivation and as a source for classical allusions used in writing light verse, were published in large numbers from around the late seventeenth century.

Most students of nō chant *(su-utai)* in the Kamigata area were linked to the Fukuō school (also known as the Kyoto Kanze school). The history of this school shows that its practices were not sufficiently flexible to accommodate the rapidly increasing numbers of students who wished to study nō chant. Internal troubles and the publication of unauthorized texts resulted in excommunication of pupils and the migration of students to the head school in Edo. At first, dissatisfied students could not simply break all ties to the Kyoto school and join the main Edo family. Instead one finds forms of double allegiance and provisional membership. Nevertheless, by the nineteenth century, the Kyoto Kanze school had been all but absorbed by the main Edo school.

Whether aware of their own power or not, the Edo-period commoner classes wielded considerable influence in the development of many types of performing arts. This is true even for the nō, which is often claimed to have been off limits to all but the warrior stratum.

CHAPTER 10

SOCIAL STRATA AND MUSIC

Analyzing the relation of social strata to Edo-period music is not easy. Many musical forms of this age were the shared cultural property of village communities and constituted a music of the social base with no specific carrier. Popular songs, for example, were sung by a broad public that crossed class lines. Other songs were associated with types of labor, while performances of certain genres of accompanied dance or dialogue were limited to a specific small group or to certain villages. Annual rituals or festivals such as the *bon* dance present yet other problems. Whatever the genre, a discussion of the relationship of social strata to Edo-period music calls for an analysis of the transformations occurring within Edo-period society.

Japanese folk performing arts witnessed remarkable development during the Edo period. Communities that previously lacked music of their own now came to possess some; areas that had been heir to archaic, undeveloped forms found these forms driven out by new, superior ones. Once new genres were firmly accepted, they changed but little. Eventually they became the stable cultural property of the base level of society. Upper-class music, by contrast, which functioned mainly as a leisure pursuit, was usually transmitted by *iemoto*. The development of an *iemoto* system during the Edo period allowed upper-class musical genres to spread to a broad sector of the population. This diffusion poses interesting problems concerning class consciousness, class transformation, and class tensions.

Music Shared by Social Classes

Rigorous distinctions of social status were enforced during the Edo period. The ruling classes monopolized certain types of food, clothing, and shelter, as well as forms of culture. Music was no exception. Nevertheless, at the start of the Edo period the cultural gap between the ruling class and the commoners was still narrow. Although the rulers constructed luxurious residences, flaunted their financial power, and erected castle towers from which they could literally gaze down upon the public, the culture of the period remained essentially unstratified. Rulers and ruled engaged in much cultural exchange and shared many concerns.

As castle towns were built throughout the land, warriors tended to leave sites of production to concentrate around each daimyo. Warriors thereby became urban idlers and, eventually, transformed themselves into a new aristocracy. This ennoblement did not, of course, occur overnight. Food, clothing, and housing might improve quickly, but culture often remained similar to that of the commoners. Even the plebeian kabuki was presented at Edo castle. Toward the end of his life, the third shogun Iemitsu (1604–1651) often delighted in such performances, which featured actors from the major Edo theaters. Records in the *Matsudaira Yamato no kami nikki* (Diary of the Governor of Yamato)[1] show that kabuki actors and other performers were also invited to play at daimyo residences until the Genroku period (1688–1704). In short, during the early years of the Edo period, rulers easily came into contact with commoner culture.

Conversely, in this environment commoners greatly developed their skills. Throughout Japan, artisans and performers of the commoner class, including Izumo no Okuni (b. 1572), the reputed founder of kabuki, were creating new artistic genres. Rural inhabitants thronged to the capital in search of new opportunities. When such individuals gained sufficient confidence, they often called themselves *tenka ichi:* the best in the world. *Tenka ichi* masters soon existed in such numbers that in the seventh month of 1682 the bakufu issued an edict prohibiting people from designating themselves in this way.[2] From this cultural environment, in which creation and appreciation were a communal effort shared by both high and low, some outstanding musical compositions emerged. One of these was the *koto* piece *Rokudan no shirabe.* This masterpiece, whose composer is uncertain, may have been written as early as the 1630s.

The poetic meter known as *kinsei kouta-chō* ("early-modern short song meter") was yet another remarkable product of this age. This meter contains twenty-six syllables, which can be divided into units of seven, seven, seven, and five syllables. These units can, in turn, be divided into even smaller segments of (3–4), (4–3), (3–4), and (5) syllables. Early forms of *kinsei kouta-chō* appear in the *Kanginshū,*[3] a collection of songs from the middle of the Muromachi period (1333–1573). During this age, so-called Muromachi *kouta* (short

Maker of musical instruments. He is working on a *koto;* in the back are a *biwa* and a *shamisen.* From *Jinrin kinmōzui.*

songs) were popular. Somewhat later, another type of song known as
ryūtatsu kouta appeared.[4] Both of these genres often made use of the
kinsei kouta-chō. By the Kan'ei period (1624–1644) songs using the 7–
7–7–5 meter had become highly fashionable. Even today this meter
remains one of the most popular Japanese poetic forms. It reappears
in many Japanese "hit songs" of the twentieth century: "Kachūsha no
uta" (Katusha's Song),[5] sung by Matsui Sumako; "Tōkyō kōshin-
kyoku" (Tokyo March);[6] "Ringo no uta" (Apple Song);[7] and countless others.

Fujita Tokutarō has studied the early history of the *kinsei kouta-chō*
in some detail.[8] He points out that the first and third seven-syllable
units of the *kinsei kouta-chō* are both grouped in a 3–4 syllable pattern. When words in this meter are set to music, the melody is usually characterized by the presence of a rest at the start of these seven-
syllable units (see figure below).[9] Songs of the upper classes show no
such rests. Instead, the first syllable is extended, creating an elegant
effect not found in songs of the lower classes. Many short songs of
the Muromachi period were associated with the upper stratum of
warriors or the clergy and were sung in a refined manner. Hence the
opening rest is usually lacking. In time, however, the *kinsei kouta-chō*
was enjoyed by both high and low. Here, too, the gap between the
cultures of different social classes remained narrow.

Musical Genres of the Ruling Class

As the warriors moved to urban areas and wished to assert their position of authority, they quickly set about clarifying class boundaries.
Old aristocratic cultural traditions of the ancient imperial capital of
Kyoto were revived. By the third decade of the seventeenth century,
the movement to restore both Heian-period court culture and traditional Kamakura and Muromachi warrior culture was in full swing.
One of the old traditions monopolized by the upper stratum of warriors was nō drama. Only the warriors were officially permitted to
stage danced performances of nō. The warriors greatly enjoyed

Rhythmic pattern of the *kinsei kouta-chō*.

dancing nō dances, performing the chants, and playing the flute and drums.

Gagaku (court music), which had nearly disappeared during the period of civil wars, was also revitalized. This music accompanied bakufu or court rituals and various annual ceremonies. *Gagaku* thus became a fixed, formalized, ruling-class music.[10] The bakufu established an ensemble known as the "musicians of the three areas" *(sanbō gakunin)*. In 1665 the military government granted this group an annual stipend of 2,000 *koku* of rice. Fifty-one musicians were employed: seventeen each from the Kyoto court, the "southern capital" of Nara (the Kōfukuji Temple and Kasuga Shrine), and the Osaka Tennōji Temple. Some of these musicians stemmed from houses that served as hereditary teachers of the *shō* (mouth organ), the *hichiriki* (a double-reed wind instrument), and the *fue* (or *ryūteki*, transverse flute). Besides these "master" houses, families of "superior art" *(jōgei-ke)* and "middle-level art" *(chūgei-ke)* existed as well. Disciples of each house took examinations on *shō, hichiriki,* or *fue* to become the next generation of official performers. These examinations were open; any candidate who received the requisite number of votes was rewarded with the appropriate qualification. Examination results, which show the grades awarded to each contestant on each occasion, are still extant today. From these one learns that the first examination was held in 1665; subsequent judgings took place every four years. The format of these examinations remained unchanged until the end of the Edo period.

Ruling-class privilege was also revealed in the official sanction given to the *komusō* system of the Fuke sect of Zen Buddhism. *Komusō* were masterless, *shakuhachi*-playing samurai who roamed the land outfitted with their "three seals" and "three tools."[11] Unlike other monks, they did not recite sutras; nor did they perform funerals or memorial services. The bakufu officially sanctioned the *komusō* organization during the Enpō period (1673–1681) to control the large number of masterless samurai *(rōnin)*. The urgency of the *rōnin* problem had become obvious after the "Keian Incident" of 1651 in which a group of disgruntled warriors plotted the overthrow of the bakufu.

The Fuke sect was headquartered at two temples: the Ichigetsuji (in Kogane, Shimōsa province) and the Reihōji (in Ōme, Musashi province). The sect's authority relied on a document known as the *Komusō okite-gaki* (Regulations of the *Komusō*),[12] supposedly bestowed upon the association by Tokugawa Ieyasu. Mikami Sanji has shown that this document was a forgery; but the bakufu was itself probably aware of this fact.[13] In any case, with its official government backing and the exclusion of commoners from its ranks, the Fuke sect could regulate the transmission of *shakuhachi* music. This music thereby became the privilege of the samurai class.

Such cultural policies were designed to polarize social classes and to establish the cultural hegemony of the rulers. By the middle of the Edo period, innumerable social and cultural distinctions had been systematized. As a result, *gagaku* and nō developed little. *Gagaku* had already become a kind of cultural fossil long before the Edo period, but nō had seen vigorous creative activity until the days of Hideyoshi (1536–1598). Once the ruling classes of Edo monopolized nō, however, all creative activity came to a halt. The genre was formalized; a canon of "classics" was established. Both *gagaku* and nō now came under the control of specific houses that oversaw the propagation of the repertory as a "house art" *(iegei)*.

Iemoto Systems of Nō and *Gagaku*

In the distant past, early forms of nō had been performed by many troupes spread over a large geographical area. During the Edo period these troupes and their styles congealed to become what was known as the "four troupes *(za)* and one school *(ryū)*" of Yamato. These organizations served the bakufu and were closely tied to warrior society. Each of the "four *za* and one *ryū*" possessed its own internally coherent manner of acting and music. Hence disputes over how to perform nō did not arise. Even within each *za*, responsibilities were clearly defined: some houses were in charge of main *(shite)* roles, others performed supporting *(waki)* roles, and yet others specialized in musical accompaniment *(hayashi)*. This division of labor gained momentum from the middle of the Edo period.

Gagaku presented a somewhat different case. Before the Edo period, performance rights seem not to have been the subject of much concern. During the turbulent era of civil wars, rights over the repertory were left largely undefined. Troubles began to arise once the *gagaku* repertory became an *iegei*—that is, the possession and monopoly of certain houses. In 1771, for example, Kubo Chikanaka (1734–1809) filed a lawsuit when he discovered that Kubo Mitsushige (1739–1812) was giving *hichiriki* lessons. Mitsushige was denied the right to instruct and was forced to submit a written apology. In 1787 the Ōno house fought with the Hayashi house over the rights to the dance known as *umai*,[14] but this dispute remained unresolved. In 1801, Hayashi Hironao, a *gagaku* musician from the Osaka Tennōji, maneuvered to obtain permission for his family to perform the *batōmai,* a dance that had hitherto been the rightful *iegei* of the Shiba family. Similar incidents occurred constantly.

As each house established an *iemoto* system for marketing its *iegei,* traditional cultural forms underwent revision and conventionalization. Kanze Motoakira (1725–1774), the fifteenth *iemoto* of the Kanze school of nō, set about improving the economic position of his school by revising Kanze-school nō texts (1765). Similarly, in 1814 the Ue house of musicians from Nara revised their traditional *gagaku* practices.

Iemoto Systems and the *Chōnin*

From around the Genroku period, the number of wealthy *chōnin* increased rapidly. Since *chōnin* were nominally subordinate to the warrior class, they could not flaunt their own social ascent. Instead, they developed a typically Japanese means for breaking through class barriers. This break was highly passive, but it enabled the *chōnin* to step out of their social class and enter a cultural world in which social rank was of little concern. This form of escape soon became fashionable within *chōnin* society at large; it then spread even to provincial farm villages.

In the distant past, Japanese commoners could sometimes rise to high positions; but by the Edo period a rise in social status was nearly impossible. Unlike China, Japan had no official examination system that allowed talented individuals from a broad spectrum of society to rise in the social hierarchy. Impenetrable social barriers thus forced the *chōnin* to direct their efforts elsewhere. As a result, they created vigorous, powerful cultural communities. Within this "world apart," the *chōnin* could ignore the limitations of their lowly social status. Here they could break with reality and rise to become members of a community of "cultured individuals." This was the secret of the popularity of the *iemoto* system during the Edo period.

The possibility of breaking with reality was to some extent already known during earlier times, both in and out of Japan. Christianity, for example, offered an analogous scheme: by being baptized and receiving a Christian name, believers could enter a "world apart." Buddhists, too, could become acolytes at a temple and hope to turn out a great priest. A similar logic was at work when Japanese courtesans broke with their past and became goddesses of song and dance. Women of the pleasure quarters assumed elegant names derived from famous courtesans of the past or from the fifty-four chapters of the *Tale of Genji.* "Genji names," for example, included Usugumo

(Wreath of Cloud), Hatsune (The First Warbler), Wakamurasaki (Light Purple), Kagaribi (Flares), and the like. The pleasure quarters even had their own special language, a jargon known as *sato kotoba*.

Japanese ascetics and pilgrims, too, made a break with reality when they donned white uniforms and journeyed to the three Kumano shrines, the "three shrines of Dewa," the "thirty-three Kannon of the western provinces," or the "eighty-eight holy sites of Shikoku." Much the same held true for participants in the San'ō and Kanda festivals in Edo. These celebrations were riotously popular because they substituted chaotic freedom for the usual social order. Here people reverted to their common human essence; equality in status was symbolized by *yukata* uniforms. Festivals and pilgrimages, lotteries, mass flights to the great shrine at Ise, or excursions to bustling quarters of the city were all sources of passionate enthusiasm because social reality was thereby momentarily obliterated.

Such breaks with reality were commonplace and represented the wisdom of an oppressed populace. The break enacted was but a fleeting one, usually lasting only a few days. Such liberation could not yet satisfy a *chōnin* class that had matured into the culturally dominant force of the age. The logic of continuous liberation was not discovered until the middle of the Edo period. This logic emerged from within the cultural communities of the *iemoto* system.

The San'ō festival on the fifteenth day of the sixth month. From *Tōto saijiki*.

The phenomenon of "bamboo names" *(chikumei)*, the names assumed by *shakuhachi* performers, provide a good example. As we have seen, the organization of the *komusō* occupied a unique position in Japanese musical life during the early Edo period. The *komusō* were not above engaging in disorderly brawls or robbing law-abiding citizens of their belongings. The influx of hoodlums and ne'er-do-wells into the *komusō* community turned the temples of this organization into little more than a hangout for gangsters. The bakufu responded by issuing frequent prohibitions. In 1759, all peasants and *chōnin* were again banned from entering the ranks of *komusō*. Since the official regulations of the *komusō* (the *Komusō okitegaki*) already excluded peasants and *chōnin*, the Fuke sect had no alternative but to concede to these demands.

The bakufu, however, also forbade the issuance of *chikumei* to *shakuhachi* players. This order met with stubborn resistance from the sect. In the seventh month of 1759 Shōzan, a monk from the Reihōji, presented a protest to the bakufu. Shōzan noted that renowned *chōnin* masters of the *shakuhachi* had appeared; some of these were even serving as teachers. As *chōnin*, such men were not qualified to become bona-fide *komusō*. But *chōnin* performers ardently desired an artist's name; the temple had responded to such wishes by granting *chikumei*. These names, Shōzan argued, had nothing to do with the qualifications of a *komusō*. *Chikumei* served only as a symbol testifying to the bearer's virtuosity as a *shakuhachi* performer.

Students of the famous teacher Kurosawa Kinko (1710–1771), for example, had been awarded the *chikumei* Kinna, Kinsa, Kinshō, Kinpū, and the like. Kinko was a renowned *shakuhachi* master in charge of teaching the Fuke *shakuhachi* at studios known as *fukiawase-sho;* he also manufactured *shakuhachi*. A document entitled *Chōka jūkyo shakuhachi shinan-sha seimei narabi ni fukiawase-sho mei* (Names of Teaching Studios and *Shakuhachi* Teachers Living in Townsman Quarters), submitted by both the Reihōji and Ichigetsuji temples to the Edo town magistrate in 1768, shows that Kinko was operating five teaching studios in the city. Kinko commanded a large following, but he was only one of many respected *shakuhachi* teachers active at the time. In 1785, at the studio attached to the Kyoto Myōanji, nineteen teachers—Kokyō, Ryōun, Kofū, Kichō, Rozan, and others—were giving lessons. Kinko, Kokyō, Ryōun, and their colleagues were so-called *machi shishō*, "town teachers." The Ichigetsuji, Reihōji, and Myōanji temples corresponded to their *iemoto*. These "town teachers" were surrounded by many *chōnin*, some of whom were sufficiently skillful to earn a *chikumei*.

A similar phenomenon can be found in the community of Edo

gidayū chanters. Amateurs who wished to learn this form of *jōruri* chanting appeared in the city during the first few decades of the eighteenth century. By the middle of the century, *gidayū* had become highly popular. One community of *gidayū* devotees supported Toyotake-style chant. Toyotake chant had initially appeared in Osaka; its golden age lasted until the middle of the eighteenth century. During the Kyōhō period (1716–1736) the chanter Toyotake Hizen no Jō (1704–1758), the top student of the Osaka chanter Toyotake Echizen no Shōjo (1681–1764), came to Edo to perform and teach. To control the correct transmission of his tradition he compiled a register of students. This document, entitled "Hōkyoku fuji no kodama" (The Supreme Reverberation of Toyotake Chant, published in 1755),[15] shows that Hizen no Jō had 218 disciples, 196 of whom lived within the city of Edo. Most of these students were *chōnin* from the *shitamachi* area.[16] Some eighteen—Mojitayū, Shumetayū, Nakatayū, Wakasadayū, and others—served as "town teachers."[17] These teachers in turn had many students with names such as Rikitayū, Akashidayū, Uratadayū, Sumatayū, and so on. Some disciples did not assume a *tayū* name, preferring instead to identify themselves by some other fanciful appellation: Kumakichi from Shiba Mishima-chō, Soden of Ningyō-chō, or Yogiku of Tomizawa-chō.

Other forms of *jōruri* were popular as well. A debate over various *jōruri* styles is recorded in Ondōsha's *Jōruri sangoku-shi* (The *Jōruri* Tale of the Three Kingdoms, published in 1755).[18] Here one reads that old man Hakubee prefers the venerable, elegant *tosa bushi* style; his son, the cultured young master, likes *katō bushi;* Chōkurō, the shop manager, favors *gidayū bushi;* and Hankichi, a lowly clerk, is so passionately fond of *bungo bushi* styles that he would risk losing his job to pursue this art.

In communities dedicated to artistic genres, participants could assume a *haikai* name, a nō chanter's name, a *chikumei*, or a *gidayū* name. In each case the individual entered a realm outside of everyday social reality. A student in the *iemoto* system who demonstrated outstanding technical command or who became a senior member might, in the hierarchy of this miniature society, rise to a position of high rank. This in turn allowed such a person to become a figure of authority within the cultural world at large.

During the mid-Edo period, many people wished to devote their lives to artistic leisure pursuits and break with everyday social reality. The *iemoto* system, which was a result of such demand, was nothing less than a revolutionary change in methods of Japanese cultural transmission. During the medieval era and earlier, some families had either passed on a venerable old *iegei* to their own descendants or, occasionally, created new *iegei*. From the middle of the Edo period, however, the establishment of *iemoto* systems allowed such families to control a huge population of disciples. But why were class barriers overcome only passively? Why was there no general movement of breaking down real class barriers in Japan? These important questions touch on the fundamental nature of Japanese society and cannot be analyzed in detail here. Instead, I should like to contain the discussion to the field of music and mention a somewhat related issue: the complete lack of development of traditional Japanese choral singing.

In Japan, folk songs were at times sung in groups; Buddhist dances invoking Amida and the midsummer *bon* dance were also accompanied by group chant or song. But such musical styles were not true choral singing; the singers merely sang in unison. Moreover, folk performing arts that featured group singing were not leisure pursuits: they were annual rituals limited to specific days of the year and to certain set locations. In other words, occupational associations or groups of rural inhabitants did not possess the kind of musical communal property that Europeans had in their choral music—that is, a leisure pursuit in which each member sings one part in order to recreate an ensemble work that is the common property of society. Japanese society did not develop this kind of communal form of music, however, or any other analogous communal forms of culture.

That choral singing failed to develop within the *iemoto* system may have been the result of the one-to-one format of student/teacher relations. Regardless of the number of people organized within a cultural community, the *iemoto* system remained a series of student/teacher dyads. Japanese culture in general did not develop the kind of teamwork in which each person functions as a distinctly individuated member of a community. Instead, each isolated member of the *iemoto* system sought individual transformation and personal progress.

Iemoto Systems and the Spread of *Gagaku* and Nō

Let us now turn to the end of the Edo period, by which time class divisions had become extremely rigid. When, for example, in 1819, the daughter of the Tokugawa Kii family passed by the kabuki theater and caught a glimpse of the seventh Danjūrō's performance of *Sukeroku,* she was confined to her province and her samurai attendant was sentenced to disembowelment. Severe punishment lay in store for anyone who openly broke through cultural class barriers. As a result, the culture of the privileged social strata continued to stagnate. By contrast, the culture of the ruled classes, transmitted through huge *iemoto* systems, expanded and developed.

The case of *gagaku* is instructive. As we have seen, *gagaku* served as the instrumental music of the imperial court and the privileged echelons of society surrounding the bakufu until the middle of the Edo period. In performances of instrumental pieces, the emperor and several dozen higher courtiers and court musicians joined forces to create a large orchestra numbering as many as one hundred members. Court dances *(bugaku)* were performed to this accompaniment. Accepted wisdom has long held that *gagaku* and *bugaku* were entirely off limits to commoners and that, unlike the genres of *kiyomoto* or *tokiwazu*, court music had no *iemoto* system. Most scholars contend that although commoners came into contact with *gagaku* when certain temples and shrines performed their rites, no commoner actually played the *fue* or the *hichiriki*.

In fact, during the last two decades of the eighteenth century, families of official musicians of the "three directions" (Nara, Osaka, Kyoto) accepted commoners as students of the *shō*, the *hichiriki*, and the *fue*. Even the major secret works were passed on to such disciples. A list of students of the Toyohara family, a house of official Kyoto musicians, shows that for three generations—from Fumiaki (1783–1840) to Kageaki (1812–1848) and Toyoaki (1816–1860), that is, from 1796 until the last days of the bakufu—some 571 students received instruction. A similar list from the Tsuji family, a house of official Nara musicians, records the names of 535 disciples of Noriyoshi (1789–1845) and Norisada II (1832–1863) starting from 1799. Most students came from Kyoto, Edo, Owari, Yamato, Mino, Ise, and Ōmi; others came from more distant provinces. The majority of disciples were warriors, but others were clerics or *chōnin*. Even peasants can be found among the listed students. In the case of the Toyohara family, *chōnin* and peasants accounted for 119 individuals, some 20 percent of the total; in the case of the Tsuji family, some 10 percent stemmed from these two strata. Wealthy *chōnin* from towns along the Tōkaidō highway entertained themselves by forming cultural groups dedicated to playing the instruments of the *gagaku* ensemble.

Nō, too, was popular among the commoner classes. As we saw in Chapter 9, from the early part of the Edo period *utai* was frequently learned by wealthy peasants and merchants. During the later years of the period, *utai* became highly fashionable and spread to a huge population of commoners. Many towns and villages founded associations devoted to such chanting. Each of the official nō troupes was to some extent organized as an *iemoto* system.

Despite restrictions that, for example, prohibited commoners

from performing *gagaku* and nō as stage arts, Edo-period commoners continued to expand their cultural horizons. By doing so, this
populace succeeded in creating a "world apart" of unprecedented
breadth and depth.

Popular Performing Arts

Finally, let us turn briefly to the golden age of popular performing
arts during the late Edo period. The class nature of the music associated with annual rituals and festivals, or with professional performers of the lowest social stratum, underwent little change during the
first half of the Edo period. By the end of the period, however, great
transformations had taken place, boosting popular performing arts
to a high level of prominence. As a result, many professional performers from Edo and other urban centers succeeded in making a
name for themselves. Members of the lowest social strata used their
talents to overcome class barriers.

Many popular performers could be seen at *yose* (variety halls).
These small theaters became highly popular during the nineteenth
century. *Yose* performing arts included comic monologues, *sandai-
banashi* (monologues in which the audience offered three themes
for the performer to combine into a humorous story), riddle improvising, "eight-role art" (in which one performer took on numerous
roles and performed simultaneously on several instruments), mimicry, conjuring, top-spinning tricks, dancing, and women's *gidayū*
chanting. Street performers included acrobats, top spinners, "quick-
draw" sword artists, "basket jumpers," and others. On festival days at
temples, shrines, and other bustling spots in the city, acrobats, street
performers, and showmen often set up small huts for their shows.

Most shows took place during the daytime. In fact, almost all the
pastimes of the Edo period—the kabuki, the puppet theater with its
jōruri chanting, the performances of storytellers—took place during
daylight hours. *Yose,* however, featured cheap nighttime shows. These
performances were directed at an audience of urban day-laborers.
Many *yose* featured programs of comic monologues *(rakugo);* others
specialized in dancing, conjuring, or "eight-role art." The existence
of a large variety of *yose* genres allowed these houses to flourish even
when they stood side by side.

Individuals with surprising abilities emerged from the urban
areas—at times from within the working-class audience itself. Performers honed their skills before a lively and appreciative public that
viewed the acts at close range. Performers who did not come up to

scratch were showered with abuse. As a result, *yose* performers attained an unprecedented level of skill.

Most of these virtuosi stemmed from the social base. Through their art, performers could rise in society. Until the mid-Edo period, such artists would have spent their entire lives toiling at the bottom of society. By the end of the period, however, the cultural marketplace allowed geniuses of lowly birth to develop their abilities. Later, when international cultural exchange became possible, popular performers were among the first to go abroad as representatives of their nation.

CHAPTER 11

THE AESTHETICS OF KABUKI

The aesthetics of the kabuki theater comprises a variety of elements: hairstyles, makeup, costumes, settings, props, music, and much else. All these components deserve detailed study. In the following discussion, however, I shall limit myself to only four prominent aspects of the Edo kabuki: the aesthetic of the "street knight" *(kyōsha* or *kyōkaku);* the aesthetic of exorcism; the aesthetic of fashion; and the aesthetic of evil.

The Aesthetic of the Street Knight

Important Edoesque features entered kabuki when Ichikawa Danjūrō—Edo's greatest actor-hero and a name inherited through over a dozen generations to this very day—created the *aragoto* (bravura) style of acting. The first Ichikawa Danjūrō (1660–1704) appeared on the stage of the Edo Nakamura-za at age fourteen. In his debut performance he played the role of the young Heian-period warrior Sakata Kintoki in the play *Shitennō osanadachi* (The Birthplace of the Four Heavenly Emperors). On this occasion Danjūrō seems to have worn nonnaturalistic red and black makeup *(kumadori)* and a checkered costume fastened by a round cotton-padded ropelike sash. He earned the highest praise for his wild, energetic performances.

In the years preceding Danjūrō's debut, a form of puppet theater known as *Kinpira jōruri* was highly popular in Edo. This genre featured *aragoto*-like scenes in which Sakata Kintoki's son Kinpira engaged in superhuman feats—valiantly disposing of scores of enemies, for example, or fishing a thousand-foot whale from the sea. The *Kantō kekki monogatari* (Tales of Hot-Bloods from the Kantō Region) records that Danjūrō's performances were kabuki versions of this *Kinpira jōruri*.[1] During the seventh month of 1690 Danjūrō starred in *Kinpira kabutoron* (The Argument over Kinpira's Helmet);

A performance of *saruwaka kyōgen* "in the past." From *Edo meisho zue.*

in the eleventh month of 1700 he appeared in *Kinpira rokujō-gayoi* (Kinpira Goes to the Sixth Block).[2] One may thus assume that Danjūrō's *aragoto* grew out of the Kinpira style of puppet theater.

The rise of Ichikawa Danjūrō and *aragoto* acting cannot be understood without reference to contemporary conditions in the city of Edo. During the city's early years, warriors from throughout the country were stationed there; ambitious men from all the provinces swarmed to the capital. After the Battle of Sekigahara (1600) and the Osaka Summer Campaign (1615), many warriors found themselves suddenly out of work. These unemployed men-at-arms often became either *kabukimono*—gallants who flaunted their "deviant" appearance and speech—or *kyōkaku*, "street knights," the self-appointed guardians of the common folk. The house of Ichikawa Danjūrō, originally a warrior house from the province of Kai, was in close contact with such groups. In fact, Danjūrō's father Jūzō may himself have been a *kyōkaku*. In any case, Danjūrō's upbringing took place in an environment steeped in the chivalry of the street knight. By combining the muscular style of *Kinpira jōruri* with this spirit of gallantry, Danjūrō succeeded in creating the unique *aragoto* style of Edo kabuki.

Aragoto became the essence of the Ichikawa family's style of acting and production and was later codified by the seventh Danjūrō (1791–1859) in the "Eighteen Favorites" *(kabuki jūhachiban)*. A typical *aragoto* scene can be seen when the invincible hero Takenuki Gorō, shod in tall wooden clogs, effortlessly unsheathes a huge bamboo sword and struts around the stage. A similar effect is seen when Kamakura Gongorō Kagemasa, the hero of the play *Shibaraku* (Wait a Moment!), brandishes a sword some three yards in length and decapitates a dozen men with a single stroke. *Aragoto* style also appears in plays featuring the Soga brothers. In *Yanone* (The Arrowhead, 1725),[3] for example, Soga Gorō behaves in a highly brusque and aggressive manner.

Shibaraku was performed annually during the eleventh month. This play was a *kaomise* ("face-showing") play in which the lineup of newly contracted actors was introduced to the audience. Reduced to its essentials, *Shibaraku* is the story of a youthful superman delivering a righteous public from the clutches of evil. This play is now a fixed repertory piece, but during the Edo period this was not the case. On each occasion, the plot was slightly altered and new elements were added. When the hero Gongorō appears in *Shibaraku*, he wears a tremendous costume and a huge sword. He dons *sujikuma* makeup,[4] which gives him an almost supernatural appearance. At the very moment the play's villain is about to execute his virtuous opponents, Gongorō enters from the runway *(hanamichi)* that extends into the audience. Before the execution can take place, the shout "Wait a moment!" *(shibaraku)* is suddenly heard from behind the *agemaku*, a curtain hung at the back of the *hanamichi*. The intrepid hero then struts down the *hanamichi* thundering, *"Shibaraku! Shibaraku! Shibaraku!"* After rescuing the law-abiding citizens from the cruelty of the tyrants, he effortlessly dispatches all his adversaries with one sweep of his gigantic sword. But before engaging in this superman-like activity, Gongorō reveals his identity in a speech on the *hanamichi*. Usually toward the end of this speech, he announces that he is the superman Ichikawa Danjūrō.

Throughout the Edo period, all three Edo theaters—the Nakamura-za, the Ichimura-za, and the Morita-za—produced variations of this plot. That such repeat performances were possible speaks for the remarkable power of this *aragoto* play's theme: the defeat of evil by righteousness. The young superman Danjūrō, the pride of the city, here created a "superhuman" theatrical style that shows victims of feudal oppression liberated.

The costuming and makeup of *Shibaraku* evoke a realm of the supernatural. Stories of mysterious individuals who appear from nowhere to rescue the public are also found off the kabuki stage. In the Shimabara Rebellion of 1637, in which Christians of Amakusa rose in arms against the bakufu and its policy of religious oppression, the leader of the Christian army was supposedly a young boy named Amakusa Shirō Tokisada (1621–1638).[5] Similarly, when famines and the eruption of Mount Asama prompted a series of destructive riots in Edo during the Tenmei period (1781–1789), a rumor began to circulate that the crowd of rioters was being led by a beautiful young lad possessing spectacular strength. This young man was said to be able to fly through the air like a bird. In the Hiroshima riots of 1784, a handsome young boy was also said to have played a major role. Such stories instilled courage in the lower classes, who staged widespread and violent protests.[6]

Another example dates from the first month of 1768, some twenty years before the Tenmei disturbances. At this time riots broke out in Osaka over the registration requirements for placing a mortgage on real estate. On this occasion an illustrated pamphlet called *Umehana Niō no monbi* (Plum Blossoms: The "Gift Days" of Niō, the Deva Kings) was published. This booklet contained illustrations of a huge, all-powerful Deva King smashing the houses of the evil rich who were the source of the problem.[7] The Deva King here symbolized the feelings of the disgruntled citizenry. This publication was, of course, immediately banned. Interestingly, the Deva King was said to have wreaked havoc twenty years later in the Tenmei riots, where he supposedly appeared alongside the beautiful youth mentioned earlier.

Amakusa Shirō was a historical figure, but the others—the Tenmei youth, the Deva King of the "Plum Blossoms" pamphlet, and the Deva King of the Edo Tenmei riots—were sheer fantasy. Nevertheless, these images of supernatural power functioned as a source of spiritual support and had much in common with the young Danjūrō's fight for righteousness on the kabuki stage. Kabuki characters such as Takenuki Gorō, Sukeroku, Gongorō in *Shibaraku,* Gorō of the Soga plays and *Yanone,* and other superhuman heroes were all manifestations of this phenomenon.

The aesthetic of *aragoto* is thus a development of the themes of chivalry and righteousness—essentially the theme of "power to the weak." Such chivalry may be beautiful even when it results in death. When, for example, Banzuiin Chōbee faces his nemesis fully aware that this confrontation spells doom, the fact that his death is the result of chivalry endows Chōbee with a kind of grandeur.[8] For the spectators, who were otherwise unable to elevate themselves above the muddle of their daily lives, viewing such chivalry functioned as a kind of spiritual purification.

No doubt the street knights included depraved individuals who secretly accepted bribes from the authorities. Nevertheless, in an age that lacked a civilian police force and an adequate public law, these "gallants" were necessary to protect the weak. The true street knight risked his life in the pursuit of eliminating evil. His dedication to the cause of the law-abiding citizen allowed him to become a symbol in kabuki aesthetics. In sum, then, the aesthetic of *aragoto* was very much a product of its age. Today *aragoto* may at times appear absurdly contrived; its trivial features can hardly be overlooked. Yet during the Edo period, *aragoto* stood unrivaled in its ability to move an audience.

The Aesthetic of Exorcism

The title of this section may not be entirely appropriate, but what I wish to consider here is a phenomenon that parallels the aesthetic of the street knight. As we have seen, the aesthetic of the street knight thrives on the border between fantasy and reality. Reality was also idealized when religious activity reappeared in kabuki. The aesthetic of exorcism is best exemplified in the extended declamation *(tsurane)* of *Shibaraku* or in plays dealing with the Soga brothers—that is, in performances which functioned as a type of annual ritual for the Edo public.

Let us turn first to the *tsurane* of *Shibaraku*. When Danjūrō appears on the *hanamichi* in his superman-like role, he delivers a *tsurane* with great bravura. His efforts are invariably rewarded with a tremendous ovation. Danjūrō was of course not the only actor to perform *Shibaraku*. All three Edo theaters staged original versions of *Shibaraku* during the eleventh month. A new *tsurane* could thus be heard annually at each theater.

An outstanding example of a *tsurane* was delivered in 1796 by the fifth Danjūrō (1741–1806) at the Miyako-za (the "alternate theater" of the Nakamura-za).[9] The text of this speech survives in the *Kabuki nendai-ki* (Kabuki Annals).[10] Yet another *tsurane* was performed that year at the Kawarasaki-za (the "alternate theater" of the Morita-za) by the six-year-old Ichikawa Shinnosuke.[11] This speech was presented in the play *Itsukushima yuki no kaomise* (The "Face-Showing" in the Snow at Itsukushima),[12] which was the third section of the first historical piece on the daily program. With a loud, ringing voice the character Gendamaru Hirotsuna, the second son of the great general and poet Minamoto no Yorimasa (1104–1180), declaims:

> Hear ye, barbarians and savages to the east, west, north, and south! Hear ye, heaven and earth and all Edo! I, Ichikawa of Edo, the scion and rightful descendant of Fudō, the guardian god of Narita, protect

each and all from injury and evil. You may laugh; you may scold me as a brat spouting great nonsense from my little mouth. But by my natural disposition I rise like a demon from a terrifying tale, bursting into the house, performing impossible feats. Today, like an early-blossoming flower, I splendidly appear in my first *Shibaraku*. Need I say it? Even my father, the great Minamoto no Yorimasa, could not tame me, the intractable youth, Gendamaru Hirotsuna. This I announce to all, with the most profound respect.[13]

This *tsurane,* together with an illustration of Shinnosuke's pose, was published as a flyer that was purchased by the Edo citizenry and by provincials who wished to take home a souvenir of the city's theater. This circular perhaps functioned also as a talisman, warding off evil spirits in the year to come. For Shinnosuke's speech begins with an announcement that he will guard Edo and indeed all heaven and earth. With great bravado he proclaims his heroic origins and reveals that at age six this is his first appearance in the play *Shibaraku*. This speech is in effect an obsequy, a rite for pacifying the spirits of Edo. Hovering over this *tsurane* is the image of a beautiful young lad with superhuman abilities.

During the same month as these "face-showing" performances, ancient folk-religious ceremonies and rites were held throughout Japan to drive out evil accumulated during the year. After these rituals, prayers were then offered for welcoming in the new year. Also during the eleventh month, there were Shinto ceremonies in which a ritual dance *(kagura)* was offered to the gods at many shrines. This performance, too, functioned as a solemn rite for sending off the old year and beckoning in the new. With their fresh cast of stars, their young male lead, and the *tsurane,* eleventh-month kabuki performances also served to drive out evil.

After evil had been successfully exorcised, good luck was ushered in. "Face-showing" plays functioned in this manner as well. Together with the New Year's performances, these plays were considered particularly auspicious. Only on such special occasions did the managers of the three Edo theaters—Nakamura Kanzaburō of the Nakamura-za, Ichimura Uzaemon of the Ichimura-za, and Morita Kan'ya of the Morita-za—join their sons to perform a "lucky" play *(kotobuki kyōgen)* and the special ceremonial dance *Sanbasō*. These plays were a ritualistic "house art" unique to each theater. The *kotobuki kyōgen* at the Nakamura-za was *Saruwaka;* the Ichimura-za presented *Kaidō kudari* (Down the Highway). Even when plays were staged at the alternate theaters, the "house art" of each corresponding main theater was performed. Such traditions are carefully

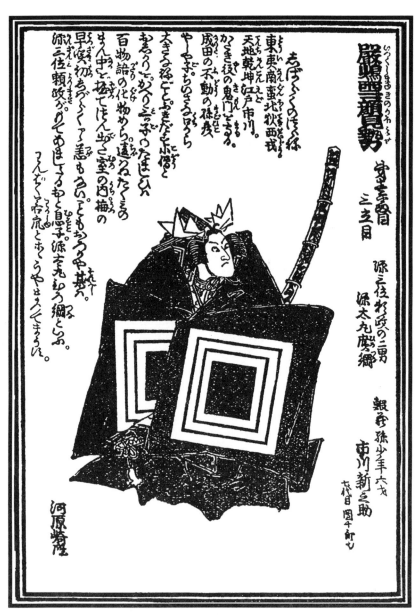

Printed flyer of the *tsurane* delivered by Ichikawa Danjūrō (Shinnosuke) as a six-year-old hero. From *Kabuki nendai-ki*.

recorded in the *Shibai-bayashi nikki* (Diary of Musical Theater Accompaniment).[14]

With their auspicious overtones, eleventh-month performances became an important, festive event for the kabuki-loving *Edokko*. The night before the curtain opened on the premiere, groups of fans staged wild festivals. During performances by Danjūrō or the female impersonator *(onnagata)* Segawa Kikunojō, fans assumed bizarre dress, lined up on the *hanamichi,* and eulogized their hero. Such activities also contributed to the sense of spiritual liberation provided by *Shibaraku* and plays featuring the deeds of the Soga brothers.

Let us turn next to the New Year's plays. At New Year's, Soga plays were performed annually at all three Edo theaters. This tradition lasted for well over a century. Like the play *Shibaraku,* the Soga plays always featured a scene in which the hero confronts the villain. Danjūrō, the protagonist and troupe head, is here cast in the role of the villain Kudō Suketsune. In the climactic scene, Kudō strikes a powerful pose on a raised platform at stage left; a line of daimyo stands in attendance on the raised platform at center stage. Summoned by their friend Asahina, the two brothers Gorō and Jūrō emerge from behind the *agemaku* curtain onto the *hanamichi.* As they make their way toward the main stage they are accompanied by *taimen sanjū* music on the *shamisen.* They then exchange a toast with Kudō. Gorō's acting and the music of the offstage ensemble *(geza)* work in tandem to bring this scene to its culmination.

Next Jūrō Sukenari, the older brother, receives the *sake* cup, as etiquette demands. The younger brother Gorō, however, bares his waist in typical *aragoto* style and turns to Kudō to give a fiery speech in which he swears revenge for his father's murder. This oration is punctuated by loud beats on the *ōdaiko* (large drum) of the *geza* ensemble. Gorō roars:

> What an auspicious day! Today my most cherished wish to meet you has finally been fulfilled. My invocations to the gods and spirits have been heard. To face you now, to confront you, this indeed is fortune's flower blossoming at last. Good luck now resides within the three houses; demons are blown out by this celestial wind, eighteen years in coming. Humbly do I accept this cup of *sake.*

At each beat of the *taiko* Gorō violently shakes his head and reinforces his fierce cross-eyed glare. This pose has a beautiful, almost breathtaking, quality. It is based on the same principles as the *aragoto* acting of the scene "Pulling the Carriage Apart" from *Sugawara denju*

Taimen Sanjū

◿ = plucked with the left hand
V = upstroke of the plectrum

Taimen sanjū played on the *shamisen* in the kabuki. From Machida Kashō, *Shamisen seikyoku ni okeru senritsu-kei no kenkyū (Tōyō ongaku kenkyū,* vol. 47), 1981.

tenarai kagami. There the three heros Umeōmaru, Matsuōmaru, and Sakuraōmaru strike a dramatic pose in which they shake their heads back and forth five times in dramatic fashion. This movement is called *itsutsu-gashira* ("five heads") and is not accompanied by dialogue. Instead, the offstage ensemble music brings this truly exquisite moment of "grand period" kabuki to its climax. After his speech, Gorō, positioned before a small offering stand, accepts the *sake* cup. Finally, after an exchange with Kudō, he is unable to restrain his anger any longer. He splinters the offering stand and smashes his *sake* cup. This act of violence invariably elicits cheers of approval and a thunderous ovation from the audience.

Soga plays were staged with the new year in mind. Their main purpose, as echoed in Gorō's speech, was to grant expression to the commoners' hopes that after many years of waiting, a terrible wrong could finally be avenged. Portrayals of the feudal ethic of loyalty had little to do with the popularity of the dramas featuring the Soga brothers or the forty-seven loyal retainers of *Chūshingura.* Instead, the Edo public was moved by witnessing scenes in which the powerless could finally slay their tyrannical oppressors. All commoners in feudal society were to some extent oppressed. As the years went by, however, commoners increasingly became aware of their own oppression. Against this historical background, the dramas of the Soga brothers and those of the loyal retainers of *Chūshingura* could take on a new and important meaning. Witnessing vendettas at the start of the year gave the populace a sense that life was starting anew.

What was displayed on the kabuki stage was, of course, no more than a potential world. But the deeds of the Soga brothers showed that potentiality could ultimately, after eighteen long years of waiting, turn into reality. The common people understood this secret. The Edo kabuki theaters, in turn, responded by staging plays that reached deep into the public's imagination.

The Aesthetic of Fashion

Before the advent of modern mass media, only cheap woodblock prints known as *kawaraban* provided the Japanese public with a modest supply of news. Information reported in such prints is often unreliable, however, which makes trends in Edo fashion difficult to research.

Edo fashions often originated in the styles of great kabuki stars. When, for example, the seventh Danjūrō wore a costume with the design of a symbol of sickle *(kama)* and the syllables *wa* and *nu*—thus spelling the word *kamawanu* ("I don't care") in rebus form—a *kamawanu* fad immediately swept through the city. This fad stimulated the production of a large variety of dyed fabrics and kimono or kerchiefs with the *kamawanu* design. Somewhat earlier, the checkered pattern of the obi used by the actor Sanokawa Ichimatsu I (1722–1762) had become a highly fashionable design. The famous mid-eighteenth-century *onnagata* Segawa Kikunojō was also a pivotal figure in determining women's fashions.[15]

Performances of Edo, Kamigata, or provincial kabuki often included ingenious advertisement. In the play *Sukeroku*, for example, Kanpera Monbee and Asagao Senbei, two retainers of the villain Ikyū, press the hero Sukeroku. When the drama reaches a point of high tension, Senbei suddenly provides comic relief. In a series of puns, he lists in quick succession the products of famous rice-cracker *(senbei)* stores in Edo. Senbei shouts at Sukeroku:

> Hey! You know-nothing simpleton . . . surely you know that the attendant to whom you speak is the lady-killer Asagao Senbei [rice crackers in the shape of a morning glory blossom]: the grandchild of Satō Senbei [sweet rice crackers], a man whose older sister is Usuyuki Senbei [rice crackers covered with white sugar]; whose brother is Konoha Senbei [rice crackers shaped like a leaf]; and whose master is Shio Senbei [salted rice crackers]![16]

This list is in effect an advertisement for the products of famous Edo *senbei* shops. *Asagao senbei,* for example, are listed at the end of the third section of a guide to Edo entitled *Edo ka no ko* (A Dappled Cloth of Edo, published 1687): "*Asagao senbei* sold at Kita Hatchōbori Dōshinchō in the shop of Fujiya Seizaemon." The same book also lists two other *senbei* shops, one selling *meriyasu senbei* and another *kuzu senbei* (crackers made with arrowroot flour). Such *senbei* shops joined forces with the kabuki to advertise their products. Similarly, when the wheat noodle *(udon)* vendor Fukuyama bumps into Kanpera Monbee in the famous "*udon* scene," this was a reference to an *udon* shop that flourished in the theater quarters at Fukiya-chō and Sakai-chō. With such advertisements kabuki theater became an important source of contemporary trends.

Major incidents that caught the public's attention were often dramatized and adapted for the kabuki stage: the arson committed by Oshichi the greengrocer's daughter,[17] sex scandals of reputedly holy monks, double suicides, or any of a number of famous vendettas. The bakufu repeatedly banned such true-to-life depictions, but playwrights found ways to circumvent government interdiction. For example, the vendetta of the loyal retainers of the play *Chūshingura* was set in the distant fourteenth-century world of the *Taiheiki* (Records of a Great Peace).[18] Audiences knew, however, that they were watching a version of the latest news. Kabuki was thus a thoroughly up-to-date form of entertainment.

The Aesthetic of Evil

During the Taishō period (1912–1926) I lived in a village on the banks of the Chigusa River, some ten kilometers upstream and to the north of the castle town of Akō in Harima province. Every year, in spring and autumn, a temporary stage was constructed for two days of "village kabuki." Various plays were produced, some so unusual they do not even appear in today's kabuki encyclopedias. I had not yet entered elementary school, but I never missed such performances, whose scenes and lines I committed solidly to memory.

When my parents or grandparents spoke of these plays, I was always fascinated. I listened closely to the comments of the adults and asked many questions. One term, however, I always failed to understand. No matter how often I was given an explanation, I simply could not grasp the expression *aku* ("evil"). As a child I often heard the grown-ups say, "Shihei's *aku* really hit the spot," or "this time Igami no Gonta's *aku* wasn't quite enough," or "it should have had more *aku!*" I had no idea of what everyone was talking about, but these early experiences made me aware that "evil" in kabuki was something very special.

Villains and evildoers are, of course, found in theater throughout the world. But the aesthetic of evil in kabuki—in particular Edo kabuki from the end of the eighteenth to the end of the nineteenth centuries—was something highly original. Although this thesis deserves to be developed at some length, here I shall simply sketch the outlines of the aesthetic of evil by considering two outstanding instances. An early example of the aesthetic of evil can be found in the creation of the role of the "villain lover." The role of Sadakurō in the fifth act of *Kanadehon chūshingura* (Chūshingura: The Treasury of Loyal Retainers)[19] had always been played in the garb of a mountain priest; Sadakurō was a villain pure and simple. But when Nakamura Nakazō I (1736–1790) performed this role, he wore a crested black kimono, thereby turning Sadakurō into a good-looking young man. The style of the "villain lover" was subsequently developed by the playwrights Tsuruya Nanboku IV (1755–1829) and Kawatake Mokuami (1816–1893). Such characters appear in Mokuami's plays *Sannin*

Kichiza (Three Men Called Kichiza)[20] and *Benten kozō* (Benten the Thief)[21] and in Nanboku's *Yotsuya kaidan* (The Ghosts of Yotsuya).[22]

Let us turn next to this last-mentioned play, *Yotsuya kaidan,* whose plot unfolds as follows. Tamiya Iemon, a "loyal retainer" of Akō, commits a murder but manages to marry the victim's daughter Oiwa by tricking her into believing that he will seek to avenge her father's killer. Soon thereafter, Iemon falls in love with Oume, the daughter of a neighbor, and he slays his wife to marry Oume. The faithful Oiwa is subjected to the most vicious treatment before being murdered, but, as a paragon of virtue, she accepts her lot without complaining. The moment she dies, however, Oiwa is transformed into the most horrible ghost imaginable. The pure, faultless victim suddenly becomes a cruel and indomitable avenger. Completely rejecting all Buddhist invocations and religious rites, she eventually succeeds in killing Iemon. Iemon arrogantly proclaims that even decapitation will not stop him, but he finally succumbs to Oiwa's powers.

One of the scenes at the start of this play takes place in the quarters of the lowest class of unlicensed prostitutes. This lowly den of vice, beyond the pale of feudal morality, is exhibited on stage. Moreover, the audience is treated to scenes of gruesome murder. Such spectacles display the essence of evil most effectively. I do not know if the author, Tsuruya Nanboku, stood opposed to contemporary feudal morality. In any case, Iemon—who is in fact one of the "loyal retainers" of the play *Chūshingura*—possesses not a shred of loyalty. He is, rather, the very epitome of treachery. Yet it would be simplistic to view Iemon as merely an "antifeudal" or "anti-Confucian" symbol. The same is true for Oiwa, the faithful wife and archetype of feudal moral behavior, who turns into a cruel demon the moment she is killed.

Rather than expressing such old concerns, the aesthetic of evil was something entirely new. Its creation owed much to the author-actor team of Kawatake Mokuami and Ichikawa Kodanji IV (1812–1866). These men collaborated on many outstanding plays, including *Sakura giminden*[23] and the *Sannin Kichiza* cited earlier. In these plays, and in other favorites such as *Benten kozō* or *Gen'yadana,*[24] evil was often portrayed as something stylish. This stylishness was embodied in the "villain lovers" and "virtuous bandits" who appear in such plays.

Evil as seen here was no longer confined to the character traits of solitary villains on the stage. Instead, it had been transformed into something that gave expression to the energy of the commoner populace. Iemon, Yosaburō, Benten Kozō, Ojō Kichiza, and others symbolized this energy. With inexorable force, no longer containable by government regulations or coercion, the culture of the commoners drove forward. Even the satirical drawings of Kuniyoshi or popular novels such as Takizawa Bakin's *Nanso Satomi hakkenden* could no longer be suppressed. Evil as found in these works had much in common with evil seen on the kabuki stage. In either case, this new type of evil was part of the explosion of commoner culture in the last decades of the Edo period.

Conclusion: Music and Other Elements

The aesthetics of kabuki includes many more important components. One of the most notable is kabuki music in all of its many forms. A remarkable musical effect occurs, for example, when Mitsuhide appears in the tenth act of *Ehon taikōki* (The Picture Book of the Meritorious Prince).[25] The moment that he declaims, "Appearing from far beyond the moonflower trellis . . . ," frogs that have been croaking incessantly suddenly fall still. The sole purpose of the croaking is to prepare this moment of tense silence. This wonderfully realistic effect is created by rubbing together two *akagai* shells.

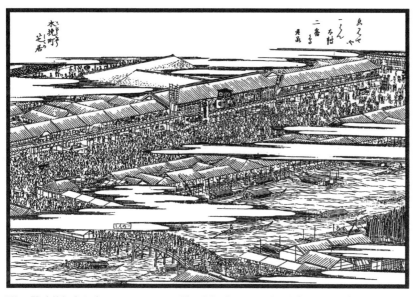

The Kobiki-chō theater quarter. The Morita-za or its "alternate theater," the Kawarasaki-za, were located here, as were numerous teahouses and restaurants. From *Edo meisho zue.*

Another dramatic effect is created by the use of the *ki* (or *hyōshigi:* wooden clappers). When Yoshitsune and Benkei perform the famous tragic scene in *Kanjinchō* (The Subscription List),[26] Benkei dances to the following text of a *nagauta* composition:

> The warrior,
>> With armor and sleeve pillow
>> As sole companions . . .
> Sometimes,
>> Adrift at sea
>> At mercy of wind and tide . . .
> Sometimes,
>> In mountain fastness,
>> Where no hoofprint breaks the white snow . . .
> While he endures it all,
>> From small evening waves of the sea,
>> Come whispers of disgrace and banishment.[27]

When he finishes his dance, Benkei moves his left foot forward and strikes a powerful pose known as an *ishinage mie* ("stone-throwing pose").[28] Precisely at this moment the *ki* are struck. This effect, which occurs only once in *Kanjinchō*, is of the utmost importance. With the line that follows, "For three long years past . . . ," the play has reached its great turning point, from which the mood suddenly relaxes.

The *kodama* (echo) pattern is yet another kind of fascinating off-stage *(geza)* music. This formula is used, for example, in the "Mountain Scene" of the play *Imoseyama onna teikin* (Mount Imo and Mount Se: An Exemplary Tale of Womanly Virtue).[29] Here the Yoshino River is imagined as flowing between the two *hanamichi*. When the daimyo Daihanji and the widow of the rival daimyo Dazai appear on opposite *hanamichi*, two *tsuzumi* players, one upstage and one downstage, perform the *kodama no aikata* ("echo interlude"), in which they echo each other's drumbeats at long intervals. Although such an effect may not be noticed by the spectators, it creates a mood of dark mountain recesses. The same pattern, a truly brilliant invention of the *geza* ensemble, can also be found in the ocean scenes of the dance piece *Shiokumi* (The Brine Ladlers)[30] and the play *Kezori* (The Barber's Assistant).[31] Later it was deftly put to use in Yamamoto Yasue's masterful performances of Kinoshita Junji's (b. 1914) play *Yūzuru* (Twilight of a Crane, 1949).

Other superb *geza* music includes the patterns accompanying snow scenes of *Sagi musume* (The Heron Maiden)[32] and *Ninokuchi mura* (Ninokuchi Village).[33] Still other wonderful music is heard in the scene "On the Banks of the Sumida River" of the play *Kamiyui Shinza*.[34] In this play the protagonist pops open his umbrella as he is about to cross the bridge. At this point one hears the *kashira-iri nami no oto* pattern, which also functions as a drum pattern for the *nagauta* ensemble's performance of the words "Blow, river winds! Up with the bamboo blind!"[35]

Other important elements of kabuki aesthetics include the manner in which the idea of *iki*—as cultivated by the courtesans of Yoshiwara and the geisha of the Fukagawa area of Edo—appears on stage in the form of costumes and props. Visual elements in general were developed to a high degree in the kabuki. To represent falling snow or cherry blossoms, for example, pieces of paper are cut into small triangles and placed in a bamboo basket that is suspended at some height. When the basket is shaken, the flakes fall, creating a beautiful effect.

The manner in which many kabuki plays are structured is also remarkable. Whereas most Western dramas have a coherent theme or plot that is maintained throughout the entire play, it is only the individual acts that form a unity in kabuki classics such as *Chūshingura* or *Yotsuya kaidan*. A climax in Western drama usually occurs at only one point in the action; but kabuki plays often have several such moments. *Chūshingura*, for example, peaks both in Act 6, "Kanpei's Suicide," and in Act 7, "The Ichiriki Brothel." *Sugawara denju tenarai kagami* (Sugawara and the Secrets of Calligraphy)[36] and *Yotsuya kaidan* are structured similarly. Many of the best-known kabuki plays thus contain a series of highly discontinuous situations: in effect, a continuity of the discontinuous.

When Tsubouchi Shōyō (1859–1935) attempted to study kabuki using modern scholarly methods, he found it to be so heterogeneous as to defy systematic analysis.[37] To be sure, kabuki aesthetics comprises a number of elements. Each of these, however, is a fascinating manifestation of Japanese style and is worthy of detailed analysis.

12

POPULAR PERFORMING ARTS: FROM EDO TO MEIJI

After the end of the Edo period, many popular performing arts underwent rapid modernization; others, however, retained the styles and forms they had assumed during the preceding age. In this short study I shall attempt to analyze the uneven development of Japanese popular performing arts as they passed from the last years of the Edo period into the Meiji period (1868–1912).

Types of Popular Performing Arts

Research by Haneda Yoshiaki, Fukuda Sadayoshi, Shimizu Ikutarō, Matsuda Michio, Tsurumi Shunsuke, and others has shown that popular arts are best divided into two categories: one includes genres in which the process of appreciation is also a process of creation; the other comprises arts in which an audience delights in performances presented by others.[1] Here I should like to limit myself to the latter genres: quick-paced, interesting, and inexpensive performances that often relied on master/apprentice relations for passing on the required skills. Many Japanese popular performing arts boast a long tradition, but it was not until the Edo period that a great variety of such arts reached a large public. The golden age of popular performing arts followed the Kasei period (1804–1830) and lasted to the very end of the Edo period.

Details of popular amusements and performing arts can be found in many contemporary records: the *Bukō nenpyō* (Chronicles of Edo [1849–1878], by Saitō Gesshin [1804–1878], supplemented by Kitamura Nobuyo [1783–1856] and Sekine Shisei [1825–1893]); the *Misemono zasshi* (Miscellaneous Records of Spectacles, by Kodera Gyokuchō, written in 1828–1833 and containing information on events from 1814 to 1833); the *Kōto gosui* (Naps in the Imperial Capital, by Nishizawa Ippōken, published in 1850); the *Kiki no manimani*

(As I Heard It, by Kitamura Nobuyo, recording events in Edo from 1781 to 1853); the *Dōchō tosetsu* (Reports from the Streets, by Ōsato Shinsai, recording events from 1825 to 1830); and the *Morisada mankō* (Morisada's Miscellany, by Kitagawa Morisada, written from the 1830s to the 1860s). On the basis of such records, one may compile the following list of popular arts and diversions flourishing from around the Kasei period until the end of the Edo period. Although some of the documents used to produce this list are not from Edo, nearly all the arts listed here were performed in the capital:

1. *Tricks and acrobatics (kyokugei)*
   Illusionists
   Conjuring
   Mechanical contraptions
   Water-driven contraptions
   "Takeda's new contraption"
   Acrobatics
   Equestrian feats *(kyokuba)*
   Top-spinning tricks
   Acrobatic *shamisen* performances
   Performances with bamboo castanets
   Fan tricks
   Performances with masks *(hyakume, hyaku manako)*

2. *Special abilities (tokugi)*
   Foot tricks
   Horse tricks
   "Eight-role art" *(hachiningei:* one performer takes on eight roles)
   "Fifteen-role art"
   "Eighteen-role art"
   "One-hundred-role art"
   Streamer flying *(noborisashi)*

3. *Mimicry (monomane)*
   Impersonators
   Birdcall imitations
   Grimacing (mimicking famous people)
   Gesturing
   Mime plays

4. *Dance (buyō)*
   Chinaman's dance
   Nagasaki snake dance

Edo geisha dance
Holy dance of the Izumo Grand Shrine
Sumiyoshi dance
Daikagura (lion dance)

5. *Narrative arts*
Punch-line stories
Light, witty stories
Edifying old tales
"Topic of the day" stories
Trio of storytellers reciting "topic of the day" stories
Narration while performing tricks using mechanical contraptions
Riddle improvising
Battle narratives
Chongare bushi (popular narratives accompanied on *shamisen*)
Ukare bushi (similar to *chongare bushi*)
Ahodara sutra (humorous satiric verses recited in the manner of a
    sutra; performed by itinerant pseudo-monks to the accom-
    paniment of a wooden drum)
Saimon, sekkyō (homilies or recitation)

6. *Theatricals and* jōruri
Farces
Teriha kyōgen (nō drama performed in kabuki style, including
    popular songs and dances)
Comic shows or plays with monkeys
Improvised comedies
Shadow images
Magic lantern shows
Puppet shows
Women's *gidayū*
Parlor *jōruri*
Other forms of *jōruri*

The types of entertainment listed here were often performed on temporary stages for crowds that gathered at festivals, fairs, and anniversaries. Shows were frequently staged at popular spots in the city: at Shijō in Kyoto; Dōtonbori and Naniwa Shinchi in Osaka; Ryōgoku Hirokōji, Ueno Yamashita, and Asakusa Okuyama in Edo; and Ōsu or the grounds of the Seijuin Temple in Nagoya. More or less permanent stages existed at *yoseba* or *yose* (variety halls).

Performances also took place on the street. Top-spinners, for example, performed both on the stage and in the streets. Street performers included "sword unsheathers" *(iai-nuki)*, jesters *(nodaiko)*, strolling musicians, conjurer-acrobats *(mamezō)*, Buddhist exorcisers, preachers, and sermonizers. Some street performances were originally of folk origin: comic dialogues *(manzai)*; the *daikagura* lion dance and music; the auspicious Daikoku dance; and the *shamisen* playing and singing of women known as *torioi*, who made their rounds at New Year's.

I shall leave the precise description of these arts to the various reference books on these genres.[2] Here I wish to consider other issues: the reception of such arts by the contemporary masses; the social status or class of the audiences; the relation of supply and demand between the performers and their audience; the relations of the provinces to the three major urban centers; and the ways in which the various shows were managed. In particular, I should like to chart the course taken by popular performing arts in their transition from the Edo period to modern times.

Edo-Period Performers

Let us turn first to the reception of popular performing arts by the masses. Popular success was usually governed by two criteria: the skill and virtuosity of the performer and the originality or amount of planning of the performance. Let us consider some examples.

The *Bukō nenpyō* (Chronicles of Edo) records the following information for 1857:

> From the first day of the new year, Hayatake Torakichi from Osaka performed solo top-spinning tricks, conjuring, acrobatics, tightrope walking, and a medley of other feats near Ryōgoku Bridge. This drew huge crowds of spectators. From around the third month, a man named Sakurazuna Komajū and his three young disciples Kōkichi, Fukumatsu, and Sukesaburō came from Osaka to perform in the same manner as Hayatake. These artistes displayed their abilities at the Sensōji Temple at [Asakusa] Okuyama. Crowds of spectators thronged to these performances, which continued until the end of the fifth month.[3]

Sakurazuna Komajū obviously possessed skills unusual enough to allow him to stage highly popular performances for five months. No doubt, Hayatake and Sakurazuna were both superb acrobats.

Similar shows took place at the Seijuin in Nagoya. Shows at this temple sometimes featured mimicry *(monomane)*. An entry for the twenty-second day of the seventh month of 1831 in the *Misemono zasshi* gives a very favorable description of the performers and their skills:

Asao Torakichi
Azuma Uzō: mimics well-known birdcalls, performs fan tricks, and
    plays the castanets *(yotsudake)*
Utagawa Fukunosuke
Azuma Kamenosuke
Utagawa Hyakujirō
Yoshikawa Senpachi: acrobatic *shamisen* performances using a ladle
    or an egg as plectrum
Azuma Sennosuke

The above-mentioned Senpachi is a true virtuoso on the *shamisen*. He can play using only one or two strings of the instrument or while holding the instrument on his head. He can even reproduce the sound of a *koto* and can perform in ways that sound like a duet (a good and a bad player, two good players, or two bad players). He also performs many other marvelous and curious feats. Uzō is also an extremely skilled performer of the castanets; the way he inserts effects into theatricals is phenomenal. He too performs various marvelous tricks with a fan.[4]

Such arts were brought to perfection within the framework of strict master/disciple relationships. After many years of apprenticeship, students acquired a rock-solid mastery of their skill. This skill, and not the intricacy of the magic tricks performed, was the key to success. The conjurer-acrobat known as Mamezō, for example, who performed on the street for the general public, used only simple props. Hence much emphasis was placed on the skill and dexterity of Mamezō's performances. Mamezō first requested his audience to throw coins. Shouting "I won't do it till you throw some more!" he waited until enough money had been collected. Then, at lightning speed, he jumped through a basketlike tube through which sword blades protruded or into which burning candles had been placed. Mamezō swallowed or disgorged swords and needles and performed any number of other fantastic feats.

Other popular performers included the top-spinner Matsui Gensui and the foot-trick specialist Mushōken Kamekichi. Yet another great virtuoso, whose clever and original performances were rewarded with great public acclaim, was the riddle-improviser Dodoitsubō Senka (1796–1852). A section of the *Shichū fūbun kaki-*

A "basket jumper" *(kagonuke).* From *Wakan sansai zue* (Pictures of the Three Realms in Japan and China), 1713.

utsushi (A Copy of Accounts of Manners in the City) from the fifth month of 1846 offers a contemporary account of Dodoitsubō's performances at *yoseba* in Edo:

> The so-called storyteller *(hanashika)* Dodoitsubō Senka improvises comic riddles on themes posed by his audience. He accompanies his

Dodoitsubō Senka. From the title page of *Azuma-jiman meijin totchiriton.* Reprinted in Mitamura Engyo, ed., *Kawaraban no hayariuta.*

performances on the *shamisen*. For this he has earned an extraordinary reputation. He now appears at a well-traversed spot near Ryōgoku Bridge, in the precincts of the Yushima Tenjin Shrine, and at one other location. To make his daily rounds to these three spots, he hires a palanquin and two or three carriers. For these performances he earns some 7 or 8 *ryō* per day.[5]

Dodoitsubō's reputation, which allowed him to earn a huge sum of money, was not simply based on his storytelling skills. His popularity also relied on his ability to thematize the everyday concerns of his audience.

Dodoitsubō's art, an impromptu affair of short duration, required instantaneous reactions. Other virtuosi, however, produced stationary exhibits. The "living figures" *(iki-ningyō)* of Matsumoto Kisaburō were one particularly celebrated example. An 1855 entry of the *Bukō nenpyō* records that

> from the eighteenth day of the second month an eighty-day temple fair *(kaichō)* took place at the Sensōji Temple [in Asakusa] in which a figure of the god Kannon was unveiled. . . . At the same time, "living figures" from Osaka were put on display at Asakusa Okuyama. These figures were manufactured by Matsumoto Kisaburō from Bingo in Kumamoto; they are said to be made, not of wood or clay, but rather of papier-mâché. Many figures were exhibited: inhabitants of the island of long arms, the island of long legs, the land of perforated chests, the land of no stomachs, and figures from other exotic lands. Figures of courtesans from the Maruyama area [of Nagasaki] were also displayed. All of these figures, both men and women, are completely lifelike.[6]

According to the sculptor Takamura Kōun (1852–1934), who saw these "living figures" as a young man, Matsumoto crafted his creations at age twenty-eight. These masterpieces stunned the doll-makers and sculptors of Edo. In one particularly popular exhibit

> [a figure of] a geisha from the Maruyama area was seen naked in a bathhouse setting. Behind her was a young servant girl holding a kind of washcloth. The geisha appeared to be about to enter the water, with a towel just barely covering her private parts. Two more figures had just come out of the water and were arranging their hair and putting on makeup in front of a mirror. This exhibit was very enchanting; the figures of this display were especially highly praised.[7]

Kōun and Edo sculptors were obviously impressed by Matsumoto's superb craftsmanship. But the reason for the success of the exhibits must be sought elsewhere: in the novelty of the idea of creating a set of figures that, though stationary, showed a kind of striptease act. Also unique was the idea of transforming the scene of an *ukiyo-e* into sculpture.

The success of performing arts at the end of the Edo period relied mainly on the level of virtuosity, the originality of a performance or a conception, and the degree to which an audience could find its concerns expressed in an art. Performers who could fulfill these conditions were eagerly sought by the *yose* and other show houses. At such theaters, virtuosi turned their art into a commodity that could be sold at a premium. If the foregoing conditions were met, an artist could achieve great popularity on the stages of Edo, Kyoto, and Osaka. Circumstances varied, of course: some performers polished their art in these three cities; others, such as Matsumoto Kisaburō, came to the city as a kind of dark horse from the provinces. Yet others were invited from the provinces to appear in the cities.

More examples of contemporary performances can be found in Kodera Gyokuchō's *Misemono zasshi*. This volume includes records of performers who came to Nagoya from throughout Japan. In the eighth month of 1821, the storyteller *(kōshakushi)* Zuiun from Asakusa (Edo) came to Nagoya to perform the *Taihei gishin-den* (The Legend of Faithful Retainers During the Time of Great Peace).[8] Also during the eighth month, the Asakusa shellwork artist Ōtsuka Kanzō exhibited his work in Nagoya after having toured Kyoto and Osaka.[9] In the fourth month of 1823, performances of *Kojitsu ima monogatari shin-ju-butsu shōdan* (Modern Tales of Old Truths: Shinto, Confucian, and Buddhist Comic Stories) as told by Utei Enba (1743–1822), Iwai Kanehachi, Seiryūtei Bayū, and Bandō Masakichi scored a great hit. A second run took place during the sixth month of the same year.[10] In the second month of 1824, performances by the raconteurs Utei Enba, Sanshōtei Senkichi, Seiryūtei Masakichi, Sanshōtei Kiraku, and Futabatei Keiba were tremendously popular.[11] From the fourteenth day of the third month, performances of "eight-role art" given by Ushijima Tozan, the founder of the Ushijima school of *hachiningei,* were added to this program.

Several years later, in the ninth month of 1828, performances of *sannin kakeai ukiyo-banashi* (a trio of storytellers telling "topic of the day" stories) were given by Kashiwaya Tomematsu and his two brothers Inomatsu and Yasomatsu. These shows found great favor among the public and ran for three months.[12] Then, during the seventh month of 1831, Dodoitsubō Senka appeared in a show entitled *Kokkei-banashi yūri gijō* (comic stories of the theater and brothels) and performed "punch-line stories," "topic-of-the-day" duets, and "*yoshikono* songs improvised on three topics."[13] This latter genre was probably the same as the riddle improvising mentioned earlier. In any case, all of these performances were highly successful and enjoyed long runs.

The third month of 1834 featured a performance of *tokiwazu* chant by Komoji-dayū and his disciples.[14] Other Nagoya exhibits worthy of note included acrobats and "Takeda mechanical contraptions" from Osaka, as well as the water contraptions *(mizu karakuri)* of Sakurai Shigesuke and Takei Yoshima from Kyoto. Such touring exhibits were very common. In many cases a Nagoya show manager engaged performers from Edo, Kyoto, or Osaka to appear in his theater. But tours were not limited to the cities. As we have seen in Chapter 7, theatrical performances took place throughout Japan. Both in urban areas and in rural villages, performing arts were staged before a highly responsive public.

Let us turn next to the show manager or promoter and examine the social and economic context of late Edo-period performing arts. Managers and promoters usually did not possess enough capital to turn performances of popular performing arts into profitable show troupes. As noted earlier, shows were usually staged at *yose* or in small, temporary playhouses hastily built at popular spots. Profits were usually small. For example, Matsumoto Kisaburō's final masterpiece, the 1874–1875 exhibit of "living figures" representing thirty-three famous sites of the "western pilgrimage route," was said to have been wildly successful. But according to Takamura Kōun, the total number of spectators was a mere 7,500 people.[15]

The practices of Kawashima Kayū, a Kasei-period (1804–1830) master of "eight-role art," are recorded in Sekine Shisei's *Shisei airoku:*

[Kawashima's] fee for going to a parlor *(zashiki)* was 1 *ryō* per day; for a performance at his home he charged a basic fee of forty-eight coppers per person. If the audience numbered over one hundred people he expanded his home to accommodate up to one hundred and fifty people. When this production earned a high reputation he put on a show at a teahouse *(machiai-jaya)* at Gensuke-chō (Hikage-chō) in Shiba. Here his audience supposedly numbered over three hundred people a day. Later he built a playhouse within the grounds of the Shiba Shinmei shrine. At this location he let the conjurer Harusuke perform an introductory act, but he performed the finale himself. Admission was one hundred coppers per person.[16]

From this description we learn that as the size of Kayū's audience increased, his performance space expanded accordingly. It remains unclear, however, whether a third party—a promoter or manager who hired Kayū—was involved or whether Kayū functioned as his own show manager and promoter. Since Kayū utilized his own home as a theater, however, he presumably operated both in the capacity of performer and promoter.

The use of private residences as unofficial *yose* may have been the result of government regulations prohibiting many types of performing arts. Official *yose* were limited to the "four arts" or "four skills": tales of times past; war and battle stories; lectures on practical ethics *(shingaku);* and lectures on Shinto. Private homes may thus have functioned as *yose* for other genres. In any case, Kayū's practice was probably not the rule. Although written somewhat later, San'yūtei Itchō's *Mandan Meiji shonen* (Tales of the Early Meiji Years) records that

> in those days there were three major theaters in Ryōgoku: the "San-jitei," run by Chōemon of Yanagibashi; the "Hayashiya," run by Otoemon, a lumber carrier who lives near Ryōgoku; and the plasterer Itarō's "Koriba" on the other side of Ryōgoku Bridge, known for [*rakugo* performer San'yūtei] Enchō's daytime performances, which were highly successful for seven years. These were the three top theaters.[17]

Here lumber carriers and plasterers functioned as playhouse managers and promoters. The following excerpt from the *Bukō nenpyō,* recording events of 1866, reveals that Kintarō, a boss of the fire brigade, ran one of the largest *yoseba* in Edo:

> Kintarō, the head of the fire brigade *(hikeshi ninpu no kashira)*—the head of the *"se"* group of firemen *(tobi)* who put out fires in the ward—resides at Yoko-chō, to the east of the third block of Minami Denma-chō, and is running a *yoseba*. His professional name *(yagō)* is Sanomatsu. This theater has a frontage of sixty-nine feet and a depth of over fifty-four feet. The stage is over twenty-four feet in size and is surrounded on all three sides by two levels of galleries. Kabuki plays staged here are acted by both young boys (aged between eleven and seventeen) and young girls. These actors do not speak. Instead, they move their mouths to the words of the *jōruri* recitation. Thus they are nicknamed "living figures" *(iki-ningyō)*. This theater is known as the best of Edo's large *yose;* every day spectators come here in droves.

But from the end of the third month performances were halted because of a legal violation for which a fine was levied. The best young male actors performing here were named Komajaku, Tamago, and Komajirō.[18]

Fireman Kintarō was obviously running a grand, profitable show. In fact, ambitious productions of popular performing arts had already appeared earlier. According to the *Kitamachi bugyō-sho shichū torishimari-gakari jōshinsho* (Written Report of the City Law-Enforcement Officials Submitted to the Northern Town Magistrate) of the tenth month of 1841, puppet theater performed to *jōruri* accompaniment was being staged at *yose* in *chōnin* quarters in 1829. Because such performances fell outside the scope of the officially sanctioned "four skills," they were banned. The report mentions, however, that shows closely resembling the puppet theater were recently again being advertised as featuring "large props" or "large contraptions." As a result, the official puppet theater house was falling on hard times.[19]

Evidently the rise of the *yose* was already a threat to the authorized theaters before the Tenpō Reforms of the early 1840s. After the reforms, things hardly improved for these theaters. According to the *Machi bugyō jōshinsho* (Written Report Submitted to the City Magistrate) of the seventh day of the fifth month of 1847, the official kabuki theaters at Saruwaka-chō continued to flourish, but the audience for the puppet theater had dwindled to the vanishing point. Inviting famous performers from Kyoto was of no avail; promoters were nowhere to be found. The document reports that chanters, *shamisen* accompanists, and others who had previously been associated with the puppet theater had begun to work for the *yose*, where puppet theater accompanied by "parlor *jōruri*" was highly popular.[20]

The success of these nighttime shows rested on their informality, low cost, and inherent interest. Audiences especially enjoyed watching female performers reciting *jōruri*. Already in 1805 laws had been issued banning the practice of staging shows in which groups of five or six girls performed *jōruri*.[21] Later, during the seventh month of 1841, the authorities lamented that it was not right to send one's daughter onto the *yose* stage as a *jōruri* performer and then live an easy life from the profits.[22] But as the earlier-mentioned document from the tenth month of 1841 shows, little heed was paid to contemporary laws banning women's *jōruri* performances.[23] *Chōnin* women relied on such appearances as a source of income. This form of recitation—also called *musume gidayū* (girl's *gidayū*) or *yose jōruri*—was performed at *yose,* on shrine grounds, and in many other locations throughout the city.

Yose managers were generally members of the Edo commoner populace; they staged shows simply by hiring available performers.[24] Although one gains a vague idea of the size of the audience from the type of records cited earlier, no accurate statistics or concrete historical evidence is extant. Little is known about the number and precise nature of the *yose* or their distribution within the city of Edo. One of the few useful studies is Sekine Mokuan's *Kōdan rakugo konjakutan* (Old and New Tales of Comic Narrative and Storytelling), which gives statistics on the number of *yose* during certain years. According to Sekine, there were 75 *yose* in 1815 and 125 in the late 1820s. In 1842 the Tenpō Reforms limited the number of officially sanctioned *yose* in the city proper to a mere 15. But by 1844 business permits had been issued to over 60, and by 1845 their number had swelled to more than 700. In 1854, some 220 *yose* were offering war stories; another 162 featured other types of storytellers. Later, the fortunes of the *yose* declined: by 1880 there were 163; in 1884 there were 87; and by 1901 their numbers had shrunk to 78.[25]

The most famous *yose* were concentrated in the downtown area of Edo: Kanda, Nihonbashi, Kyōbashi, Shiba, Shitaya, Asakusa, and Fukagawa. Others were scattered around the uptown area: in Kōjimachi, Azabu, Akasaka, Yotsuya, Ushigome, Koishikawa, and Hongō. Edo *yose* managers—plasterers, lumber carriers, firemen, in short, members of the working class—probably staged their shows simply by converting permanent structures that were used for other purposes during the daytime into nighttime *yose*. Such edifices were in effect the communal property of the citizenry. This communal quality of *yose* was one of their most important characteristics. Performances heard and seen in these theaters were the very soul of the working class. Within the walls of the *yose* the citizens could enjoy a form of public entertainment they had created for themselves.

Who, then, was the *yose* audience? Such a question is difficult to answer precisely, but information found in the *Shichū torishimari ruishū* (Documents Concerning Law Enforcement in the City) allows one to make inferences. According to the *Onmitsu mawari jōshinsho* (Written Report of Spies; seventh month of 1841), provincial warriors stationed in Edo flocked to performances in which women and children appeared on stage. Occasionally samurai even fell in love with the women, whom they accompanied to and from the *yose* and treated as mistresses. Sometimes these relationships progressed to the point where, despite the man's warrior status, an elopement was the result. Disobeying the laws and behaving in such a manner was, according to this document, hardly to be condoned.[26]

Other pertinent information can be gleaned from a section of the *Shichū fūbunsho* (Document on Manners in the City) dating from the second month of 1847. By this time the prohibitions of the Tenpō Reforms had been relaxed, and many *yose* were again in operation. This report notes that unlike the official "four arts," women's *jōruri* was still subject to strict prohibitions. Nevertheless, under the pretext of offering "unaccompanied recitations" or "recitals," performances of women's *jōruri* had again been taking place quite openly since the previous spring. The document continues by noting that except for the genre "tales of times past," the "four arts," which during the days of the Tenpō Reforms had enjoyed a brief resurgence, were in a steep decline. Farces, in essence no different from kabuki, were now being performed at the *yose* as well. The cheap price of an admission ticket and the convenience of nighttime performances allowed both men and women to attend. Women were especially numerous. In sum, the *yose* were prospering throughout the city.[27]

Although these historical materials refer only to the kind of *yose* that featured "parlor *jōruri*" *(zashiki jōruri)* or "women's *jōruri*" *(onna jōruri)*, they seem to portray a general trend. In any case, audiences who packed these show houses included warriors and commoners from Edo or the suburbs. Unmarried men and women from the Edo working class especially enjoyed visiting the *yose* where they could hear comic monologues, riddle improvising, "eight-role art," and much else. Audience members also included visitors to the city from nearby villages. Such sightseers often came to the city primarily to attend temple fairs and festivals.

The Transition to Meiji

I should now like to turn to the transformation of popular performing arts after the start of the Meiji period. Most performing arts followed one of three paths into the modern era. Some were transformed into commercial stage productions or forms of mass media; these arts thereby exposed themselves to the effects of modern capital and to foreign influence. Other arts simply disappeared, the victim of modernization. Yet others remained relatively unchanged.

The first category can be subdivided into two types: arts whose transformation was limited to the manner of presentation (an art might be altered and modernized, becoming a stage show or a kind of mass medium, but the art itself was left intact) and arts whose fundamental character was altered. Both types of change pose important questions that are still of relevance today. Of particular interest is the change brought about by the infusion of capital. During the great upheavals accompanying the Meiji Restoration, Japanese capital was still undeveloped. Hence the first major consolidation of popular performing arts into commercial productions was the result of foreign capital. An event of epoch-making significance occurred in 1866, when an American identified in the *Bukō nenpyō* as "Benkutsu" hired many outstanding performers for an international tour.[28] These performers were given two-year contracts and sent touring the United States and Europe. This event appears to have been highly newsworthy. Indeed, the *Bukō nenpyō* gives a detailed account of the names of the various performers and their repertory:[29]

> This year [1866] top-spinners, acrobats, sleight-of-hand artists, and the like were hired by an American to go to his country. These performers (names given below) performed their respective arts in Yokohama this spring, when, at the request of the American "Benkutsu," they were contracted for two years, from the ninth month of this year until the tenth month of the year after next.

- Top-spinners: from the third block of Tawaramachi in Asakusa, Matsui Gensui, his wife Hana, their daughters Mitsu and Saki, their son Kunitarō, age seven.
- Sleight-of-hand artists: from Arai-chō in north Honjo, Yanagawa Chōjūrō; from Aioi-chō in Kanda, Sumidagawa Namigorō and his wife Koman; from the same house, Namishichi.
- Tightrope walkers: Namigorō's son Towakichi; on *shamisen*, Namigorō's younger sister Tora.
- Top-spinners: from the ward before the Ryūhō-ji in Asakusa, Matsui Kikujirō's daughter Tsune, age eight (put inside a top); from the same house, Matsugorō.
- Lion stunts *(shishi no kyoku),* commonly known as *kakubee-jishi no kyoku:* from the same house as above, Umekichi and Matsujū.
- Strong men, and foot jugglers: from the second block of Kyōmachi in Yoshiwara, Hamaikari Sadakichi and his adopted son Nagakichi (assistant balanced above) from the same house as Umekichi; from Koishikawa Shirakabe-chō, the helper Ichitarō and an assistant (balanced overhead) Ryūnosuke; from the first block of Minami-denma-chō, Kichibee's son Kanekichi; on flute, from Koishikawa Kami-tomisaka-chō, Rinzō; on drums, from Tsumagoi-chō, Shigematsu and others.

The program is as follows:

Sleight-of-Hand
- Disappearing wooden doll in the shape of Sanbasō [a figure of an old man who brings luck; originally from a nō drama]—later turns into a curtain twelve feet long on four sides.
- Princess doll—turns into a lit dragon lantern.
- Figure of a Chinese child—turns into a *daruma* figure with a head eighteen inches in length.
- Flat-headed wooden figure commonly known as Fukusuke—turns into a moon-faced woman five feet tall.
- Figure of a ceremonial court dancer—turns into a flower cart two feet in height.
- Spring-driven mechanism—puppeteer.
- Spring-driven contraption—an egg from which a mythical bird hatches.
- Small bird (in a Japanese palanquin) on the way to its wedding.
- Water-driven contraption—jewel of a thousand and ten thousand felicitations.
- Water-driven contraption—Yodogawa rattan blind.
- Water-driven contraption—double-tiered flower stand.
- Basket of all the world's sights and sounds.[30]
- The rage of the lion in the nō play "Stone Bridge" *(Shakkyō)*—tied down with four ropes.
- Breakaway stunts from the top of a sliding door.
- Tightrope walking.
- Butterfly tricks—replicas of butterflies are made to fly in various ways; at the end, real butterflies are released.

Foot Tricks
- Stunts in which three ladders are climbed.
- Stunts in which large streamers are held and balanced.
- Breakaway stunts with a ladder that is balanced.
- Stunts in which a bamboo pole is balanced.
- Foot juggling of a large barrel that has been cut in half.
- Stunts on a stone platform.
- Stunts in which a large vessel holding water is balanced.
- Stunts in which a large ladder is balanced.
- Stunts in which a large wooden bathtub is balanced and dropped.
- Stunts in which a *sake* barrel is balanced. (In all these stunts a small child may be balanced overhead.)[31]
- Stunts in which several small tubs are balanced (called *hane-mushi*).

Top Spinning[32]
- One large top—twenty-two inches and weighing forty-five pounds.
- A strand of jute yarn—weighing fourteen pounds.
- One twelve-inch top—weighing 3.7 ounces [sic].
- Four boxes, one foot square, decorated with black maki-e.
- Festival lantern—opens on four sides to display a replica of a peony; two feet in height, eighteen inches in width.
- Battledore trick tops.
- "Crossing the stone bridge"—ladders four feet in height, two feet on all four sides.
- Large top—splits in half to reveal Tsune, a girl who performs a dance; three-and-a-half feet in size.
- "Tenjin shrine"—these are riddles.
- Urashima wooden figure—crossing the coral; five feet in height, four feet in width.
- Cuckoo—opens on four sides; seven feet [sic] in length, six inches square.
- Basket-jumping top—[the tubular basket is] twenty-seven feet long [sic], one foot in diameter.
- Clock—twenty inches high, eight-and-a-half feet wide.
- Lottery doll—powered by a spring.
- Five-tiered top—eight inches high.
- Paper lantern top—becomes a lit one-foot Odawara lantern.
- Multiple tops—thirty-five.
- Swords—tops pass along sword blades.

These records list two dozen performers, including top-spinners, magicians, acrobats, and pedalists, and others. A group of fourteen performers, including Matsui Gensui, had set sail from Yokohama on December 2, 1866, on the English steamer *Nepaul.* After stopping in Shanghai and Hong Kong the party arrived in Southampton on February 2, 1867, and held their first performance on February 11. In Paris they were joined by members of the Hamaikari troupe; together they all performed at the Paris Exposition in July 1867.[33]

These early tours served as models for what was to become a steady stream of tours by performers hired by foreign managers. Miyaoka Kenji's *Ikoku henro tabi geinin shimatsu-sho* (Explanation of Performers Touring Foreign Countries) mentions many performers, managers, and tours:

> 1866: Several acrobats from the troupe "Satsuma" were hired by a British entrepreneur and departed from Nagasaki.

1866 (end): The troupe of Hamaikari Sadakichi was hired by the American entrepreneur [Thomas] Maguire and left for Paris on the eastward route.

1867 (June 3): The "Mikado" acrobat troupe (led by Gōnosuke) performed for three days at the Maguire's Academy of Music in San Francisco. (This group must have left Japan around the beginning of May 1867.)

Azuma-no-Suke spinning a barrel. From *Moji-e zukushi* (A List of Letter-Pictures), published in the Kyōhō period, 1716–1736. Azuma's body is drawn with the letters that spell his name. Reprinted in Asakura Musei, *Misemono kenkyū.*

1867 (June 5): A party of twenty-four members of the Osaka show troupe "Great Dragon" arrives in San Francisco.

1867 (June 9): The Great Dragon troupe performs at the Metropolitan Theater in San Francisco (promoted by Baldwin, Gilbert and Co.).

1867 (July 21): Matsui Gensui's troupe performs at the Théâtre de France Imperial. Somewhat later, Hamaikari Sadakichi's troupe performs at the Cirque Napoleon. The first performance is attended by the Japanese envoy and representative to the exposition, Tokugawa Akitake ([1853–1910], the younger brother of Yoshinobu [1837–1913]), who makes a congratulatory donation of 2,500 francs.

1867 (July 24): Thirty-one members of the troupe led by Hayatake Torakichi set sail from Yokohama on the *Colorado.* They arrive in San Francisco on August 18.

1867 (September 18): Hayatake Torakichi's troupe performs at the Metropolitan Theater in San Francisco. (The promoter was a Portuguese named Da Roza.)

1869: The sleight-of-hand artist Yanagawa Chōjūrō, who had earlier gone to Europe with the troupe of Matsui Gensui, tours Europe and returns home.

1869 (February 8): Articles appear indicating that Daikagura Maruichi, Masukagami Isokichi, and others are touring Europe.

1869 (June 5): The "Satsuma" troupe performs stunts in New York.

1870–1876: Matsui Gensui XVII (real name: Matsumoto Yoshigorō) tours England and America. Around this time the foot juggler Mitsuda Takijirō also tours abroad.

1878?: Hattori Shōkyoku (later known as Shōkyokusai Ten'ichi) is hired in Nagasaki by the American magician Jonesu [Jonas?], whom he joins on tours abroad. Hattori returns to Japan in 1882.

1882: While performing at the Ekōin at Ryōgoku, Kagami Sentarō X is contracted for two years by the "Cirque Chiarini," an equestrian troupe from Italy that is on an Asian tour. Kagami returns to Japan in 1884.

1887: The troupe of Shōkyokusai Ten'ichi (ten members) displays its magic in Shanghai.

1890 (October): Kitamura Fukumatsu from Ōsaka forms the troupe "Kitamura-gumi," which specializes in performances abroad. Leading a group of five performers he departs for a round-the-world tour. (By around 1904–1905 the membership of this troupe had swelled to sixty-one.)

1891 (October): The equestrian acrobatic troupe of Kawamura Komajirō is on tour in the West Indies.

1894: The jester *(hōkan)* Sakuragawa Sueji, the comedian *(rakugoka)* Yanagiya Uryū, and a number of others travel to America.

1894: Kagami Sentarō X is hired by the Haamusuri [Harmston?] equestrian acrobatic troupe, with whom he again tours Asia.

Besides these tours, storytellers *(kōdan)* and reciters of *saimon, ukarebushi, gidayū,* and *kiyomoto* also went abroad, often at their own expense.

Miyaoka has sifted through the few available historical documents to present the story of foreign tours undertaken by such performers. He shows that unlike the ambassadors, envoys, and students sent abroad by the bakufu and the Meiji government, these performers were later consigned to obscurity. Why was this the case? Although it is perhaps a debatable view, I believe that the main reason lies in the feudal economic consciousness of Japanese performers. This consciousness lagged far behind the times, thereby laying itself open to the practices of ruthless European and American entrepreneurs who knew modern capitalism and could exploit these virtuosi. Japanese performers could not yet properly transform their art into a commodity; moreover, they showed an almost complete lack of knowledge of international conditions. As a result, popular performers were not showered with honors on their return. Instead, they were left behind in Japan's rush toward modernization.

Let us now turn to the transformations in popular performing arts brought about by the mass media. An example can be found in the talks of the famous *yose* raconteur San'yūtei Enchō (1839–1900), which were serialized in newspapers and magazines and even published as books. Such forms were perhaps not yet a true "mass medium," but such publications did earn a large readership. A few years ago, at an anniversary held for Enchō at the Zenshōan in the Yanaka area of Tokyo, Fujiura Tomitarō, the *iemoto* of the San'yūtei school of *rakugo,* mentioned that Fukuzawa Yukichi (1835–1901) had brought his students to Enchō's performances at Enchō's lecture hall. Fukuzawa's evaluation of these performances remains unclear, but he may have wanted his students to listen to Enchō's style of speaking. Perhaps he felt that Enchō's talks constituted a new, modern type of speech.

The case of the Tachikawa Bunko paperback books, which were highly popular from the end of Meiji to the Taishō period, is also illustrative. Adachi Kan'ichi has argued that the publisher, Tachikawa Kumajirō, paid authors Tamada Gyokushūsai (1856–1921) and Yamada Suijin a pittance for their work, condemning them to a life of poverty while he himself reaped huge profits.[34] Although storytelling had made its way into the printed media, innovation seems to have been limited to the ways publishers ran their business. Authors, too, were left behind on the road to modernization.

Comic narratives, storytelling, and many other *yose* arts were hardly affected by the arrival of the Meiji period; they thus fit into the third category cited earlier. But the introduction of Japanese and foreign capital caused traditional arts to undergo lopsided development. When promoters and publishers supplied capital and initiated new business practices, an important element that touched the very essence of popular arts was gradually lost: the active participation of the masses. Popular arts were no longer forms that thrived as part of the everyday lives of working-class people. Only the commercial side of these arts developed. The spread of films, radio, and television only aggravated such tendencies.

Here too the lack of a modern consciouness was a major obstacle. Performers' "artistic temperament" was itself partly responsible for steering the arts into an impasse. A good example of such a temperament was that of the renowned sleight-of-hand artist Yanagawa Itchōsai. According to the *Bukō nenpyō,* Yanagawa went to America in 1866. Thereafter, he inherited the name Itchōsai III and remained a highly acclaimed conjurer. In July 1892, the Meiji emperor attended Itchōsai's performance at the residence of Marquis Nabeshima. On this occasion, "lion stunts," "gold-of-the-Dōjōji-Temple tricks," and a trick showing a "goldfish passing through a sphere" were performed. These were all traditional Yanagawa "house arts." Oka Onitarō (1872–1943) describes Itchōsai's demeanor after this command performance: "As a true Edo performer [he] had absolutely no intention of using his accolades to make money; Itchōsai still displayed nothing more than his reputation as the one and only Itchōsai."[35] Even after returning home from his long tours of Europe and America, Itchōsai retained the old-fashioned, highly refined "house arts" of his school and showed no trace of an entrepreneur's consciousness. He seems to have had no interest in using the honor of an imperial inspection to further his career. Oka Onitarō, a typical contemporary critic and representative of the general public, heaped praise on such an eminently respectable man, a true master performer.

Yanagawa's case is of course but one example. Nevertheless, it does appear that performers who toured Europe and America did not simply break with the traditional arts of the past. Indeed, the spirit and temperament of these performers, which had been instilled in them by the traditional master/disciple relationship, were not changed in the least. Performers had gone through long and hard periods of training, and their consciousness was impossible to transform overnight. This consciousness, however, left performers exposed to modern business practices.

After the Meiji period, Western influence was felt by popular performing arts, but its effect was surprisingly small. Imports from the West included, for example, Western-style conjuring at *yose* by Asahi Manmaro and Bankokusai Heidon.[36] Later, Kitensai Shōichi was also highly praised for his Western-style magic shows.[37] Jugglers, acrobats, and magicians who toured Europe and America were also probably subjected to Western influence. These performers may have learned and imported Western-style tricks. From the early Meiji period, European and American performers (some in equestrian acrobat troupes) also toured Japan. Yet Western influence remained limited, for the general public did not undergo any major transformation. Even artists who had toured abroad—for example, Yanagawa Itchōsai—remained untouched by the transition from Edo to Meiji.

Continuity of traditional performing arts was aided by the idea of "spheres of influence" of show promoters. Power relations in the world of popular performing arts survived the Meiji Restoration almost completely intact. From Edo through Meiji, for example, all of Asakusa Okuyama stood under the control of Shinmon Tatsugorō (real name: Machida Jinzaemon). The restoration had little effect on the rights of such bosses. Daimyo, too, maintained much of their authority; traditional prerogative could then be deftly put to use by performers. At the start of the Meiji period, for example, Awashima Chingaku (1823–1889), father of the writer Awashima Kangetsu (1859–1916), wished to open a peep show named "spectacles of the world" at Okuyama. To circumvent Shinmon Tatsugorō's control, Chingaku posted a sign claiming that he was officially working for the daimyo of Mito. This ploy proved to be effective: Shinmon did not interfere.[38]

Change and continuity were thus not mutually exclusive. Instead of engaging in direct confrontation, Edo and Meiji coexisted. Such was the case of the performances of Takezawa Tōji. An entry in the *Bukō nenpyō* notes that Tōji scored a great success with his top-spinning tricks and his spring-driven contraptions, which he exhibited at Ryōgoku Nishi-hirokōji from the spring to the fall of 1844.[39] In the third month of 1849, Tōji's son Manjirō took the name Tōji, and both father and son gave a repeat performance that drew even bigger crowds.[40] In his *Kōjirō yobanashi* (Night Tales at the Kōjirō) Okamoto Kidō recounts how Tōji II brilliantly danced *Yakkodako* suspended over the heads of the spectators at the kabuki theater.[41] Here the skills of the Edo period were carried over into the Meiji era.

Conclusion

In closing I should like to mention once again the audience that patronized popular performing arts. An insight into the public's mentality can be gained from Tanabe Wakao's autobiography, *Haiyū* (Actor). Tanabe recollects making his way to the capital from rural Niigata around 1904. During his apprenticeship at a confectioner's shop at Goken-chō in Kanda, a senior employee took Tanabe to view various troupes. Tanabe saw the Aoe-za at Asakusa, the stunts of a female acrobat who balanced on a ball at Edogawa, and theatrical performances at the Tokiwa-za (seen from third-floor standing-room tiers). In these passages of *Haiyū,* Tanabe transmits the thrill he felt—the joy of one who was momentarily liberated from the hardships of life.[42] With the passing of time, theaters were modernized: lighting changed from paper lanterns to oil lamps and then to incandescent or fluorescent lighting. But the basic lifestyle of the public remained almost unchanged.

The transition from Edo to Meiji brought little change in the relation of the popular performing arts to the general public. The mode of reception of these arts did not change; nor did the fundamental nature of the arts themselves. Conspicuous modernization took place only on the supply side of performances, as arts were transformed into stage shows. The contradictions resulting from this change were responsible for many of the problems that were to plague these arts.

AFTERWORD

I am very happy that a selection of my work on Edo-period culture is now available to an English-speaking readership. The studies included in this volume are for the most part introductory in nature, although some chapters—for example, those on Edo-period nō or cuisine—treat subjects largely ignored outside of Japan. I hope that a broad range of readers will find something useful in this book.

During the 1960s and 1970s a group of scholars known as the "Edo Chōnin Kenkyūkai" and I began to utilize a huge number of Edo-period resources to build a solid basis for the study of Edo-period culture. I believe we succeeded in making a good start, but much more remains to be done. Today, many researchers unfortunately take the easy way out, merely applying trendy new theories to old misinformation. All the while, invaluable Edo-period historical materials gather dust on library shelves.

Let me give an example of the kind of work that appears to me both timely and worthwhile. For the last few years I have been engaged in examining the work of Edo-period tea masters, who produced many beautiful bamboo tea ladles *(chashaku)* and covers. These priceless creations are examples of highly refined but essentially functional artifacts. I have carefully examined and measured thousands of outstanding Edo-period ladles in order to discover the secrets of a truly beautiful ladle and cover. Using this information and my own sense of proportion and beauty, I have carved over five thousand such ladles myself. In a recent exhibition, I displayed a small proportion of my best creations, along with related examples of my brushwork and painting. In the near future I plan to publish a book on the tea ladles and covers of Edo-period tea masters. Such research will, I believe, enrich our understanding, not just of tea ladles, but of the aesthetics of the tea ceremony and, by extension, Japanese culture in general.

Today Edo-period culture presents as fascinating and fertile an area of inquiry as ever. As international borders gradually break down, there is no reason why such research should take place only in Japan. Museums and archives in many parts of the world house countless superb examples of Edo-period culture. I hope that the present volume will stimulate the reexamination of such artifacts or documents and thereby contribute to the growth of Edo-period cultural studies.

I would like to extend my warmest appreciation to the translator, Gerald Groemer, himself an outstanding scholar of Edo-period culture. Without his efforts over many years this volume would never have materialized. While working on this translation, Groemer was in constant contact with me, making sure that any deviations from the original reflected accurately what I wished to say. Moreover, Groemer has rechecked all my sources. This painstaking undertaking, only too rarely emulated by Japanese scholars, has allowed him to correct several errors found in the originals. I should also like to thank the University of Hawai'i Press for agreeing to publish this volume and thus allowing my work to reach a large reading public.

NISHIYAMA MATSUNOSUKE

NOTES

Translator's Introduction

1. This book is included as volume 1 of Nishiyama's collected major writings: *Nishiyama Matsunosuke chosakushū*, 7 vols. (Tokyo: Yoshikawa Kōbunkan, 1982–1987).

2. For a rather weak attempt at an ahistorical "sociological" analysis see Francis L. K. Hsu, *Iemoto: The Heart of Japan*. An outline of some of Nishiyama's ideas on the subject can be found in Benito Ortolani, "Iemoto." Additional studies in English include P. G. O'Neill, "Organization and Authority in the Traditional Arts," which emphasizes the nō; Cathleen Read and David Locke, "An Analysis of the Yamada-ryū Sōkyoku Iemoto System," which treats *koto* music; Nakamura Matazo, *Kabuki Backstage, Onstage: An Actor's Life*, pp. 37–47, which explains the *iemoto* system as it exists in the kabuki today; and *Fenway Court: 1992 (Competition and Collaboration: Hereditary Schools in Japanese Culture)*, which presents studies on a variety of *iemoto* systems in visual and performing arts.

3. Nishiyama Matsunosuke, *Iemoto no kenkyū*, p. 16.

4. A thorough discussion can be found in Nishiyama Matsunosuke, "Kinsei yūgei-ron."

Introduction: The Study of Edo-Period Culture

1. Kagoshima Juzō (1897–1982) was a poet and a sculptor of paper dolls.

2. See Nishiyama Matsunosuke, "Kaei bunka shiron," pp. 50–51.

3. This painting is considered a secret divinity of awesome power. It is stored at the Miidera (formally known as Onjōji), a temple of the Tendai sect in Ōtsu, Shiga prefecture.

4. Swords from the house of Aoe of Kurashiki in Bitchū province date back to the Heian period. The house of Osafune was active during the middle Kamakura period and was located in Bizen province. Mitsutada and his son Nagamitsu are especially renowned.

5. By Matsudaira Naonori (1642–1695).

6. By Yanagisawa Nobutoki (1724–1792), the grandson of the powerful bakufu figure Yanagisawa Yoshiyasu (1658–1714).

7. By Moriyama Takamori (1738–1815).

8. The book is by Li Xian (1408–1466). A copy published in Kyoto (by Kanaya Chōbee) in 1713 is in the possession of the National Diet Library.

9. See Nishiyama Matsunosuke, "Meikō hanran to meijingei."

10. For designs see *Kosode moyō hiinagata hon shūsei.*

Chapter 1

1. All places ending with *-hashi* or *-bashi* are bridges. Many bridges led directly to gates (*-gomon* or *-mon*).

2. See Fujino Tamotsu, *Bakuhan taisei-shi no kenkyū: kenryoku kōzō no kaku-ritsu to tenkai.*

3. Based on records found in the *Tōkyō-shi shikō* (Documents of the History of Tokyo).

4. For the source of Table 1.3 see Nishiyama Matsunosuke, "Edo bunka no kitei," pp. 92–93.

5. For a translation of these laws see John Carey Hall, "The Laws with Regard to the Emperor's Palace," in *Japanese Feudal Law*, pp. 80–97. Article 7, however, is mysteriously missing.

6. This legal code in fifty-one articles is also known as *Goseibai shikimoku.* A translation ("Institutes of Judicature") can be found in John Carey Hall, *Japanese Feudal Law*, pp. 3–44.

7. Translated in John Carey Hall, *Japanese Feudal Law*, pp. 288–308.

8. Wooden swords or poles had been common; the bamboo sword *(shi-nai)* had the advantage of not causing severe injury to one's opponent.

9. In the *Kyū bakufu hikitsugi-sho* (in the possession of the National Diet Library).

10. The Zōjōji is a high-ranking temple of the Pure Land sect, located since 1598 in what is today the Minato ward of Tokyo. The temple was designated in 1590 as the family temple of the Tokugawa.

11. The origin of *saya-ate* can be traced at least to the play *Fuwa*, the first performance of which starred Ichikawa Danjūrō I and took place in 1680 at the Ichimura-za in Edo. The same title was given to many similar scenes including a notable one in the play *Ukiyozuka hiyoku no inazuma* by Tsuruya Nanboku IV, first performed at the Ichimura-za in 1823.

Chapter 2

1. See Nishiyama Matsunosuke, "Kōki Edo chōnin no bunka seikatsu"; and Hamada Giichirō, "Edo-Tōkyōjin no katagi/ninjō."

2. *Tsūgen sōmagaki*, p. 357.

3. *Eda sangoju*, pp. 241 and 248.

4. *Chirizuka dan,* p. 248.

5. See Chiba Osamu, ed., *Shodai Senryū senku-shū,* pp. 5–11; see also Yamazawa Hideo, "Manku awase."

6. This list, a parody of contemporary actor rankings, is included in the book *Gakuju hissō* (Collected Writings on Auspicious Pleasures, by the Owari samurai Kawamura Hide'ei), now in the possession of the Nagoya-shi Tsurumai Chūō Toshokan.

7. Cited in Noda Hisao, "Hōreki no shoto no bungakuteki ichi genshō," p. 242.

8. The full title of this play is *Sukeroku yukari no Edo-zakura.* Ichikawa Danjūrō II (1688–1758) first performed a version of it in 1713 at the Edo Yamamura-za. For an English translation see James R. Brandon, "Sukeroku, the Flower of Edo," in *Kabuki: Five Classic Plays.*

Chapter 3

1. Originally published in 1930. See also the sequel " 'Iki' no honshitsu" (The Essence of *Iki*).

2. Many plays treat this subject. A famous version written by Chikamatsu Hanji (1725–1783) is *Osome Hisamatsu shinpan utazaimon,* first performed in the original puppet version in 1780 at the Osaka Takemoto-za and then adapted for the kabuki. Another well-known kabuki version is *Osome Hisamatsu ukina no yomiuri* by Tsuruya Nanboku IV, first performed in 1813 at the Edo Morita-za.

3. Kuki, " 'Iki' no kōzō," p. 18.

4. See Nakamura Yukihiko, "Tsū to bungaku"; Mizuno Minoru, " 'Tsū' no bungakuteki kōsatsu"; Uzuki Hiroshi, "Tsū: sharebon no shudai to shuchō o megutte."

5. Pp. 39–55.

6. *Kumo no itomaki,* p. 281.

Chapter 4

1. *Hōgu kago,* pp. 251–253.

2. For details see Konta Yōzō, "Edo no shuppan shihon."

3. See Hosono Masanobu, *Shiba Kōkan,* pp. 39–41.

4. *Kinsei mono no hon Edo sakusha burui,* p. 58.

5. Compiled by Ōta Nanpo. A complete copy is in the possession of Tsukuba University.

Chapter 5

1. Table 5.1 is based on records found in the *Tōkyō-shi shikō.*

2. *Saitō Gesshin nikki* (copies in the possession of Tokyo University,

Waseda University, and the Dai Tōkyū Kinen Bunko). For extracts see Nishiyama Matsunosuke, "Saitō Gesshin Nikki."

3. For more detail see Nishiyama Matsunosuke, "Edo no nanushi Saitō
Gesshin," pp. 459–511.

4. Kannon (more fully, Kanzeon Bosatsu; Skt. Avalokiteśvara) is the goddess of mercy; Shōden (more fully, Daishō kangiten; Skt. Nandikeśvara) is
thought to bring riches and good health.

5. Bishamonten (Skt. Vaiśravaṇa) is one of the four heavenly emperors.

6. Tenjin ("heavenly god") is a deification of Sugawara no Michizane
(845–903) as the god of wisdom.

7. In Japan Konpira (Skt. Kumbhīra) is the god who protects seafarers.

8. Or Enma-ō (Skt. Yamarāja).

9. Myōkensama or Myōken Bosatsu (Skt. Sudarśana) is the deification
(in female form) of the Great Bear. She is, among other things, the protector of the land and bringer of good luck.

10. See Jippensha Ikku, *Roku Amida mōde.*

11. Umewaka-maru is a semifictional character who appears in the nō
play *Sumidagawa.* The invocation to this twelve-year-old child took place at
the Mokuboji, a temple at Mukōjima.

12. Kishimojin or Kishibojin (Skt. Hāritī) is the goddess of childbearing
and child rearing. The most famous Kishimojin of Edo was at Zōshigaya.

13. *Morisada mankō,* vol. 2, p. 271.

14. See Inobe Shigeo, *Fuji no shinkō,* pp. 345–346.

15. *Tōto saijiki,* vol. 2, p. 75.

16. See Miura Ieyoshi, *Fuji shinkō to Fuji-kō.*

17. Gozu Tennō. This Buddhist deity of hell, enshrined at many temples
throughout Japan, was the protector of the Gion Monastery (Gion Shōja) in
Kyoto and was believed to ward off disease and evil.

18. Tanabata is a festival that explains the midsummer brightness of the
stars Vega and Altair on either side of the Milky Way by the myth of a cow-
herd who is able to cross the river to meet his beloved Weaving Maid on the
seventh day of the seventh month.

19. Fudō or Fudō Myōō (Skt. Acala) is a fiery deity that expresses great
wrath and power. Together with Kannon, Fudō was one of the most widely
worshiped gods of the Edo period.

20. For a detailed description see Nishiyama Matsunosuke, "Edo no
nanushi Saitō Gesshin," pp. 436–445.

21. Kinoe-ne refers to a certain day according to the Sino-Japanese lunar
calendar. The exact meaning of Hattengū is not entirely clear. This name
appears in Gesshin's diary from the eleventh month of 1862. See Nishiyama
Matsunosuke, "Edo no machi nanushi Saitō Gesshin," p. 498.

22. The Rat Festival *(nematsuri)* was held in honor of the god Daikoku,
one of the "seven lucky gods" *(shichi fukujin).* Usually rice with *azuki* beans
was cooked on this day, but Gesshin's family prepared rice cooked in tea
(chameshi).

23. Since there are twelve horary signs in the Chinese calendar, the same
sign occurs once every twelve days.

24. The deification of Katō Kiyomasa (1562–1611), a powerful daimyo of the early Edo period.

25. See *Narukami*. Translated by James R. Brandon as "Saint Narukami and the God Fudō (see *Kabuki: Five Classic Plays*). Aizen Myōō (Skt. Rāgarāja) purified a believer's feelings of love and lust; this deity was often worshiped by dyers and prostitutes.

Chapter 6

1. See Nishiyama Matsunosuke, *Iemoto no kenkyū*, p. 121.

2. Statistics compiled by Hiruma Hisashi.

3. See Nishiyama Matsunosuke, *Iemoto no kenkyū*, pp. 395–396.

4. Ibid., pp. 435 and 446.

5. See Haga Noboru, *Bakumatsu kokugaku no tenkai;* "Kigyōchi machikata no bunka: Kiryū, Ashikaga, Ojiya, Shiozawa no baai"; and "Mikawa Yoshida-han no kokugakusha no katsudō."

6. See Watanabe Ichirō, "Kinsei Echigo ni okeru chijimi-nuno san-ichiba no seiritsu to sono hen'yō." Watanabe's article is extremely difficult to obtain. Some of the data he collected are reproduced in Fujino Tamotsu, *Bakuhan taisei-shi no kenkyū: kenryoku kōzō no kakuritsu to tenkai*, pp. 621–622.

7. For a complete listing of the names and origin of contributors see "Harimaze byōbu: kokusho shōmei nayose-chō", in Miya Eiji, ed., *Suzuki Bokushi shiryō-shū*, pp. 279–286.

8. See Suzuki Bokushi Kenshōkai, *Bokushi*, p. 112.

9. See *Eisei kiroku-shū*, pp. 33–34.

10. See Nishiyama Matsunosuke, "Kinsei bunka-shi kenkyū-hō ni kan-suru shiron."

11. See Miki Yōkichirō, ed., *Awa ai-fu (Shiwa zusetsu hen)*, p. 128.

12. Furushima Toshio, *Edo jidai no shōhin ryūtsū to kōtsū: Shinshū chūma no kenkyū*, pp. 139 and 148.

13. See Sugae Masumi, *Sugae Masumi yūranki*.

14. *Hokuetsu seppu*, pp. 82–85, 182–187.

15. Suzuki Bokushi, *Eisei kiroku-shū*, pp. 57–58.

16. Three versions, two of them dated 1855, are in the possession of the National Diet Library.

17. In the possession of Watanabe Ichirō.

18. First performed in 1823 at the Edo Morita-za as part of the piece *Yamato-gana tamuke no itsumoji;* composed by Kiyomoto Saibee I; text by Masuyama Kinpachi.

19. Full title: *Nochi no tsuki shuen no shimadai*. First performed at the Edo Nakamura-za in 1828; composed by Kineya Saburōsuke IV (later Kineya Rokuzaemon X) and Kishizawa Shikisa; text by Segawa Jokō II.

20. *Kisen* also exists in a *nagauta* version composed by Kineya Rokuzaemon X. The *kiyomoto* version was composed by Kiyomoto Saibee I; text by Matsumoto Kōji; first performed in 1831 at the Edo Nakamura-za. *Sumiyoshi odori* (also *Taihei sumiyoshi odori* or *Ukiyo kairaishi*) is said to have been

taken from an earlier *geki bushi* work. A record of a performance in 1807 exists.

21. See Machida Kashō, *Min'yō genryū-kō: "Esashi oiwake" to "Sado okesa";* and "Haiya Bushi to Okesa Bushi."

22. See Gunji Masakatsu, *Kyōdo geinō,* pp. 86–90.

23. Furushima Toshio, *Nihon nōgyō-shi,* p. 341.

24. Sekijima Hisao, "Tokugawa makki no nōson jinushi no shōhi seikatsu."

Chapter 7

1. *Sannin Kichiza kuruwa no hatsugai,* pp. 115–116.

2. *Morisada Mankō,* vol. 1, p. 208.

3. *Kōshoku gonin onna,* p. 231. In English see Wm. Theodore de Bary, trans., *Five Women Who Loved Love,* p. 62.

4. *Yōmei tennō shokunin kagami,* pp. 104–105.

5. *Hōei no rakusho,* pp. 311–312.

6. For greater detail on the *iemoto* of *manzai* see Nishiyama Matsunosuke, *Iemoto monogatari,* pp. 92–100.

7. See for example *Haifū yanagidaru,* p. 669; Negishi Senryū, ed., *Kosenryū jiten,* vol. 1, p. 82. Later sources often give the location of the "*saizō* market" as Nihonbashi, not Edobashi.

8. For a detailed discussion of the *iemoto* of the *daikagura* see Nishiyama Matsunosuke, *Iemoto monogatari,* pp. 111–123.

9. Map 7.1 is based on *Shiojiri* (Salt-Making Sand Heaps), vol. 16 (fasc. 76), p. 118.

10. *Wakashima-za ikkan,* p. 923.

11. Ibid., p. 933.

12. Ibid., p. 923.

13. *Hokuetsu seppu,* p. 182.

14. *Wakashima-za ikkan,* p. 914.

15. Ibid., p. 918.

16. Ibid., pp. 930–932.

17. Ibid., p. 923.

18. Today only the eighth act, also known as *Moritsuna jin'ya,* is performed. The play was written for puppets by Chikamatsu Hanji in 1769 and adapted for the kabuki the following year.

19. This title refers to a whole lineage of plays, versions of which were written on many occasions. A famous example is *Kiyomizu Seigen rokudō meguri,* written in 1762 by Takeda Jizō and Namiki Ōsuke.

20. By Takeda Izumo and his assistants; first performed in 1747 in its puppet version and adapted for the kabuki soon after.

21. By Takeda Izumo and his assistants; first performed as a puppet play in Osaka in 1734 and then adapted for the kabuki.

22. See *Wakashima-za ikkan,* pp. 922 and 938.

23. Ibid., p. 931.

24. *Kumano mōde*, pp. 74–75.

25. *Seiritsuen zuihitsu*, vol. 3, sec. 57.

26. *Wakashima-za ikkan*, p. 910.

27. *Aoto zōshi hana no nishiki-e*, p. 116; see Samuel L. Leiter, ed. and trans., "Benten Kozō," pp. 41–42.

28. Written for puppets by Suga Sensuke; first performed in Osaka in 1776 and later adapted for kabuki; also known as *Katsuragawa* or *Ohan Chōemon*.

29. Also known as *Ohan Chōemon;* text by Sakurada Jisuke II; music by Kiyosawa Mankichi (later Kiyomoto Saibee); first performed at the Edo Nakamura-za in 1819.

30. *Michiyuki shian no hoka*, p. 359.

31. The full formal title of this piece is *Hanabutai kasumi no saruhiki;* text by Nakamura Jūsuke; music by Kishizawa Shikisa V; first performed in 1838 at the Edo Ichimura-za.

32. *Hanabutai kasumi no saruhiki*, p. 54.

33. First performed in its puppet version on June 20, 1703. The play (with the first scene omitted) has been translated by Donald Keene.

34. This verse and the following two are taken from the start of the *goeika* entitled *Saigoku sanjūsan-ban junrei uta* (Pilgrimage Song of the Thirty-Three Sites of the Western Land). This poem gives descriptions of each of the thirty-three stops on the tour. See *Saigoku sanjūsan-ban junrei uta*, pp. 450–453.

35. *Keisei Awa no Naruto*, p. 645; "Saigoku sanjūsan-ban junrei uta," p. 450.

36. See pp. 72–75. Nishiyama quotes the entire section, but innumerable puns and allusions defy translation.

37. According to this legend, a hungry Kūkai saw an old woman washing greens. He begged her to share some with him, but she refused. From that day on, the villagers were miraculously unable to eat such greens.

38. Through his miraculous powers, Kūkai made the water of the river disappear.

39. *Nijūyohai junpai zue*, p. 353. An "Iwata obi" is a sash worn by pregnant women.

Chapter 8

1. *Jōzan kidan*, vol. 1, pp. 102–103.

2. "Seven-five-three" *(shichi-go-san)* refers to the number of dishes presented on the three trays served at a formal meal. A somewhat less luxurious "five-three-three" meal typically contains the following dishes:

Main Tray

1. *Tsubo* (cooked vegetables and potato served in a bowl with a lid)
2. *Mukō* (*mukōzuke:* vinegared fish or vegetables)
3. *Miso* soup
4. Rice (up to three bowls may be consumed)
5. Pickled vegetables

Tray 2
1. Clear soup
2. *Choku* (boiled vegetables with dressing)
3. *Hira* (a mix of five kinds of boiled vegetables from land and sea served in a flat bowl with a lid)

Tray 3
1. Salty soup
2. *Sashimi* (raw fish)
3. Mix of boiled vegetables, chicken, seafood, and the like

Tray 4 contains a sizable broiled fish.
Tray 5 contains assorted side dishes that, along with the fish on tray 4, may be taken home by the guest.

These dishes are arranged as follows:

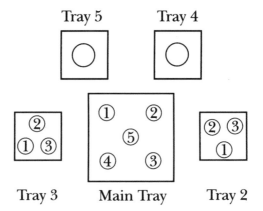

3. Compiled ca. 905; translated by Laurel Rasplica Rodd with Mary Catherine Henkenius.
4. *Suzuki-bōchō,* pp. 394–395.
5. *Fuzumō,* p. 242.
6. In the possession of the Kobe Municipal Museum of Art *(Kōbe shiritsu bijutsukan).*
7. *Kissa ōrai,* pp. 122–125.
8. *Imai Sōkyū chanoyu kakinuki,* pp. 35–36.
9. *Kamiya Sōtan nikki,* pp. 226–227.
10. Ibid., pp. 289–290.
11. *Nanbōroku,* p. 15. For Nishiyama's discussion of this work see Nishiyama Matsunosuke, " 'Nanbōroku' ni tsuite."

12. *Gunsho ruijū,* vol. 19, no. 368, *inshoku-bu.*

13. *Tokugawa jikki,* vol. 3, pp. 579–582.

14. *Shūgi gaisho,* p. 107.

15. *Minkan seiyō,* p. 100.

16. The following report is taken from the *Kawachi no kuni Kusaka-mura moto shōya Nagazaemon shozō kiroku* (Records Belonging to Nagazaemon, Ex-Headman of Kusaka Village in Kawachi Province), in the possession of the Kyoto University Library.

17. Dishes are frequently named by the vessel in which they are served. A *choku* is a small bowl usually containing raw fish or a vinegared dish. For explanations of *tsubo* and *hira* see note 2.

18. *Kyūki seishoku-hō shūsho,* p. 377.

19. The following information is taken from the diary of Yamagata Heiemon Shigeyoshi, a copy of which is in the possession of Kobayashi Shigeru.

20. During the Edo period a song called "Tsukuda bushi" was often sung by geisha while boating to and from Yoshiwara on the Sumida River. The instrumental music following the song has become an interlude often used as a setting for river scenes in the kabuki.

21. *Kanten kenbunki,* p. 321.

22. *Saikaku oki miyage,* p. 88.

23. *Kinsei kiseki-kō,* p. 324.

24. This book seems to have been mostly identical with the *Kokon ryōri-shū,* probably published between 1669 and 1674.

25. *Kumo no itomaki,* pp. 287–288.

26. *Morisada mankō,* vol. 2, p. 432.

27. *Yoku kuu* can refer to the fact that tweezers grip well and also that something is good to eat. See *Kōto gosui,* pp. 540–541.

28. *Fukijizai,* p. 368.

29. Ibid.

30. *Ryōri monogatari,* pp. 30–31.

31. "Soba no mukashi-banashi," p. 168.

32. Ibid., p. 170.

Chapter 9

1. Sendai-shi shi hensan iinkai, "Sendai han shoki no nō ni tsuite," p. 44.

2. Ibid., p. 45.

3. *Okina,* literally "Old Man," is a group of archaic, semireligious dances.

4. Sendai-shi shi hensan iinkai, p. 61 ("Kōzan kōji-ke kiroku").

5. I have been unable to determine the meaning of the word "Takuren."

6. This inscription includes a phrase whose meaning remains obscure.

7. Ikenouchi Nobuyoshi, *Nōgaku seisuiki,* vol. 1, p. 174.

8. See Nonomura Kaizō, *Nōgaku kokonki,* pp. 241–272.

9. Ibid., p. 254.

10. Omote Akira, "Utai-kō."

11. The diary covers the years 1693 to 1706. Kawachiya Yoshimasa's real name was Tsuboi Yoshimasa.

12. *Kawachiya Yoshimasa kyūki*, p. 35.

13. Ibid., p. 35.

14. Wakita Osamu, "Jinai-machi no kōzō to tenkai," p. 3.

15. *Kawachiya Yoshimasa kyūki*, pp. 351–352.

16. Ibid., p. 352.

17. Wakita, "Jinai-machi no kōzō to tenkai," pp. 5–6.

18. Ejima Ihee, *Kurumaya-hon no kenkyū*, p. 8.

19. *Genroku taiheiki*, p. 366. *Kenkō-zuka* (A Marker for [Yoshida] Kenkō) may be the same work as the *Kenkō hōshi* cited earlier. In the *Genroku taiheiki* the reading of the title *Goshaku tenugui* is indicated as *Goshaku tenogoi*. This seems to have been a humorous type of work.

20. *Su-utai yoyo no ato*, p. 667.

21. *Saikaku oridome*, p. 329.

22. *Saikaku nagori no tomo*, chap. 5, sec. 4 (pp. 228–230).

23. Murata Atsushi, "Saikaku mugaku monmō no setsu." For Saikaku's *haikai* verses see *Saikaku ōyakazu chūshaku*.

24. Yamazaki Gakudō, "Yōkyoku to haiku."

25. *Kawachiya Yoshimasa kyūki*, p. 96.

26. Also *Kawachi no kuni kagami meisho-ki*. The list of poets can be found on pp. 405–409. Yoshimasa's poems appear on pp. 338, 341, 344, 351, and 368.

27. *Kawachiya Yoshimasa kyūki*, p. 96.

28. By Sasaki Haruyuki.

29. Nonomura Kaizō, "Kyō-Kanze no yurai," in *Nōgaku kokonki*, pp. 243–305.

30. *Su-utai yoyo no ato*, p. 670.

31. Ibid., p. 673.

32. Ibid., p. 677.

33. Ibid., pp. 671–672.

34. Ibid., p. 673.

35. From *Itazura uta jujuden* (in the possession of Asano Masanobu). The complete citation is reproduced in Nishiyama Matsunosuke, *Iemoto no kenkyū*, p. 320 (n. 45).

36. *Nōgaku kokonki*, p. 166. Author's note: The shrines in question include the Ōmiya Jinja in Miki, the Tanikami Jinja in Yamada, the Saita Jinja in Asakawa, the Ōmiya Jinja in Shimomura, the Misaka Jinja in Shijimi, the Tonohata Jinja in Kuchiyokawa, the Ōtoshi Jinja in Ogihara, the Kurumi Jinja in Toyochi, and a certain shrine in Ōkawase.

37. *Su-utai yoyo no ato*, pp. 377–380.

Chapter 10

1. This diary spans the period from 1658 to 1695. See Wakatsuki Yasuji, *Kinsei shoki kokugeki no kenkyū*. For a critical discussion see Takeuchi Michitaka, *Kinsei geinō-shi no kenkyū*, pp. 90–98.

2. *Ofuregaki kanpō shūsei* (art. 2051), p. 1004.

3. Compiled in 1518. An English translation by Frank Hoff is entitled *Like a Boat in a Storm: A Century of Song in Japan.*

4. Also *ryūtatsu bushi.* This was a popular song greatly in vogue around 1600. Its name stems from the Nichiren priest Ryūtatsu, who reputedly first wrote this type of song.

5. Written in 1914; lyrics by Shimamura Hōgetsu and Sōma Gofū; music by Nakayama Shinpei.

6. Words by Noguchi Ujō; music by Nakayama Shinpei; written in 1929.

7. Written in 1945; lyrics by Satō Hachirō; music by Makime Tadashi.

8. See Fujita Tokutarō, *Kinsei kayō no kenkyū,* pp. 97–120.

9. Ibid., pp. 104–109.

10. A detailed discussion of the *gagaku* organizations can be found in Nishiyama Matsunosuke, *Iemoto no kenkyū,* pp. 160–259.

11. The "three seals" *(san'in)* were actually three licenses: a *honsoku* (the *komusō's* license and most important document); a *kai'in* (personal identification papers); and a *tsūin* (travel permit). The "three tools" were the *komusō's* typical basketlike hat *(tengai),* his priest's stole, and the *shakuhachi* itself.

12. This document is also known as the *Keichō okite-gaki* (Governmental Decree of the Keichō Period [1596–1615]). See Nishiyama Matsunosuke, *Iemoto no kenkyū,* pp. 514–520; in English, see Kamisangō Yūkō, "The Shakuhachi—Its History and Development," pp. 103–107.

13. Mikami Sanji, "Fuke-shū ni tsuite." Mikami's arguments are outlined in Nishiyama Matsunosuke, *Iemoto no kenkyū,* pp. 517–518.

14. A court dance accompanied by Korean-style music.

15. "Hōkyoku fuji no kodama," pp. 45–48.

16. See Nishiyama Matsunosuke, "Kinsei toshi no seikatsu," and Engeki kenkyūkai, ed., *Mikan jōruri geiron shū.*

17. "Hōkyoku fuji no kodama," pp. 45–48.

18. See Takano Tatsuyuki, *Nihon kayōshi,* pp. 983–986.

Chapter 11

1. The author and date of this work are unknown. On Ichikawa Danjūrō see *Kantō kekki monogatari,* pp. 332–333.

2. *Kabuki nenpyō,* vol. 1, pp. 174 and 252.

3. Translated by Laurence Kominz in "Ya no Ne: The Genesis of a Kabuki Aragoto Classic."

4. Patterns of *kumadori* can be found illustrated in Ruth M. Shaver, *Kabuki Costume.* For *sujikuma* two red lines sweep upward from the inner corners of the eyebrows where they meet at the upper end of the nose. Curved red lines run from the outside tip of each eyebrow down past the eyes and back to the sides of the face. Another pair of curved red lines runs from the wings to the nose under each cheek.

5. For a vivid description see Ivan Morris, *The Nobility of Failure: Tragic Heroes in the History of Japan,* pp. 143–179.

6. See Takeuchi Makoto, "Tenmei no uchikowashi."

7. The illustration is reproduced in Kōta Naritomo, *Edo to Ōsaka*, p. 63.

8. Chōbee was an Edo *kyōkaku* who lived in Asakusa; he seems to have died in the 1650s. Chōbee appears in many plays, including *Banzui Chōbee shōjin manaita* (written by Sakurada Jisuke I [1734–1806]; first performed in 1803 at the Edo Nakamura-za) and *Kiwametsuki Banzui Chōbee* (by Kawatake Mokuami; first performed in 1881 at the Tokyo Haruki-za).

9. An "alternate theater" (*hikae yagura*, literally "alternate tower") was used in cases where a theater manager of one of the three Edo theaters could for some reason not produce plays at his regular theater.

10. See *Kabuki nendai-ki*, p. 531.

11. Grandson of Ebizō (Danjūrō V); he later became the seventh Danjūrō.

12. By Sakurada Jisuke I and Muraoka Kōji (fl. 1789–1818).

13. *Kabuki nendai-ki*, p. 530.

14. For a detailed discussion see Nishiyama Matsunosuke, "Shibai-bayashi nikki."

15. On kabuki costumes see Ruth M. Shaver, *Kabuki Costume*.

16. This elaborate pun is left untranslated in Brandon's English performing version of *Sukeroku*. For a note on where it should occur, see James R. Brandon, *Kabuki: Five Classic Plays*, p. 70.

17. Many variants of this story exist. A well-known version can be found in Ihara Saikaku's novel *Kōshoku gonin onna* (*Five Women Who Loved Love*, 1683; translated by de Bary). The first recorded kabuki performance took place at the Osaka Arashi San'emon-za in 1706. Thereafter countless kabuki versions have been staged in Edo and elsewhere.

18. Translated by Helen Craig McCullough.

19. This play, commonly known simply as *Chūshingura*, was originally created in 1748 as a puppet play by Takeda Izumo II (1691–1756) and his assistants. The puppet version has been translated by Donald Keene as *Chūshingura: The Treasury of Loyal Retainers*. For more information and an English kabuki performing version see James R. Brandon, ed., *Chūshingura: Studies in Kabuki and the Puppet Theater*.

20. The full title of this play, first performed at the Edo Ichimura-za in 1860, is *Sannin Kichiza kuruwa no hatsugai* (Three Rogues Called Kichiza at the Licensed Quarters).

21. First performed at the Edo Ichimura-za in 1862, the play is also known as *Shiranami gonin otoko* (The Story of Five Notorious Thieves); the full title is *Aoto zōshi hana no nishiki-e*. The last two acts, including the famous "Hamamatsu no ba" (Scene at Hamamatsu), are often performed independently. See Samuel L. Leiter, ed. and trans., "Benten Kozō"; see also Earle Ernst, ed., "Benten the Thief," in *Three Japanese Plays from the Traditional Theatre*, pp. 145–199.

22. The full title is *Tōkaidō Yotsuya kaidan*. This play was written by Tsuruya Nanboku IV and first performed at the Edo Nakamura-za in 1825.

23. Also known as *Sakura Sōgorō* and *Higashiyama Sakura sōshi*, this play was written by Segawa Jokō III (1806–1881) and first performed in 1851 at

the Edo Nakamura-za. The play was revised in 1861 by Kawatake Mokuami for Ichikawa Kodanji IV.

24. A section of the play known as *Kirare Yosa* or, more fully, as *Yo wa nasake ukina no yokogushi;* written by Segawa Jokō III and first performed in 1853 at the Edo Nakamura-za; translated into English by Adolphe Clarence Scott as *Genyadana: A Japanese Kabuki Play.*

25. The "meritorious prince" refers to Hideyoshi. This play was originally created for the puppet theater by Chikamatsu Yanagi (1762–1803) in 1799. The tenth act, commonly called the "Amagasaki Scene," is the only part of the play still in the repertoire.

26. This play is one of the most popular plays of the Ichikawa house's repertory of "Eighteen Favorites." It was adapted by Namiki Gohei III (1789–1855) from the nō play *Ataka* and first performed by Ichikawa Ebizō (later the eighth Danjūrō) in 1840 at the Edo Kawarasaki-za. For a translation see James R. Brandon and Tamako Niwa, *Kabuki Plays.*

27. *Nagauta* music by Kineya Rokusaburō IV (1779–1855). See Brandon and Niwa, *Kabuki Plays,* pp. 41–42.

28. This *mie* indicates that Yoshitsune's fortunes are being dashed to earth in the same way. See Brandon and Niwa, *Kabuki Plays,* p. 42.

29. Written for puppets by Chikamatsu Hanji and his assistants and first staged in 1771. One of the unique features of this play is the use of not one but two *hanamichi.* For a detailed study in English of the puppet version see C. Andrew Gerstle, Kiyoshi Inobe, and William Malm, *Theater as Music: The Bunraku Play "Mt. Imo and Mt. Se: An Exemplary Tale of Womanly Virtue."*

30. This *nagauta* constitutes a section of the dance piece *Shichimai-tsuzuki hana no sugata-e* (music by Kineya Shōjirō II [d. 1820], text by Sakurada Jisuke II [1768–1829]). The first performance took place at the Edo Ichimura-za in 1811 with Bandō Mitsugorō III (1775–1831) in the lead role.

31. Various kabuki versions of this play, based on Chikamatsu Monzaemon's 1718 *jōruri* piece *Hakata kojorō namimakura,* have been performed since 1776.

32. This is the title of a *nagauta* included in the dance piece *Yanagi ni hina shochō no saezuri* (music by Fujita Kichiji I [1714–1771] and Kineya Chūjirō I). The first performance took place at the Edo Ichimura-za in 1762.

33. This is the last third of the play *Koibikyaku Yamato ōrai,* which is based on the *jōruri* piece *Keisei koibikyaku.* This piece is in turn based on the latter half of Chikamatsu Monzaemon's *Meido no hikyaku* (translated by Donald Keene as "The Courier for Hell"). Kabuki versions have been performed at least since 1797.

34. Written by Kawatake Mokuami and first performed in 1873 at the Edo Ichimura-za. The full title is *Tsuyu kosode mukashi hachijō.*

35. For a transcription see the musical example in Chapter 8. Note, however, that the drum pattern used in this performance is not *kashira-iri nami no oto* but simply *nami no oto.* (*Kashira-iri nami no oto* would include an extra beat at the start of the pattern.)

36. Written as a puppet play by Takeda Izumo II and his assistants and

first performed in 1746 at the Osaka Takemoto-za. By the following year the work was being performed in Edo as kabuki. The puppet version has been translated into English by Stanleigh H. Jones, *Sugawara and the Secrets of Calligraphy.*

37. In English see Tsubouchi Shōyō and Yamamoto Jirō, *History and Characteristics of Kabuki: The Japanese Classical Drama.*

Chapter 12

1. See Fukuda Sadayoshi, *Minshū to engei;* Shimizu Ikutarō, "Taishū goraku ni tsuite"; Matsuda Michio, "Goraku no ichizuke"; Tsurumi Shunsuke, *Taishū geijutsu.*

2. See, for example, Miyoshi Ikkō, ed., *Edo-Tōkyō fūzokugo jiten,* and Asakura Musei, *Misemono kenkyū.* For a good discussion in English of some of these genres see Andrew L. Markus, "The Carnival of Edo: *Misemono* Spectacles from Contemporary Accounts."

3. *Bukō nenpyō,* vol. 2, p. 159.

4. *Misemono zasshi,* vol. 1, p. 389.

5. *Shichū fūbun kakiutsushi,* p. 489.

6. *Bukō nenpyō,* vol. 2, pp. 143–144.

7. Cited by Miyoshi Ikkō, ed., *Edo-Tōkyō fūzokugo jiten,* p. 249. I have been unable to locate the original passage in *Kōun kaikodan.*

8. *Misemono zasshi,* vol. 1, p. 306. The plot of this story no doubt concerned the deeds of the faithful retainers of the *Chūshingura* story.

9. Ibid.

10. Ibid., vol. 1, pp. 324–325. The correct reading of the title is unclear.

11. Ibid., vol. 1, p. 330.

12. Ibid., vol. 1, pp. 361–364.

13. Ibid., vol. 1, p. 388. The correct reading of the show's title is unclear *(Kokkei-banashi kuruwa shibai?).*

14. Ibid., vol. 2, pp. 19–20.

15. Cited in Miyoshi Ikkō, ed., *Edo-Tōkyō fūzokugo jiten,* p. 251.

16. *Shisei airoku,* vol. 202, pp. 60–62.

17. *Mandan Meiji shonen,* p. 559.

18. *Bukō nenpyō,* vol. 2, p. 203.

19. *Kitamachi bugyō-sho shichū torishimari-gakari jōshinsho,* p. 236.

20. *Machi bugyō jōshinsho,* pp. 34–35.

21. See *Kitamachi bugyō-sho shichū torishimari-gakari jōshinsho,* p. 236.

22. *Rinji mawari jōshinsho,* p. 17.

23. *Kitamachi bugyō-sho shichū torishimari-gakari jōshinsho,* p. 236.

24. See Hiruma Hisashi, "Seiritsu-ki ni okeru rakugo no shakaiteki kiban."

25. Sekine Mokuan, *Kōdan rakugo konjakutan,* pp. 102–103.

26. *Onmitsu mawari jōshinsho,* p. 212.

27. *Shichū fūbunsho,* pp. 9–10.

28. In the passages that follow I have tried as far as possible to convert

non-Japanese names from *katakana* syllabary to the correct romanized spelling. In cases where I have been unable to determine the spelling of a name, I have given a transliteration of the *katakana* version and followed this by a guess in parentheses. "Benkutsu" is Edward Banks. The tour in question is one undertaken by the troupe of Hamaikari Sadakichi. This tour, which first took the troupe to America, was organized by a "Professor" Richard Risley who hired Banks. According to the San Francisco paper *Daily Dramatic Chronicle* of January 3, 1867, Banks was an official at the U.S. embassy in Kanagawa and spoke Japanese. I have corrected some of Miyaoka's account below.

29. *Bukō nenpyō*, vol. 2, pp. 207–209. The exact nature of many of these tricks remains obscure. Several of the dimensions given for objects seem highly unlikely, and "Tora" should probably read "Tou," but I have reproduced what is recorded. It should be noted, however, that although Yanagawa Chōjūrō as well as Matsui Gensui and his family did go on tour in 1866, this was not the four arranged by Edward Banks.

30. In this stunt a seemingly infinite number of objects was produced from a (bottomless) basket and held up for display.

31. For descriptions of some of these stunts see Miyaoka Kenji, *Ikoku henro tabi geinin shimatsu-sho*, p. 26.

32. This section appears to be an inventory of what was taken abroad, rather than a list of tricks.

33. Matsui Gensui's performances at the Paris Exposition are recorded in some detail in *Shibusawa Eiichi tai-futsu nikki* (Diary of Shibusawa Eiichi [1840–1931] During His Stay in France), pp. 119–135.

34. See Adachi Kan'ichi, "Tachikawa bunko no tanjō."

35. Oka Onitarō, "Shogei mukashibanashi," p. 322.

36. Ibid., p. 326.

37. Ibid.

38. Miyoshi Ikkō, *Edo-Tōkyō fūzokugo jiten*, p. 301.

39. *Bukō nenpyō*, vol. 2, p. 103.

40. Ibid., vol. 2, p. 117. It should be noted that the syllable *"ji"* in the name of the father is often written with a different character than the one used in the name of the son. The activities of Tōji II are described in Yamamoto Shōgetsu, *Meiji sesō hyaku-banashi* (One Hundred Tales of Meiji Times), pp. 220–221.

41. Yamamoto Shōgetsu, *Meiji sesō hyaku-banashi*, p. 186. The full title of this tokiwazu dance piece is *Yakkodako sato no harukaze*. The text is by Kawatake Mokuami (first performed in 1893).

42. Tanabe Wakao, *Haiyū*, p. 7.

GLOSSARY

agemaku Curtain hung over the rear entrance to the *hanamichi* in the kabuki theater.

ageya Houses of entertainment to which courtesans went when called by customers; intermediary houses.

akahon Literally "red (covered) books"—short illustrated books, mostly for children, popular especially during the opening decades of the eighteenth century.

akanuke Unpretentious urbanity, elegance, polished manners—considered by some to be an essential ingredient of *iki*.

aragoto "Rough" kabuki acting style, particularly as developed by Ichikawa Danjūrō, that features nonnaturalistic makeup and grandiose, exaggerated, vigorously masculine deportment.

azuma nishiki-e See *ukiyo-e*.

bakufu Literally "tent government"—the military government of Japan. During the Edo period the Tokugawa family ruled the land and thus its government is known as the Tokugawa bakufu. Earlier bakufu were established by the Minamoto family (Kamakura bakufu, 1185–1333) and the Ashikaga family (Muromachi bakufu, 1333–1573).

bikuni Itinerant nuns who, by the Edo period, were also known to engage in prostitution.

binzasara Clapper or rattle made of a dozen or more thin boards loosely tied together. The instrument is held on both sides and produces a sound when the boards are suddenly brought together.

bitai Allure, coquetry, flirtatiousness—considered an essential ingredient of *iki*.

biwa Four-stringed lute, played with a large plectrum, heard in *gagaku* and often used to accompany battle tales and other historical narratives.

bon A midsummer festival when the souls of the dead are believed to return for a visit to this world. *Bon* dancing is one of the most common folk dance genres throughout Japan. It is usually accompanied by drums, flutes, and song.

bonseki The creation of miniature landscape-like scenes in a tray by using rocks and sand.

bonten Sacred poles with a paper streamers, located at the top (left and right) of a kabuki theater tower.

bu   A gold or silver coin equal in value to a quarter of a *ryō*.

bugaku   Court dances. See *gagaku*.

bukan   Registries containing information on military households. *Bukan* were often printed in book form and sold to the general public.

bungo bushi   A form of *jōruri* performed by the chanter Miyakoji Bungo no jō from around the second decade of the eighteenth century; banned by the Edo city magistrate in 1736.

bunjin-ga   "Literati painting," or "literary men's painting," originally influenced by eighteenth-century Chinese painting. Many of the artists were Confucian scholars, poets, and calligraphers who sought to be individualistic in their painting.

choku   A dish—usually of boiled vegetables with dressing.

chongare bushi   A form of popular narrative often chanted to *shamisen* accompaniment by itinerant performers.

chōnin   Townsperson—including members of both the artisan and merchant strata of Edo-period society.

daijin   Ostentatiously wealthy patrons of the pleasure quarters.

daimyo   Major feudal lords with holdings of over 10,000 *koku* of rice. Daimyo were divided by the Tokugawa bakufu into various groups based on types of vassalage. The most important division was between *shinpan* (collateral houses), *fudai* (hereditary vassalage lords), and *tozama* ("outside lords").

daishōkai   Calendar designing and printing events.

dangibon   "Sermon books"—somewhat humorous books critical of contemporary society. Many were published between the 1750s and 1770s.

degaichō   See *kaichō*.

dōshin   Low-ranking peace officer, rated at 30 *koku* of rice, who worked under the *yoriki*.

eboshi   Tall black lacquered hats worn by nobles in court dress.

Echigo *chijimi*   A type of strong ramie fabric produced mainly in and around Ojiya village of Echigo province.

Edo-dana   Edo branch shops of businesses with headquarters in the Kamigata area or elsewhere.

Edo-e   See *ukiyo-e*.

Edokko   The prototypical Edo citizen.

enkyoku   Long "banquet songs" popular in the court and among the military nobility during the Kamakura and Muromachi periods.

fudai   See daimyo.

fudasashi   Originally rice brokers who saw to the conversion of warriors' rice stipends into cash, *fudasashi* eventually became de facto financial agents offering loans to warriors with the rice stipend as collateral. Many were renowned for being extremely wealthy.

fudoki   Books describing the geography and cultural characteristics of various areas of Japan.

fue   Transverse flute usually made of bamboo. Numerous types are used in *gagaku*, nō, and folk music genres.

gagaku   Court music of an ensemble featuring transverse flutes (*fue*, more accurately *ryūteki* and *komabue),* a double-reed oboe-like instrument *(hichiriki),* a free-reed mouth organ *(shō),* a four-stringed lute played with a large plectrum *(biwa),* and other string and percussion instruments. Music by this ensemble (without strings) was often used to accompany dance *(bugaku).*

gakunin Musicians of court *gagaku* ensembles.

gannin bōzu Quasi-religious mendicants who performed various genres of popular song and dance.

geki bushi A form of *jōruri* recitation developed in Edo by Satsuma Geki around the 1680s. *Geki bushi* declined greatly in popularity after the 1740s.

geza An offstage musical ensemble in the kabuki theater that includes many percussion instruments, flute, *shamisen,* and other instruments.

gidayū (bushi) *Jōruri* recitation, usually accompanied on *shamisen,* as developed by the chanter Takemoto Gidayū (1651–1714).

Gion-bayashi Festival music featuring percussion and flutes, as heard at the Gion Festival in Kyoto.

goeika A genre of song sung by Buddhist believers, especially pilgrims.

gokenin Household retainers. See *hatamoto.*

gosekku The five major festivals of the year in traditional Japan.

goze Blind itinerant female performers.

hachiningei "Eight-man art"—one man performing in an acrobatic manner to sound like an eight-man band.

haikai Light verse of the Edo period. Derived from linked verse *(renga)* of the medieval era, it became popular because it was free of most of the rigid stylistic and topical conventions that had governed linked verse. One offshoot of *haikai* was the 5–7–5 syllable satiric verse known as *senryū.* In their form, if not their content, *senryū* look like the more serious haiku.

hakama Pleated skirtlike trousers.

hanamichi A raised passageway of the kabuki theater, about five feet in width, that runs from stage right on a right angle through the auditorium to the rear of the orchestra.

hanashibon Books of comic tales popular throughout the Edo period.

hanashika Performer of monologue, usually comic in nature.

handayū bushi A style of *jōruri* invented by Edo Handayū and popular from the last years of the seventeenth to the latter half of the eighteenth centuries.

hari Spirit, pride, strength of character—seen by some as an essential ingredient of *iki.*

harugoma Auspicious New Year's performance by itinerant singer-dancers wielding a prop shaped like a small horse head on a stick.

hatamoto Bannermen. Both bannermen and household retainers *(gokenin)* were under the direct command of the shogun. Both had an assessed income of less than 10,000 *koku* of rice, but *hatamoto* were occasionally granted an audience with the shogun whereas *gokenin* were not. In 1722 the total number of bannermen stood at 5,205; household retainers numbered 17,399.

hatamoto yakko   See *kyōkaku*.

hayashi kata   The instrumental ensemble or its performers in the nō drama.

hichiriki   A double-reed bamboo aerophone, approximately seven inches in length, with nine finger holes: seven in front, two in the back. See *gagaku*.

hira   A dish—usually a mix of boiled vegetables.

hitatare   Large, square-cut coat, with cord-laced sleeves, worn with *hakama*. Often worn by samurai and courtiers as court attire.

honzōgaku   The study of plants and other natural artifacts, especially their medicinal properties.

hyōshigi   Also *ki*. Wooden clappers used in kabuki to mark the drawing of the curtain, the entrance of characters, climaxes in the action, and the like.

iainuki   Popular performance featuring the dramatic unsheathing of a huge sword.

Igamono   Samurai, usually from Iga province (today Mie prefecture), who served as retainers of the bakufu as guards, overseers of minor construction projects, and the like.

iegei   A "house art" or family tradition. During the Edo period, *iegei* were often passed on to disciples through the *iemoto* system.

iemoto system   A hierarchical system in which a real or nominal family head *(iemoto)* passes on a "house art" to disciples who in turn may have their own pupils.

iki   Refinement, stylishness, smartness, chic. Considered by some to consist essentially of the qualities of *bitai, akanuke,* and *hari*.

iki ningyō   Highly realistic figures made of papier-mâché.

jitsugaku   Pragmatic learning—as opposed to the abstract learning associated with most forms of Confucianism. *Jitsugaku* often focused on agriculture, industry, or business.

jōruri   Musical recitation, usually accompanied on the *shamisen* and often heard in the puppet and kabuki theaters. Many subgenres exist: *gidayū bushi, tosa bushi, geki bushi, bungo bushi, handayū bushi, katō bushi, tokiwazu bushi, tomimoto bushi, kiyomoto bushi, shinnai bushi,* and others.

kabuki   One of the most representative forms of theater of the Edo period, kabuki featured a variety of dramatic genres, dance, and music. Permanent troupes were highly popular among the citizenry in all the major urban areas; traveling troupes found great support in rural areas.

kabukimono   Early Edo-period individuals who swaggered through the streets flaunting "deviant" manners.

kaichō   Temple fairs featuring the display of a sacred object that was usually kept from view. When the object was from another temple, this fair was known as *degaichō*. Many popular forms of entertainment could be found at the sites of such "unveilings."

kakubee (-jishi)   Children's itinerant acrobat troupes from Echigo province.

kamabarai   Shamans who came to exorcise or purify the hearth on the last day of each month and especially before the start of the new year.

kamishimo Samurai's formal costume consisting of skirtlike trousers (*hakama*) and a jumper with broad winglike shoulders; worn over a *kosode* or other type of kimono.

kami-yashiki "Upper residence." While in Edo, a daimyo's family usually lived in the "upper residence"; retired daimyo and their successors often lived in the *naka-yashiki* ("middle residence"); *shimo-yashiki* ("lower residences") often served as depots for goods from home provinces and provided gardens and ponds for a respite. Besides these residences, daimyo occasionally owned yet other residences for various purposes.

kamuro Young girls who acted as helpers to the courtesans of the pleasure quarters.

kanjin nō Originally, nō plays staged on temple or shrine grounds in order to collect funds for religious purposes. Later this function was merely a pretense, as funds went to the theater operator. Staging such a performance usually required permission from government authorities.

kaomise (kyōgen) "Face-showing" play in the Edo kabuki, held during the eleventh month of the year, at which the actors contracted for the ensuing season were introduced to the audience.

kare sansui One of the most typical traditional forms of Japanese gardens, featuring rocks and sand rather than ponds and streams.

karitaku Temporary brothels or houses of entertainment hastily built when the licensed quarters had been damaged or destroyed by earthquake, flood, or fire.

kata Form, pattern, or series of prescribed movements.

katō bushi A form of jōruri developed around the second decade of the eighteenth century by Masumi Katō. Popular especially in the following half century, this genre was often considered to be one of the most Edoesque *jōruri* styles.

kemari A game in which a small balllike object is kicked from person to person; popular among courtiers.

ki See *hyōshigi*.

kibyōshi Literally "yellow-covered book." Popular especially around 1770–1805, it usually dealt with popular matters, sometimes in a satirical manner. Many were illustrated, some even in color.

kinpira jōruri Musical narrative genre, popular in Edo before the Genroku period, that often featured the superhuman exploits of the hero Sakata Kintoki.

kō Cooperative associations, often of members of the same religious affiliation, usually for the purpose of funding pilgrimages or financing other projects.

kōdan Storytelling or narration, often taking place in *yose*. Many featured historical plots, battle tales, tales of revenge, and the like. Before the Meiji period, they were often called *kōshaku*.

kokkeibon "Humorous books"—well-told, entertaining stories popular throughout the nineteenth century.

koku Measure for rice. One *koku* equals 47.654 U.S. gallons, 5.119 U.S. bushels, or approximately 180 liters.

kokugaku "National learning"—that is, Japanese learning, often of a Neo-Shintoist type. Popular from the middle of the Edo period, this philosophy sought to discover the Japanese national spirit in the classic literature of Japan.

komon Fine-patterned fabrics often used for *kamishimo* and women's kimono.

komusō *Shakuhachi*-playing itinerant monks associated with the Fuke sect of Zen Buddhism.

koshaku (shi) Storyteller. See *kōdan*.

kosode Small-sleeved kimono, often made of silk, worn by both men and women. During the Edo period the vertical length of the sleeves increased; their horizontal length, however, remained more or less the same, never covering the wrists.

kotsuzumi Small hourglass-shaped laced drum used in nō and other genres.

kudarimono Wares that "came down"—that is, were exported from the Kamigata area to Edo. Until the mid-eighteenth century these wares were generally considered superior to Edo wares.

kugutsushi Puppeteers who manipulated one-man puppets, often while dancing, singing, or chanting narratives.

kuramae "Before the granary"—an area near the bakufu's rice granary at Asakusa.

kusemai Form of accompanied dance, popular from the fourteenth to sixteenth centuries, that includes long narratives sung to drum accompaniment as well as dances by performers wearing *hitatare*, *suikan*, and *eboshi*. Elements of *kusemai* were later incorporated into the nō drama.

kyōka Literally "crazy verses"—satirical or humorous poems in 5–7–5–7–7 syllable form. Most *kyōka* poets assumed pseudonyms that included complex puns or literary allusions. These names are usually untranslatable; many are humorous only if the incompatibility of the semantic and phonetic values of the Sino-Japanese ideographs is sensed. Some authors chose to parody older poets: thus Hamabe no Kurohito ("dark man on the waterfront") is probably a spoof on Yamabe no Akahito, a Nara-period poet. Other names may allude to personal conditions: Yadoya no Meshimori, for example, means "servant at the inn" and refers to the fact that the poet ran an inn at Kodenma-chō in Edo.

kyōkaku Also known as *kyōsha* or *otokodate*, the *kyōkaku* were "street knights," or self-appointed defenders of the commoners, whose "chivalrous" activities, gambling, and fighting were often prohibited by the bakufu. Samurai of the *hatamoto* and *gokenin* strata were the main participants in one kind of group, whose members were called *hatamoto yakko*; *chōnin* formed yet other groups, whose members were known as *machi yakko*.

kyōsha See *kyōkaku*.

kyōshi Comic poems in Chinese.

machi Also read *chō*. A ward in the city of Edo.

machiai-jaya "Rendezvous teahouse" to which a geisha could be called for entertaining customers.

machi geisha "Town geisha"—the geisha outside the licensed quarters of Yoshiwara, in particular the women working in houses of entertainment in the Fukagawa area.

machi shishō "Town teachers"—local teachers who instructed the townspeople in leisure pursuits such as music, flower arranging, tea ceremony, and the like.

machi yakko See *kyōkaku*.

maimai Itinerant performance of dance that may have its roots in the medieval ballad drama known as *kōwakamai*.

mamezō A type of conjurer/acrobat.

manzai Comic and auspicious dialogues performed by itinerants.

Meiji Restoration The establishment of imperial rule in 1867 after the fall of the Tokugawa bakufu.

Meireki fire The fire that destroyed the greater part of the city of Edo in the first month of 1657. Casualties are estimated at 100,000. After the fire the layout and appearance of the city changed drastically.

mikoshi Portable floatlike shrines housing a Shinto deity and paraded through the streets on festive occasions.

mitsuke "Approach"—the outside section of large-scale gates of the shogun's castle. Edo castle contained some thirty-six *mitsuke*, all manned by guards.

mizu karakuri Contraptions, often dolllike in shape, that move by the force of water.

monzenmachi Areas of the city "before temple gates."

mukō or *mukōzuke* A dish—usually vinegared fish or vegetables.

nagauta More precisely *Edo nagauta*—an important vocal musical genre featuring accompaniment on *shamisen*, percussion, and flute. *Nagauta* were often heard together with kabuki dance plays, but purely musical works exist as well.

naka-yashiki "Middle residence." See *kami-yashiki*.

nanushi More accurately *machi nanushi*—city ward representatives, mainly in charge of the transmission and enforcement of orders from the city magistrate's office as transmitted by the city elders *(machi doshiyori)*.

ninjōbon Novels from around 1818–1867 dealing with "human feelings" and contemporary customs, especially within the pleasure quarters.

nishiki-e See *ukiyo-e*.

nō One of the most representative forms of theater of the Kamakura and Muromachi periods, nō is a elaborate synthesis of dramatic, musical, and visual elements.

nodaiko Semiprofessional jesters who entertained at parties and gatherings.

noshime Plain kimono, with a striped pattern across the midriff, worn as an underrobe to *kamishimo* and other formal garments.

nukemairi See *okagemairi*.

o Honorific prefix.

ōdaiko Large drum used in a variety of musical genres.

ogie bushi Song type, accompanied on *shamisen*, originally deriving from *nagauta* and highly popular in the 1770s. Invented by Ogie Royū (d. 1787).

okagemairi   Also known as *nukemairi*. Sudden mass pilgrimages to the great shrine at Ise. Most participants were members of the commoner class, who often had not received permission to go. The largest *okagemairi*, with some two or three million participants each, occurred in 1650, 1705, 1771, and 1830.

ōkawa   Large double-headed laced drum used in nō.

ōkubi-e   Half-length or head and shoulders *ukiyo-e* portraits, in particular those drawn by Utamaro.

onnagata   Female impersonators in the kabuki.

otokodate   See *kyōkaku*.

otoshibanashi   See *rakugo*.

ōtsu-e bushi   Type of popular song common throughout Japan from the early nineteenth century.

rakugo   Comic narrative often heard at the *yose*. Also *otoshibanashi*.

rangaku   Literally "Dutch learning" but referring to Western learning of the middle and later Edo period in general, when most available books on the subject were in Dutch; includes medicine, astronomy, geography, natural sciences, and much else.

renga   Linked verse. *Renga* sequences were often composed by two poets alternately (or consecutively) writing 5–7–5 and 7–7 syllable links of verse and stringing them together. This form of verse can be found as early as the Heian period (794–1185) and reached its height after the fourteenth century.

rōjū   Senior councillors of the bakufu.

rōnin   Masterless samurai.

ryō   A valuable gold coin whose value and exchange rates with silver and copper varied.

ryū   Also *ryūha*. School or style of an art—often associated with the "house art" taught by a family organized as an *iemoto* system.

ryūha   See *ryū*.

ryūtatsu kouta   Popular early Edo-period song genre started by the priest Takasabu Ryūtatsu (1527–1611).

saimon   Popular narrative genre, originally of religious purport, but later usually dealing with love suicides. Often accompanied by shaking a priest's staff (with metal rings attached) and blowing on a conch shell.

sake   Japanese rice wine.

sandai-banashi   Monologue, often comic, on three topics posed by the audience. Often performed in the *yose*.

sankin kōtai   System of "alternate attendance" in which daimyo and many of their retainers were forced to move between their regional domain and their Edo residences, usually in alternate years. Wives and children of daimyo lived in Edo permanently as de facto hostages of the bakufu.

sekizoro   Itinerant exorcisers who performed auspicious song and dance.

sekkyō   Form of musical recitation originating from Buddhist homilies and particularly popular during the early Edo period.

senjafuda Votive slips pasted on temples by pilgrims, often printed with artistically pleasing designs.

senryū Satiric, witty verse highly popular from the late eighteenth century. Most *senryū* are in 5–7–5 syllable form, but some 7–7 syllable verses exist as well. See *haikai*.

shakuhachi An end-blown bamboo flute often associated with the Fuke sect of Zen Buddhism. The standard instrument is 1.8 feet in length and has five finger holes (four in front, one in the back).

shamisen A three-stringed banjo-like lute, usually played with a large plectrum, used in chamber music and to accompany *jōruri, nagauta,* and many other popular Edo-period song and narrative genres.

sharebon Literally "smart books." Popular especially between 1764 and 1788, many featured plots about the pleasure quarter and its customers.

shibai-jaya The "theater teahouse" provided tickets and information to patrons of the theater and was a popular spot for refreshments or meals between acts.

shichi genkin A seven-stringed zither.

shimo-yashiki "Lower residence." See *kami-yashiki*.

shinden-zukuri A style of architecture that reached perfection in the Heian period, when it was used mainly for the residences of the aristocracy and high-ranking Buddhist clerics. Along with the later *shoin-zukuri*, the *shinden-zukuri* is considered one of the two major Japanese styles of residential architecture.

shingaku Ethics associated with the teachings of Ishida Baigan (1685–1744). Containing Confucian, Buddhist, Shinto, and Taoist elements and stressing virtue in everyday life, it was highly popular among the commoners, especially the merchant class.

shinnai (bushi) A popular style of *jōruri*. Often featuring love suicides and not associated with kabuki, it was invented by Tsuruga Wakasa no Jō (1717–1786).

shitamachi The "downtown" or "low city" area of Edo/Tokyo and the site of most of the townspeople's homes and shops. Located roughly between the shogun's castle in the west and the Sumida River and bay on the east.

shite Lead role in the nō.

shō A reed mouth organ usually with seventeen thin bamboo pipes, of which fifteen produce a sound when the player exhales or inhales through the mouthpiece of the instrument. Often used to play harmonies of five or six pitches. See *gagaku*.

shoin-zukuri Domestic architectural style of the medieval era. See *shinden-zukuri*.

soba Buckwheat noodles eaten with broth either hot or cold.

suikan Nobleman's court robe, usually made of white silk.

suō Man's costume with wide-sleeved top garment and long skirtlike trousers. During the Muromachi period (1333–1573) it was often worn by commoners, but from the Edo period it became ceremonial costume for warriors.

suzu   Short metal staff with small bells that jingled when shaken.

tachiyaku   Lead actor of male roles in the kabuki theater.

taiko   Large drum.

tatami   Thick straw mats with cloth borders used in Japanese residences as floor covering.

tate oyama   Lead female impersonator in the kabuki theater.

tayū   "Master"—used as an honorific title by courtesans, nō masters, itinerant performers, and others. May also be used to refer to a nō actor who plays lead roles.

tenja   Judge or teacher of verse—during the Edo period, generally a master of *haikai* or *senryū*.

Tenpō Reforms   Reforms instigated between 1841 and 1843 by the *rōjū* Mizuno Echizen no Kami Tadakuni in the hopes of strengthening the bakufu. Mizuno dismantled guilds of wholesalers, lowered or froze prices, stressed austerity in consumption, and attempted to stop immoral activities. These reforms ended in almost total failure.

terakoya   Elementary schools associated with a Buddhist temple. Pupils, generally twenty to thirty in a class, were usually commoners. Most schools taught little more than reading and writing, and sometimes arithmetic (use of the abacus).

tokiwazu   A style of *jōruri*, started by Tokiwazu Mojitayū (1709–1781), that was highly popular and closely linked to the kabuki theater.

tokonoma   An alcove or recess in a Japanese room in which a hanging scroll or other ornament may be put on display.

Tokugawa bakufu   *See* bakufu.

tomimoto   Style of *jōruri* started by Tomimoto Buzen no Jō (1716–1764), who broke away from the *tokiwazu* style to start his own school.

torioi   Female singer-*shamisen* performers who made the rounds especially in the city of Edo at New Year's. Although usually outcastes, they were often considered stylish.

Tosa bushi   A form of *jōruri* popular from the 1660s to the 1680s.

tozama   *See* daimyo.

tsū   "Savoir faire"—chiefly the pattern of behavior of the knowledgeable, refined visitor to the pleasure quarter.

tsubo   A dish—usually of cooked vegetables and potato.

tsūjin   Also *tsūkaku*. "Connoisseur" or "man of taste"—that is, a man who understood the customs and practices of the pleasure quarter.

udon   Wheat noodles usually eaten hot with broth.

ukarebushi   Light song genre of the late Edo period often heard in the *yose*.

ukiyo-e   Literally, "pictures of the floating world." Polychrome *ukiyo-e* (*nishiki-e*, "brocade pictures") made in Edo during the late eighteenth and nineteenth centuries were particularly renowned and were sometimes known as *Edo-e* ("Edo pictures") or *Azuma nishiki-e* ("brocade pictures of the east"). *Ukiyo-e* often featured portraits of famous actors or courtesans but might also include scenes from everyday life, famous places, or landscapes.

umai   Genre of court dance accompanied by *gagaku*.

wabicha   A style of tea ceremony stressing an elegant, quiet mood bordering on sadness. This style, which was particularly popular during the last quarter of the sixteenth century, was brought to perfection by Sen no Rikyū (1522–1599).

waki   Supporting role in the nō drama.

yagura   Wooden tower, often built over a theater entrance. Dyed cloth with the theater operator's family crest imprinted in white was wrapped around this edifice, which served as a type of advertisement and showed that the operator had an official permit to run a theater.

yakuharai   Itinerant exorcisers.

yamanote   The "uptown" or "high city" area of Edo/Tokyo as opposed to the "downtown" *(shitamachi)* area. This hilly area described a semicircle around the *shitamachi* and was the site of many warrior residences.

yomihon   Voluminous "reading books" popular from around the middle of the eighteenth century until the end of the Edo period. Many featured didactic plots of a Confucian or Buddhist nature.

yoriki   Assistant magistrates and legal specialists in the city administration with a rating of 200 *koku* of rice. There were generally twenty-five *yoriki* in Edo.

yose (ba)   Variety halls, highly popular among the middle and lower classes in nineteenth-century Edo. Genres performed at *yose* included comic monologues, various forms of narration and music, conjuring, magic lantern shows, and much else.

yotsudake   Castanets made of two slabs of bamboo. A pair is held in each hand and sounded, usually while dancing.

yūgei   Leisure pursuits.

zamoto   Troupe leader.

SELECTED REFERENCES

Sources in Japanese

Edo-Period and Other Early Sources

Akiyama kikō (Suzuki Bokushi). Miya Eiji, ed., *Akiyama kikō, Yanabegusa* (*Tōyō bunko*, vol. 186), pp. 1–172. Tokyo: Heibonsha, 1971.

Aoto zōshi hana no nishiki-e (Kawatake Mokuami). Kawatake Toshio et al., eds., *Meisaku kabuki zenshū*, vol. 11, pp. 79–126. Tokyo: Tōkyō Sōgen Shinsha, 1969.

Ashiya Dōman ōuchi kagami (Takeda Izumo and assistants). Kawatake Toshio et al., eds., *Meisaku kabuki zenshū*, vol. 3, pp. 109–135. Tokyo: Tōkyō Sōgen Shinsha, 1968.

Azuma kagami. Kokusho Kankōkai, ed. 3 vols. Tokyo: Kokusho Kankōkai, 1915; reprinted in 1968.

Bankoku shinwa (Morishima Chūryō). In the possession of the National Diet Library.

Banpō ryōri himitsu-bako. Yoshii Motoko, ed., *(Honkoku) Edo jidai ryōri-hon shūsei*, vol. 5, pp. 77–156. Tokyo: Rinsen Shoten, 1980.

Banzuiin Chōbee shōjin manaita (Sakurada Jisuke). Toita Yasuji et al., eds., *Meisaku kabuki zenshū*, vol. 15, pp. 53–126. Tokyo: Tōkyō Sōgen Shinsha, 1969.

Bukō nenpyō (Saitō Gesshin). Kaneko Mitsuharu, ed. 2 vols. *(Tōyō bunko)*. Tokyo: Heibonsha, 1968.

Bunbuku chagama (Jippensha Ikku). In the possession of the Tōkyō Toritsu Chūō Toshokan (Kaga Collection).

Butsurui hinshitsu (Hiraga Gennai). Masamune Tsuruo, ed., *Nihon koten zenshū*, 3rd series, vol. 16. Tokyo: Nihon Koten Zenshū Kankō-kai, 1928.

Chirizuka dan (Ogawa Kendō). Iwamoto Sashichi, ed., *Enseki Jisshū*, vol. 1, pp. 237–279. Tokyo: Kokusho Kankōkai, 1907–1908; reprinted by Tōkyō Shuppan in 1976.

Daikon ryōri hiden shō [*Shokoku meisan daikon ryōri hidensho*] (Kitodō Shujin). Yoshii Motoko, ed., *(Honkoku) Edo jidai ryōri-hon shūsei*, vol. 5, pp. 195–226. Tokyo: Rinsen Shoten, 1980.

Dōchō tosetsu (Ōsato Shinsai). Mitamura Engyo, ed., *Sohaku jisshu* (3 vols.), vol. 2, pp. 209–393. Tokyo: Chūō Kōronsha, 1978.

Eda sangoju (Ishikawa Sen). *Kinsei bungei sōsho,* vol. 6, pp. 230–252. Tokyo: Kokusho Kankōkai, 1911.

Edo ka no ko (Fujita Rihee). In the possession of the National Diet Library.

Edo meisho-ki (Asai Ryōi). Edo Sōsho Kankōkai, ed., *Edo sōsho,* vol. 2, pp. 1–160. Tokyo: Meicho Kankōkai, 1964; reprint.

Edo meisho zue (Saitō Gesshin). Miura Tadashi, ed., 4 vols. Tokyo: Yūhōdō Shoten, 1913.

Edo ryōri-tsū taizen (Yaoya Zenshirō). Geinōshi Kenkyūkai, ed., *Nihon shomin bunka shiryō shūsei,* vol. 10, pp. 543–560. Tokyo: San'ichi Shobō, 1977.

Edo sunago (Kikuoka Senryō). Koike Shōtarō, ed. Tokyo: Tōkyōdō, 1976.

Edo suzume (Kinkō Entsū; illus. Hishikawa Moronobu). *Nihon zuihitsu taisei daisan-ki,* vol. 10, pp. 44–285. Tokyo: Yoshikawa Kōbunkan, 1974.

Ehon taikōki (Chikamatsu Yanagi). Toita Yasuji et al., eds., *Meisaku kabuki zenshū,* vol. 5, pp. 351–374. *(Myōshinji no ba, Amagasaki no ba).* Tokyo: Tōkyō Sōgen Shinsha, 1970. The original *jōruri* version can be found in Yūda Yoshio, ed., *Bunraku jōruri-shū (Nihon koten bungaku taikei,* vol. 99), pp. 351–370. Tokyo: Iwanami Shoten, 1965.

Eisei kiroku-shū (Suzuki Bokushi). Miya Eiji et al., eds., *Suzuki Bokushi zenshū: ge (shiryō-hen),* pp. 11–100. Tokyo: Chūō Kōronsha, 1983.

En'yū nikki (Yanagisawa Nobutoki). Geinōshi Kenkyūkai, ed., *Nihon shomin bunka shiryō shūsei,* vol. 13, pp. 1–813. *En'yū nikki betsuroku,* pp. 817–942. Tokyo: San-ichi Shobō, 1977.

Fucha ryōri shō (Nishimura Mitatsu). Yoshii Motoko, ed., *(Honkoku) Edo jidai ryōrihon shūsei,* vol. 3, pp. 239–289. Tokyo: Rinsen Shobō, 1979.

Fukijizai (Ajari Dōjin). *Tokugawa bungei ruijū,* vol. 12, pp. 354–376. Tokyo: Kokusho Kankōkai, 1914.

Funa Benkei (Nobumitsu). Yokomichi Mario and Omote Akira, eds., *Yōkyoku shū: ge (Nihon koten bungaku taikei,* vol. 41), pp. 150–161. Tokyo: Iwanami Shoten, 1963.

Fūryū Shidōken-den (Hiraga Gennai). Nakamura Yukihiko, ed., *Nihon koten bungaku taikei,* vol. 55 *(Fūrai Sanjin shū),* pp. 153–224. Iwanami Shoten, 1961. Also in *Nihon meicho zenshū,* vol. 14 *(Kokkeibon shū),* pp. 1–54. Tokyo: Nihon Meicho Zenshū Kankōkai, 1927.

Fūzoku-tsū (Shōfūtei Shujin). *Sharebon taisei,* vol. 19, pp. 13–37. Tokyo: Chūō Kōronsha, 1983.

Fuzumō. Sasano Ken, ed., *Kyōgen-shū,* vol. 1, pp. 242–249. Tokyo: Iwanami Shoten, 1942.

Gaiyō sōkō (Zhao Yi). Shanghai: Shangwu Yinshuguan, 1957.

Genroku shojaku mokuroku. Shomoku shūran, vol. 1, pp. 134–489. Tokyo: Tōrin Shobō, 1928.

Genroku taiheiki (Miyako no Nishiki). Fujii Otoo, ed., *Ukiyo-zōshi meisaku-shū.* Tokyo: Kōdansha, 1937.

Gorin no sho (Miyamoto Musashi). Nishiyama Matsunosuke et al., eds., *Kinsei geidō-ron (Nihon shisō taikei,* vol. 61), pp. 355–394. Tokyo: Iwanami Shoten, 1972.

Gunsho ruijū (Hanawa Hokiichi, ed.). Gunsho Ruijū Kankōkai, ed., *Gunsho ruijū: dai kyūjūhen inshoku-bu*, vol. 19 (no. 368). Tokyo: Gunsho Ruijū Kankōkai, 1959–1960.

Haifū yanagidaru. Senryū zappai-shū, pp. 291–752. Tokyo: Nihon Meicho Zenshū Kankōkai, 1927.

Hakata ko-jorō nami makura (Chikamatsu Monzaemon). Shigetomo Ki, ed., *Chikamatsu jōruri-shū: jō* (*Nihon koten bungaku taikei*, vol. 49), pp. 323–354. Tokyo: Iwanami Shoten, 1958.

Hanabutai kasumi no saruhiki (Nakamura Jūsuke). Nakauchi Chōji and Tamura Nishio, eds., *Tokiwazu zenshū*, pp. 53–60. Tokyo: Nihon Ongyoku Zenshū Kankōkai, 1927.

Harimaze byōbu kokusho shōmei-chō (Suzuki Bokushi). Miya Eiji et al., eds., *Suzuki Bokushi zenshū: ge (shiryō-hen)*, pp. 359–380. Tokyo: Chūō Kōronsha, 1983.

Heihō kadensho (Yagyū Munenori). Nishiyama Matsunosuke et al., eds., *Kinsei geidō-ron* (*Nihon shisō taikei*, vol. 61), pp. 301–343. Tokyo: Iwanami Shoten, 1972.

Hitome tsutsumi. Sharebon taisei, vol. 14, pp. 177–203. Tokyo: Chūō Kōronsha, 1981.

Hōchō shiki hō. In the possession of the National Diet Library.

Hōchō shoroku (Hayashi Razan). *Nihon zuihitsu taisei daiikki*, vol. 23, pp. 337–349. Tokyo: Yoshikawa Kōbunkan, 1976.

Hōei (no) rakusho. Onchi sōsho, vol. 5, pp. 299–326. Tokyo: Hakubunkan, 1907.

Hōgu kago (Morishima Chūryō). *Nihon zuihitsu taisei daisan-ki*, vol. 8, pp. 245–262. Tokyo: Yoshikawa Kōbunkan, 1974.

Hokuetsu seppu (Suzuki Bokushi). Okada Takematsu, ed. Tokyo: Iwanami Bunko, 1989.

"Hōkyoku fuji no kodama" (excerpts). Engeki Kenkyūkai, ed., *Mikan jōruri geiron shū*, pp. 43–48. Osaka: Engeki Kenkyūkai, 1958.

Honchō tsugan (Hayashi Razan and Hayashi Gahō). 17 vols. Tokyo: Kokusho Kankōkai, 1919.

Imai Sōkyū chanoyu kakinuki (Takenami Ankyū, comp.). *Chadō koten zenshū*, vol. 10, pp. 1–64. Tokyo: Tankō Shinsha, 1961.

Imayō sekkin hiinagata (Katsushika Hokusai). Nagata Seiji, ed., *Hokusai kōgei zuan-chō*. Tokyo: Iwasaki Bijutsusha, 1983.

Imoseyama onna teikin (Chikamatsu Hanji). Yūda Yoshio, ed., *Bungaku jōruri-shū* (*Nihon koten bungaku taikei*, vol. 99), pp. 255–278. Tokyo: Iwanami Shoten, 1965. For a kabuki version see Toita Yasuji et al., eds., *Meisaku kabuki zenshū*, vol. 5, pp. 155–212. Tokyo: Tōkyō Sōgen Shinsha, 1968.

Jidai sewa ni-chō tsuzumi (Santō Kyōden). *Kibyōshi hyakushu* (*Zoku teikoku bunko*, vol. 33), pp. 491–504. Tokyo: Hakubunkan, 1909.

Jōzan kidan (Yuasa Jōzan). Suzuki Tōzō, ed. 2 vols. Tokyo: Kadokawa Shoten, 1965.

Kabuki nendai-ki. Tokyo: Hōbunkan, 1926.

Kabuki nenpyō. Ihara Toshirō, ed. 8 vols. Tokyo: Iwanami Shoten, 1956–1963.

Kagamiyama kokyō no nishiki-e (Yō Yodai). Toita Yasuji et al., eds., *Meisaku kabuki zenshū*, vol. 13, pp. 235–278. Tokyo: Tōkyō Sōgen Shinsha, 1969.

Kaidō kudari. In Saitō Gesshin, "Hyakugi jutsuryaku" (*Shin-enseki jisshu*, vol. 4, pp. 210–327), pp. 317–320. Tokyo: Chūō Kōronsha, 1981.

Kaitai shinsho (Sugita Genpaku et al., trans.). *Nihon kagaku koten zensho*, vol. 8, pp. 207–380. Tokyo: Asahi Shinbunsha, 1948.

Kaitai yakuzu (Sugita Genpaku). Tokyo: Nihon Ishi Gakkai, 1965.

Kakanpu ryakusetsu (Hiraga Gennai). *Nihon zuihitsu taisei*, 2nd series, vol. 16, pp. 237–255. Tokyo: Yoshikawa Kōbunkan, 1974.

Kamiya Sōtan nikki (Kamiya Sōtan). *Chadō koten zenshū*, vol. 6, pp. 131–382. Tokyo: Tankō Shinsha, 1958.

Kanadehon chūshingura (Takeda Izumo and assistants). Otoba Hiromu, ed., *Jōruri-shū: jō* (*Nihon koten bungaku taikei*, vol. 51), pp. 291–382. Tokyo: Iwanami Shoten, 1960. For a kabuki version see Toita Yasuji et al., eds., *Meisaku kabuki zenshū*, vol. 2, pp. 5–138. Tokyo: Tōkyō Sōgen Shinsha, 1968.

Kanbun inchi-shū. *Zokuzoku gunsho ruijū: chiri-bu*, vol. 9, pp. 1–309. Toyko: Kokusho Kankōkai, 1906.

Kan'ei shoka keizuden. Saiki Kazuma et al., eds., *Zoku gunsho ruijū kansei*, 13 vols. (in progress). Tokyo: Zoku Gunsho Ruijū Kansei-kai, 1980–1990.

Kanjinchō. Gunji Masakatsu, ed., *Kabuki jūhachiban-shū* (*Nihon bungaku taikei*, vol. 98), pp. 175–192. Tokyo: Iwanami Shoten, 1965.

Kanten kenbunki. *Enseki jisshū*, vol. 5, pp. 319–333. Tokyo: Chūō Kōronsha, 1980.

Kantō kekki monogatari (retitled *Kantō kekkeiden*). Mitamura Engyo, ed., *Mikan zuihitsu hyakushu*, vol. 6, pp. 317–374. Tokyo: Chūō Kōronsha, 1977.

Katsuragawa renri no shigarami (Suga Sensuke). Toita Yasuji et al., eds., *Meisaku kabuki zenshū*, vol. 7, pp. 177–202. Tokyo: Tōkyō Sōgen Shinsha, 1969.

Kawachi no kuni meisho kagami (Mita Jōkyū). *Kinsei bungei sōsho*, vol. 2, pp. 324–410. Tokyo: Kokusho Kankōkai, 1910.

Kawachiya Yoshimasa kyūki (Kawachiya Yoshimasa). Nomura Yutaka and Yui Kitarō, eds., *Kinsei shomin shiryō: genroku jidai ni okeru ichi shōya no kiroku.* Tokyo: Kinsei Shomin Shiryō Kankōkai, 1955.

Keisei Awa no Naruto (Chikamatsu Hanji et al.). *Chikamatsu Hanji jōruri-shū* (*Zoku teikoku bunko*, vol. 14), pp. 573–664. Tokyo: Hakubunkan, 1899.

Keiseikei (Santō Kyōden). *Sharebon taikei*, vol. 6, pp. 691–755. Tokyo: Rokugō-kan, 1931.

Kenuki. Gunji Masakatsu, ed., *Kabuki jūhachiban-shū* (*Nihon bungaku taikei*, vol. 98), pp. 233–278. Tokyo: Iwanami Shoten, 1965.

Kiki no manimani (Tanaka Taishū [Kitamura Nobuyo]). Mitamura Engyo, ed., *Mikan zuihitsu hyakushu*, vol. 6, pp. 45–221. Tokyo: Chūō Kōronsha, 1977.

Kinsei kiseki-kō (Santō Kyōden). *Nihon zuihitsu taisei*, 2nd series, vol. 6, pp. 251–376. Tokyo: Yoshikawa Kōbunkan, 1974.

Kinsei mono no hon Edo sakusha burui (Takizawa Bakin). *Onchi sōsho*, vol. 5, pp. 1–191. Tokyo: Hakubunkan, 1891.

Kissa ōrai (Gen'e). Narabayashi Tadao, ed., *Nihon no chasho*, vol. 1, pp. 83–118 (*Tōyō bunko*, vol. 201). Tokyo: Heibonsha, 1971.

Kitamachi bugyō-sho shichū torishimari-gakari jōshinsho. Tōkyō Daigaku Shiryō Hensanjo, ed., *Dai Nihon kinsei shiryō, Shichū torishimari ruishū*, vol. 1, pp. 233–245. Tokyo: Tōkyō Daigaku Shuppankai, 1959.

Kōgiroku. In the possession of Tsukuba University.

Kokin wakashū. Ozawa Masao, ed., *Nihon koten bungaku zenshū*, vol. 7. Tokyo: Shogakkan, 1971.

Kokka man'yōki (Kikumoto Gaho). Asakura Haruhiko, ed., *Kohan chishi sōsho*, vols. 1–4 (facsimile). Tokyo: Sumiya Shobō, 1969–1971.

Kokon ryōri-shū. Yoshii Motoko, ed., *(Honkoku) Edo jidai ryōrihon shūsei*, vol. 2, pp. 3–226. Tokyo: Rinsen Shobō, 1978.

Kokubyaku mizu kagami (Ishibe Kinkō). Nakamura Haruhiko, ed., *Daitōkyū kinen bunko zenpon sōkan*, vol. 5 *(kibyōshi-hen)*, pp. 359–382 (facsimile). Tokyo: Benseisha, 1976.

Kōmō zatsuwa (Morishima Chūryō). Kikuchi Toshiyoshi, ed., *Edo kagaku koten sōsho*, vol. 31 (facsimile). Tokyo: Kōwa Shuppan, 1980.

Konpira sankei meisho zue. Ikeda Yasaburō et al., eds., *Nihon meisho fūzoku-e*, vol. 14, pp. 5–126. Tokyo: Kadokawa Shoten, 1981.

Kōrin hyakuzu (Ogata Kōrin). 5 vols. Tokyo: Iwasaki Bijutsusha, 1981.

Koshijima toki no aizome (Santō Kyōden). *Kibyōshi sanjūgo shu (Nihon meicho zenshū*, vol. 11), pp. 243–272. Tokyo: Nihon Meicho Zenshū Kankōkai, 1926.

Kōshoku gonin onna (Ihara Saikaku). Tsutsumi Seiji, ed., *Nihon koten bungaku taikei (Saikaku-shū: jō*, vol. 47), pp. 219–321. Tokyo: Iwanami Shoten, 1957.

Kosode moyō hiingata hon shūsei, vol. 1. Tokyo: Gakushū Kenkyū-sha, 1974.

Kōto gosui (Nishizawa Ippōken). *Shin gunsho ruijū*, vol. 1, pp. 479–752. Tokyo: Kokusho Kankōkai, 1906.

Kumano mōde. Takano Tatsuyuki, ed., *Nihon kayō shūsei*, vol. 5, pp. 71–75. Tokyo: Shunjusha, 1928.

Kumo no itomaki (Santō Kyōzan). *Enseki jisshū*, vol. 2, pp. 271–312. Tokyo: Chūō Kōronsha, 1979.

Kyūki seishoku-hō shūsho. Ono Takeo, ed., *Nihon kinsei kiga shi*, pp. 371–386. Tokyo: Yūmei Shobō, 1987; originally published in 1935.

Kyūkō mago no tsue (Makura Undō). Ono Takeo, ed., *Nihon kinsei kiga shi*, pp. 387–418. Tokyo: Yūmei Shobō, 1987; originally published in 1935.

Machi bugyō jōshinsho. Tōkyō Daigaku Shiryō Hensanjo, ed., *Dai Nihon kinsei shiryō, Shichū torishimari ruishū*, vol. 2, pp. 19–69. Tokyo: Tōkyō Daigaku Shuppankai, 1959.

Matsudaira Yamato no kami nikki (Matsudaira Naonori). Geinōshi Kenkyūkai, ed., *Nihon shomin bunka shiryō shūsei*, vol. 12, pp. 5–628. Tokyo: San-ichi Shobō, 1977.

Michiyuki shian no hoka (Sakurada Jisuke II). Nakauchi Chōji and Tamura Nishio, eds., *Kiyomoto zenshū (Nihon ongyoku zenshū*, vol. 3), pp. 358–362. Tokyo: Nihon Ongyoku Zenshū Kankōkai, 1928.

Minkan bikōroku (Takebe Seian). Takimoto Seiichi, ed., *Nihon keizai taiten*, vol. 11, pp. 491–558. Tokyo: Meiji Bunken, 1967.

Minkan seiyō (Tanaka Kyūgū). Takimoto Seiichi, ed., *Nihon keizai taiten*, vol. 5, pp. 6–514. Tokyo: Meiji Bunken, 1965; reprint.

Misemono zasshi (Kodera Gyokuchō). Kusue Makoto, ed., *Zoku zuihitsu bungaku zenshū*, vol. 1, pp. 283–396, vol. 2, pp. 3–54. Tokyo: Zoku Zuihitsu Bungaku Zenshū Kankōkai, 1928.

Miyako meisho zue (Akizato Ritō). Takemura Toshinori, ed. Tokyo: Kadokawa Shoten, 1976.

Morisada mankō (Kitagawa Morisada). Published as *(Ruishū) kinsei fūzokushi*, 2 vols. bound together. Tokyo: Meicho Kankōkai, 1989; reprint of 1908 ed.

Moriyama Takamori nikki (Moriyama Takamori). Takeuchi Makoto and Asai Junko, eds., *Nihon toshi seikatsu shiryō-shū*, vol. 2, pp. 26–201. Tokyo: Gakushū Kenkyūsha, 1977.

Murasaki no hitomoto (Toda Mosui). *Zuihitsu bungaku senshū*, vol. 10, pp. 1–132. Tokyo: Shosaisha, 1927.

Naika sen'yō (or *Seisetsu naika sen'yō*). Translated by Udagawa Genzui. In the possession of the Tokyo Metropolitan Central Library.

Nanbōroku (Nanbō Sōkei). Nishiyama Matsunosuke, ed., *Kinsei geidō-ron* (*Nihon shisō taikei*, vol. 61), pp. 10–175. Tokyo: Iwanami Shoten, 1972.

Nankaku sensei bunshū (Hattori Nankaku). Excerpts in Rai Tsutomu, ed., *Sorai gakuha* (*Nihon shisō taikei*, vol. 37), pp. 194–245. Tokyo: Iwanami Shoten, 1972.

Nansō Satomi hakkenden (Takizawa Bakin). Koike Fujigorō, ed. 2 vols. Tokyo: Iwanami Bunko, 1990.

Narukami. Gunji Masakatsu, ed., *Kabuki jūhachiban shū* (*Nihon koten bungaku taikei*, vol. 98), pp. 194–232. Tokyo: Iwanami Shoten, 1965.

Nenashigusa (Hiraga Gennai). Nakamura Yukihiko, ed., *Fūrai Sanjin-shū* (*Nihon koten bungaku taikei*, vol. 55), pp. 33–94. Tokyo: Iwanami Shoten, 1961.

Nijūyohai junpai zue. Hayashi Hideo et al., eds., *Nihon meisho fūzoku zue*, vol. 18, pp. 294–563. Tokyo: Kadokawa Shoten, 1980.

Nitan no Shirō Fuji no hitoana kenbutsu (Santō Kyōden). *Kibyōshi hyakushu* (*Zoku teikoku bunko*, vol. 33), pp. 523–532. Tokyo: Hakubunkan, 1909.

Nochi no tsuki shuen no shimadai (Segawa Jokō II). *Tokiwazu zenshū*, pp. 251–254. Tokyo: Nihon Ongyoku Zenshū Kankōkai, 1927.

Nochi wa mukashi no monogatari (Tegara Okamochi). Iwamoto Sashichi, ed., *Enseki jisshu*, vol. 1, pp. 280–302. Tokyo: Kokusho Kankōkai, 1907–1908; reprinted by Tōkyō Shuppan in 1976. See also *Nihon zuihitsu taisei: dai san ki*, vol. 12. Tokyo: Yoshikawa Kōbunkan, 1977.

Ofuregaki kanpō shūsei. Takayanagi Shinzō and Ishii Ryōsuke, eds. Tokyo: Iwanami Shoten, 1934.

Ōmi Genji senji yakata (Chikamatsu Hanji). Toita Yasuji et al., eds., *Meisaku kabuki zenshū*, vol. 5, pp. 87–114. Tokyo: Tōkyō Sōgen Shinsha, 1970.

Ōmugaeshi bunbu no futamichi (Koikawa Harumachi). Hamada Giichirō et al., eds., *Kibyōshi/Senryū/Kyōka* (*Nihon koten bungaku zenshū*, vol. 46), pp. 159–178. Tokyo: Shōgakkan, 1971.

Onmitsu mawari jōshinsho (seventh month 1841). Tōkyō Daigaku Shiryō

Hensanjo, ed., *Dai Nihon kinsei shiryō, Shichū torishimari ruishū*, vol. 1, pp. 210–215. Tokyo: Tōkyō Daigaku Shuppankai, 1959.

Osome Hisamatsu shinpan utazaimon (Chikamatsu Hanji). Tsurumi Makoto, ed., *Jōruri-shū* (*Nihon koten bungaku taikei*, vol. 52), pp. 123–179. Tokyo: Iwanami Shoten, 1959.

Osome Hisamatsu ukina no yomiuri (Tsuruya Nanboku IV). Urayama Masao and Matsuzaki Hitoshi, eds., *Kabuki kyakuhon-shū: ge* (*Nihon koten bungaku taikei*, vol. 54), pp. 169–272. Tokyo: Iwanami Shoten, 1961.

Otogi bōko (Asai Ryōi). *Nihon meicho zenshū: kaidan meisakushū*, vol. 10, pp. 3–262. Tokyo: Nihon Meicho Zenshū Kankōkai, 1927.

Rikyū hyakkai-ki (Sen no Rikyū). *Chadō koten zenshū*, vol. 6, pp. 405–469. Tokyo: Tankō Shinsha, 1958.

Rinji mawari jōshinsho. Tōkyō Daigaku Shiryō Hensanjo, ed., *Dai Nihon kinsei shiryō, Shichū torishimari ruishū*, vol. 1, pp. 12–30. Tokyo: Tōkyō Daigaku Shuppankai, 1959.

Roku Amida mōde (Jippensha Ikku). *Kokkei meisakushū: jō* (*Zoku teikoku bunko*, vol. 25), pp. 835–946. Tokyo: Hakubunkan, 1894.

Ryōri monogatari. Yoshii Motoko, ed., *(Honkoku) Edo jidai ryōrihon shūsei*, vol. 1, pp. 3–40. Tokyo: Rinsen Shoten, 1978.

Ryōri-tsū (Yaoya Zenshirō). Yoshii Motoko, ed., *(Honkoku) Edo jidai ryōrihon shūsei*, vol. 10, pp. 3–197. Tokyo: Rinsen Shoten, 1981.

Ryūkyū banashi (Morishima Chūryō). *Edo-ki Ryūkyū mono shiryō-kan*, vol. 1, pp. 79–188 (facsimile). Tokyo: Honpō Shoseki, 1981.

Sagami nyūdō senbiki no inu (Chikamatsu Monzaemon). *Chikamatsu zenshū*, vol. 8, pp. 353–505. Tokyo: Iwanami Shoten, 1988.

Saga tennō kanro no ame (Chikamatsu Monzaemon). *Chikamatsu zenshū*, vol. 9, pp. 1–107. Tokyo: Iwanami Shoten, 1988.

Saigoku sanjūsan-sho meisho zue (1853). Hayashi Hideo et al., eds., *Nihon meisho fūzoku zue*, vol. 18, pp. 5–292. Tokyo: Kadokawa Shoten, 1980.

Saigoku sanjūsan-ban junrei uta. Takano Tatsuyuki, ed., *Nihon kayō shūsei*, vol. 4, pp. 450–453. Tokyo: Shunjusha, 1929.

Saikaku nagori no tomo (Ihara Saikaku). Asō Isoji and Fuji Akio, eds., *Saikaku nagori no tomo/Saikaku zoku tsurezure* (*Taiyaku Saikaku zenshū*, vol. 16), pp. 128–239. Tokyo: Meiji Shoin, 1977.

Saikaku oki miyage (Ihara Saikaku). Asō Isoji and Fuji Akio, eds., *Saikaku oki miyage/Yorozu no fumi hōgu* (*Taiyaku Saikaku zenshū*, vol. 15), pp. 1–137. Tokyo: Meiji Shoin, 1977.

Saikaku oridome (Ihara Saikaku). Noma Kōshin, ed., *Saikaku-shū: ge* (*Nihon koten bungaku taikei*, vol. 48), pp. 319–461. Tokyo: Iwanami Shoten, 1960.

Saikaku ōyakazu chūshaku. Maeda Kingorō, ed. 4 vols. Tokyo: Benseisha, 1987.

Sakura giminden (Segawa Jokō III). Toita Yasuji et al., eds., *Meisaku kabuki zenshū*, vol. 16, pp. 3–46. Tokyo: Tōkyō Sōgen Shinsha, 1970.

Sangoku tsūran zusetsu (Hayashi Shihei). *Dai Nihon shisō zenshū*, vol. 13, pp. 228–274. Tokyo: Dai Nihon Shisō Zenshū Kankōkai, 1932.

Sannin Kichiza kuruwa no hatsugai (Kawatake Mokuami). Imao Tetsuya, ed., *Shinchō Nihon koten shūsei*. Tokyo: Shinchōsha, 1984.

Saruwaka. In Saitō Gesshin, "Hyakugi jutsuryaku" (*Shin-enseki jisshu,* vol. 4, pp. 210–327), pp. 305–310. Tokyo: Chūō Kōronsha, 1981.

Saya-ate. Gunji Masakatsu, ed., *Kabuki jūhachiban (Nihon koten bungaku taikei,* vol. 98), pp. 166–173. Tokyo: Iwanami Shoten, 1965.

Seigaku mondo (Dazai Shundai). Rai Tsutomu, ed., *Sorai gakuha (Nihon shisō taikei,* vol. 37), pp. 57–136. Tokyo: Iwanami Shoten, 1972.

Seiritsuen zuihitsu. In the possession of the National Diet Library.

Shibai-bayashi nikki (Tanaka Denzaemon VI). *Nihon shomin bunka shiryō shūsei,* vol. 6 *(Kabuki),* pp. 531–550. Tokyo: San-ichi Shobō, 1973.

Shibaraku. Gunji Masakatsu, ed., *Kabuki jūhachiban shū (Nihon koten bungaku taisei,* vol. 98), pp. 142–164. Tokyo: Iwanami Shoten, 1965.

Shibusawa Eiichi tai-futsu nikki (Shibusawa Eiichi). Nihon Shiseki Kyōkai, ed., *Nihon shiseki kyōkai sōsho,* vol. 126. Tokyo: Tōkyō Daigaku Shuppan-kai, 1967; originally published in 1928.

Shichū fūbun kakiutsushi. Tōkyō Daigaku Shiryō Hensanjo, ed., *Dai Nihon kinsei shiryō, Shichū torishimari ruishū,* vol. 1, pp. 486–494. Tokyo: Tōkyō Daigaku Shuppankai, 1959.

Shichū fūbunsho. Tōkyō Daigaku Shiryō Hensanjo, ed., *Dai Nihon kinsei shiryō, Shichū torishimari ruishū,* vol. 2, pp. 3–18. Tokyo: Tōkyō Daigaku Shuppankai, 1959.

Shijō-ke hōchō shoroku. In the possession of the Imperial Household Agency, Dept. of Archives and Mausoleums (Kunaichō shoryōbu).

Shijō-ryū hōchōsho. Kurabayashi Seiji, ed., *Nihon ryōri hiden shūsei,* vol. 18, pp. 47–69. Tokyo: Dōbōsha, 1985.

Shikisho hōchō ryōri kirikata hidensho. Yoshii Motoko, ed., *(Honkoku) Edo jidai ryōri-hon shūsei,* vol. 1, pp. 41–180. Tokyo: Rinsen Shoten, 1978.

Shin-kage-ryū heihō mokuroku no koto (Yagyū Muneyoshi). Nishiyama Matsunosuke et al., eds., *Kinsei geidō-ron (Nihon shisō taikei,* vol. 61), pp. 345–354. Tokyo: Iwanami Shoten, 1972.

Shinkyoku shōmyō higen (Hokumonshi Bokkai Mohee). In the possession of the National Diet Library.

Shinrei yaguchi no watashi (Hiraga Gennai). Nakamura Yukihiko, ed., *Fūrai Sanjin-shū (Nihon koten bungaku taikei,* vol. 55), pp. 301–400. Tokyo: Iwanami Shoten, 1961.

Shiojiri (Amano Nobukage). *Nihon zuihitsu taisei: daisan-ki,* vols. 13–18. Tokyo: Yoshikawa Kōbunkan, 1978.

Shiokumi (Sakurada Jisuke II). Gunji Masakatsu et al., eds., *Meisaku kabuki zenshū,* vol. 24, pp. 61–6. Tokyo: Tōkyō Sōgen Shinsha, 1972.

Shisei airoku, vol. 202 (Sekine Shisei). Sekine Toshio, ed., *Sekine bunko senshū (dai ikki)* (unpaginated facsimile). Tokyo: Kyōiku Shuppan Sentaa, 1984.

Shisho koden (Dazai Shundai). In the possession of the National Diet Library.

Shōhō kuni ezu. In the possession of the Kokuritsu Kōbunshokan (Naikaku Bunko).

"Shoken-chō." *Kogidō bunko* 61–48. In the possession of the Tenri Library.

Shūgi gaisho (Kumazawa Banzan). Masamune Toshio, ed., *Banzan zenshū,* vol. 2, pp. 1–293. Tokyo: Meicho Shuppan, 1978.

Shuhanron. Yokoyama Shigeru and Matsumoto Takashi, eds., *Muromachi jidai monogatari taisei,* vol. 7, pp. 243–250. Tokyo: Kadokawa Shoten, 1979.

Shunshoku umegoyomi (Tamenaga Shunsui). Nakamura Yukihiko, ed., *Nihon koten bungaku taikei,* vol. 64, pp. 39–238. Tokyo: Iwanami Shoten, 1962.

Sonezaki shinjū (Chikamatsu Monzaemon). Shigetomo Ki, ed., *Chikamatsu jōruri-shū: jō (Nihon koten bungaku taikei,* vol. 49), pp. 17–36. Tokyo: Iwanami Shoten, 1958.

Sorai sensei gakusoku (Ogyū Sorai). *Dai Nihon shisō zenshū,* vol. 7, pp. 148–165. Tokyo: Dai Nihon Shisō Zenshū Kankōkai, 1931.

Sue tsumu hana. Aoki Nobumitsu, ed., *Sekai ai no raiburarii,* vol. 11. Tokyo: Bigakkan, 1981.

Sugae Masumi yūranki (Sugae Masumi). Uchida Takeshi and Miyamoto Tsuneichi, eds., *Tōyō bunko,* 5 vols. Tokyo: Heibonsha, 1967.

Sugawara denju tenarai kagami (Takeda Izumo and assistants). Yokoyama Tadashi, ed., *Jōruri-shū (Nihon koten bungaku zenshū),* pp. 487–630. Tokyo: Shōgakkan, 1971. For a kabuki version see Toita Yasuji et al., eds., *Meisaku kabuki zenshū,* vol. 2, pp. 139–234. Tokyo: Tōkyō Sōgen Shinsha, 1968.

Sukeroku yukari no Edo zakura. Gunji Masakatsu, ed., *Kabuki jūhachiban shū (Nihon koten bungaku taikei,* vol. 98), pp. 59–139. Tokyo: Iwanami Shoten, 1965.

Sumiyoshi odori. Nakauchi Chōji and Tamura Nishio, eds., *Kokyoku zenshū— katō, itchū, sonohachi, ogie,* pp. 45–48. Tokyo: Nihon Ongyoku Zenshū Kankōkai, 1927.

Su-utai yoyo no ato (Sasaki Haruyuki). *Nihon shomin bunka shiryō shūsei,* vol. 3, pp. 657–684. Tokyo: San-ichi Shobō, 1978.

Suzuki bōchō. Koike Hiroshi, ed., *Kyōgen-shū: jō (Nihon koten bungaku taikei,* vol. 42), pp. 391–398. Tokyo: Iwanami Shoten, 1960.

Taiheiki. Takahashi Sadaichi, ed., *Shinkō Taiheiki.* Kyoto: Shibunkaku, 1976.

Tai hyakuchin ryōri himitsu-bako. Yoshii Motoko, ed., *(Honkoku) Edo jidai ryōrihon shūsei,* vol. 5, pp. 245–276. Tokyo: Rinsen Shoten, 1980.

Tenmei nendo kyōsai nikki (Sasaki Takayuki). Ono Takeo, ed., *Nihon kinsei kiga shi,* pp. 169–194. Tokyo: Yūmei Shobō, 1987; originally published in 1935.

Tōkaidō meisho-ki (Asai Ryōi). Asakura Haruhiko, ed. 2 vols. (*Tōyō bunko,* vols. 346 and 361). Tokyo: Heibonsha, 1979.

Tōkaidō meisho zue (Akizato Ritō). *Nihon meisho zue zenshū,* vol. 5; vol. 6, pp. 555–788. Tokyo: Meisho Fukyūkai, 1975.

Tōkaidō Yotsuya kaidan (Tsuruya Nanboku). Kawatake Shigetoshi, ed. Tokyo: Iwanami Bunko, 1956.

Tokugawa jikki. Kokushi taikei, vols. 38–52. Tokyo: Yoshikawa Kōbunkan, 1930.

Tōto saijiki (Saitō Gesshin). Asakura Haruhiko, ed. 3 vols. (*Tōyō bunko,* vols. 159, 177, 221). Tokyo: Heibonsha, 1970 (vols. 1–2) and 1972 (vol. 3).

Tsūgen sōmagaki (Santō Kyōden). Mizuno Minoru, ed., *Kibyōshi sharebon shū (Nihon koten bungaku taikei,* vol. 59), pp. 353–386. Tokyo: Iwanami Shoten, 1958.

Tsuyu kosode mukashi hachijō (Kawatake Mokuami). Kawatake Toshio et al., eds., *Kabuki meisaku zenshū,* vol. 11, pp. 183–279. Tokyo: Tōkyō Sōgen Shinsha, 1969.

Wakan sansai zue (Terajima Ryōan). Vol. 4. Shimada Isao et al., eds., *Tōyō bunko,* Tokyo: Heibonsha, 1986.

Wakashima-za ikkan. Moriya Takeshi, ed., *Nihon shomin bunka shiryō shūsei,* vol. 6 *(Kabuki),* pp. 907–943. Tokyo: San-ichi Shobō, 1973.

Yamato gana tamuke no itsumoji (Masuyama Kinpachi). *Kiyomoto zenshū,* pp. 227–229. Tokyo: Seibundō, 1928.

Yanagi ni hina shochō no saezuri. Gunji Masakatsu et al., eds., *Kabuki meisaku zenshū,* vol. 19, pp. 31–42. Tokyo: Tōkyō Sōgen Shinsha, 1970.

Yanone. Gunji Masakatsu, ed., *Kabuki jūhachiban shū* (*Nihon koten bungaku taikei,* vol. 98), pp. 51–57. Tokyo: Iwanami Shoten, 1965.

Yōmei tennō shokunin kagami (Chikamatsu Monzaemon). Shuzui Kenji and Ōkubo Tadakuni, eds., *Chikamatsu jōruri shū: ge* (*Nihon koten bungaku takei,* vol. 50), pp. 58–120. Tokyo: Iwanami Shoten, 1959.

Yoshitsune senbon-zakura (Takeda Izumo and assistants). Yūda Yoshio, ed., *Bunraku jōruri-shū* (*Nihon koten bungaku taikei,* vol. 99), pp. 143–228 (excerpts). Tokyo: Iwanami Shōten, 1965. For a kabuki version see Toita Yasuji et al., eds., *Meisaku kabuki zenshū,* vol. 2, pp. 235–330. Tokyo: Tōkyō Sōgen Shinsha, 1968.

Yowanasake ukina no yokogushi (Segawa Jokō III). Toita Yasuji et al., eds., *Meisaku kabuki zenshū,* vol. 16, pp. 141–280. Tokyo: Tōkyō Sōgen Shinsha, 1970.

Twentieth-Century Sources

Adachi Kan'ichi. "Tachikawa bunko no tanjō." *Shisō no kagaku,* Oct. 1959, pp. 32–41.

Asada Denkyō. "Soba no mukashi-banashi." In Yamanaka Shio, ed., *Shumi to shikō,* pp. 161–182. Tokyo: Oka Shoin, 1929.

Asakura Musei. *Misemono kenkyū.* Tokyo: Shibunkaku, 1977; originally published in 1928.

Asō Isoji. "Iki/tsū." *Nihon bungaku kōza,* vol. 7, pp. 103–116. Tokyo: Kawade Shobō, 1954.

Chiba Osamu, ed. *Shodai Senryū senku-shū.* 2 vols. Tokyo: Iwanami Shoten, 1986.

Ejima Ihee. *Kurumaya-hon no kenkyū.* Tokyo: Kōzan Bunko, 1944.

Engeki Kenkyūkai, ed. *Mikan jōruri geiron-shū.* Osaka: Engeki Kenkyūkai, 1958.

Fujino Tamotsu. *Bakuhan taisei-shi no kenkyū: kenryoku kōzō no kakuritsu to tenkai.* Tokyo: Yoshikawa Kōbunkan, 1961.

Fujita Tokutarō. *Kinsei kayō no kenkyū.* Tokyo: Jinbun Shoin, 1937; reprinted by Benseisha in 1986.

Fukuda Sadayoshi. *Minshū to engei.* Tokyo: Iwanami Shinsho, 1953.

Furushima Toshio. *Edo jidai no shōhin ryūtsū to kōtsū: Shinshū chūma no kenkyū.* Tokyo: Ochanomizu Shobō, 1951.

———. *Nihon nōgyō-shi.* Tokyo: Iwanami Shoten, 1956.

Gunji Masakatsu. *Kyōdo geinō.* Tokyo: Sōgensha, 1958.

Haga Noboru. *Bakumatsu kokugaku no tenkai.* Tokyo: Kaku Shobō, 1963.

————. "Kigyōchi machikata no bunka: Kiryū, Ashikaga, Ojiya, Shiozawa no baai." *Hōken toshi no shomondai: Nihon no machi II,* pp. 129–166. Tokyo: Yūzankaku, 1959.

————. "Mikawa Yoshida-han no kokugakusha no katsudō." *Rekishi kyōiku* 10(11) (1962):21–27.

Hamada Giichirō. "Edo-Tōkyōjin no katagi/ninjō." *Kokubungaku kaishaku to kanshō,* special supplementary edition *(Edo-Tōkyō fūzoku-shi),* Jan. 1963.

Hiruma Hisashi. "Seiritsu-ki ni okeru rakugo no shakaiteki kiban." *Bungaku* 28(12) (1960):42–51.

Hosono Masanobu. *Shiba Kōkan.* Tokyo: Yomiuri Shinbunsha, 1974.

Iizuka Tomoichirō. "Kabuki-shi no shin kadai to shite no 'Wakashima-za ikkan.'" In Nihon Engeki Gakkai, ed., *Kabuki no shin kenkyū,* pp. 121–203. Tokyo: Chūō Kōronsha, 1952.

Ikenouchi Nobuyoshi. *Nōgaku seisuiki.* 2 vols. Tokyo: Shunjusha, 1914–1915.

Inobe Shigeo. *Fuji no shinkō.* In Sengen jinja shamusho, ed., *Fuji no kenkyū dai-san.* Tokyo: Meicho Shuppan, 1973; originally published in 1928–1929.

Kamisangō Yūkō. "The Shakuhachi—Its History and Development." In Christopher Blasdel, ed. and trans., *The Shakuhachi: A Manual for Learning,* pp. 69–132. Tokyo: Ongaku no Tomosha, 1988.

Kinoshita Junji. *Yūzuru. Kinoshita Junji sakuhin-shū,* vol. 1. Tokyo: Miraisha, 1962.

Konta Yōzō. "Edo no shuppan shihon." In Nishiyama Matsunosuke, ed., *Edo chōnin no kenkyū,* vol. 3, pp. 109–196. Tokyo: Yoshikawa Kōbunkan, 1976.

Kōta Naritomo. *Edo to Ōsaka.* Tokyo: Fuzanbō, 1942.

Kuki Shūzō. "'Iki' no honshitsu." *Kuki Shūzō zenshū,* vol. 1, pp. 87–108. Tokyo: Iwanami Shoten, 1981; originally published in 1930.

————. "'Iki' no kōzō." *Kuki Shūzō zenshū,* vol. 1, pp. 1–85. Tokyo: Iwanami Shoten, 1981; originally published in 1930.

Machida Kashō. "Haiya Bushi to Okesa Bushi." *Min'yō genryū-kō,* pp. 117–185. *Nihon no min'yō to minzoku geinō (Tōyō ongaku sensho,* vol. 1), pp. 47–185. Tokyo: Ongaku no Tomosha, 1967.

————. *Min'yō genryū-kō: "Esashi oiwake" to "Sado okesa."* Nippon Columbia AL 5047–50 (1965).

————. "Shamisen seikyoku ni okeru senritsukei no kenkyū." *Tōyō ongaku kenkyū* 47(2) (Aug. 1982).

Makino Noboru et al. *Ō-Edo mangekyō.* Tokyo: Nōsangyoson Bunka Kyōkai, 1991.

Matsuda Michio. "Goraku no ichizuke." *Shisō* (Aug. 1951):4–8.

Mikami Sanji. "Fuke-shū ni tsuite." *Shigaku zasshi* 13(4) (1902):61–76; 13(5) (1902):64–82.

Miki Yōkichirō, ed. *Awa ai-fu (Shiwa zusetsu hen).* Matsushige-machi, Tokushima-ken: Miki Sangyō, 1961.

Mitamura Engyo, ed. *Kawaraban no hayariuta.* Tokyo: Shun'yōdō, 1926.

Miura Ieyoshi. *Fuji shinkō to Fuji-kō.* Tokyo: Kōbundō, n.d. (ca. 1980).

Miya Eiji, ed. *Suzuki Bokushi shiryō-shū (Niigata-ken bunkazai chōsa hōkoku-sho,
no. 7, kiroku-hen).* Niigata: Niigata Kyōiku Iinkai, 1961.

Miyaoka Kenji. *Ikoku henro tabigeinin shimatsu-sho.* Tokyo: Shūdōsha, 1959.

Miyoshi Ikkō, ed. *Edo-Tōkyō fūzokugo jiten.* Tokyo: Seiabō, 1959.

Mizuno Minoru. " 'Tsū' no bungakuteki kōsatsu." *Edo shōsetsu ronsō,* pp. 21–
35. Tokyo: Chūō Kōronsha, 1974.

Murata Atsushi. "Saikaku mugaku monmō no setsu." *Kokugo/kokubun* 22(4)
(April 1953):79–86.

Nakamura Yukihiko. "Tsū to bungaku." *Nakamura Yukihiko chojutsu-shū,* vol.
5 *(kinsei shōsetsu yōshiki-shi kō),* pp. 279–292. Tokyo: Chūō Kōronsha,
1982.

Negishi Senryū, ed. *Kosenryū jiten,* vol. 1. Tokyo: Nihon Shinbunsha, 1955.

Nishiyama Matsunosuke. "Edo bunka no kitei." *Shichō* 62–63 (1957):85–94.

———. "Edokko." *Edo chōnin no kenkyū,* vol. 2, pp. 3–93. Tokyo: Yoshikawa
Kōbunkan, 1974.

———. "Edo no machi nanushi Saitō Gesshin." *Edo chōnin no kenkyū,* vol. 4,
pp. 395–517. Tokyo: Yoshikawa Kōbunkan, 1975.

———. *Iemoto monogatari. Nishiyama Matsunosuke chosakushū,* vol. 2, pp. 3–
255. Tokyo: Yoshikawa Kōbunkan, 1982.

———. *Iemoto no kenkyū. Nishiyama Matsunosuke chosakushū,* vol. 1. Tokyo:
Yoshikawa Kōbunkan, 1982.

———. *Iemoto-sei no tenkai. Nishiyama Matsunosuke chosakushū,* vol. 2. Tokyo:
Yoshikawa Kōbunkan, 1982.

———. "Kaei bunka shiron." *Nishiyama Matsunosuke chosakushū,* vol. 4, pp.
49–140. Tokyo: Yoshikawa Kōbunkan, 1983.

———. "Kinsei bunka-shi kenkyū-hō ni kansuru shiron." *Nishiyama Matsunosuke chosakushū,* vol. 4, pp. 189–203. Tokyo: Yoshikawa Kōbunkan, 1983.

———. "Kinsei toshi no seikatsu." *Nishiyama Matsunosuke chosakushū,* vol. 4,
pp. 260–270. Tokyo: Yoshikawa Kōbunkan, 1983.

———. "Kinsei yūgei-ron." *Kinsei geidō-ron (Nihon shisō taikei,* vol. 61), pp.
612–644. Tokyo: Iwanami Shoten, 1972.

———. "Kōki Edo chōnin no bunka seikatsu." *Nishiyama Matsunosuke chosakushū,* vol. 3, pp. 136–166. Tokyo: Yoshikawa Kōbunkan, 1983.

———. "Kuruwa." *Nishiyama Matsunosuke chosakushū,* vol. 5, pp. 1–201.
Tokyo: Yoshikawa Kōbunkan, 1985.

———. "Meikō hanran to meijingei." *Nishiyama Matsunosuke chosakushū,* vol.
5, pp. 428–444. Tokyo: Yoshikawa Kōbunkan, 1984.

———. " 'Nanbōroku' ni tsuite." *Nishiyama Matsunosuke chosakushū,* vol. 6,
pp. 180–195. Tokyo: Yoshikawa Kōbunkan, 1984.

———. "Nihonbashi." *Nishiyama Matsunosuke chosakushū,* vol. 3, pp. 167–
237. Tokyo: Yoshikawa Kōbunkan, 1983.

———. "Saitō Gesshin nikki." *Shigaku kenkyū,* pp. 1–80. Tokyo: Tōkyō
Kyōiku Daigaku bungaku-bu, 1969.

———. "Shibai-bayashi nikki." *Nishiyama Matsunosuke chosakushū,* vol. 7, pp.
281–291. Tokyo: Yoshikawa Kōbunkan, 1987.

Noda Hisao. "Hōreki no shotō no bungakuteki ichi genshō." *Kinsei shōsetsu-
shi ronkō,* pp. 237–252. Tokyo: Kaku Shobō, 1961.

Nonomura Kaizō. *Nōgaku kokonki.* Tokyo: Shun'yōdō, 1931.
Oka Onitarō. "Shogei mukashibanashi." *Azumauta,* pp. 319–362. Tokyo: Nanjinsha, 1918; reprinted, n.d.
Okamoto Kidō. "Kōjirō yobanashi." *Kidō gekidan,* pp. 91–274. Tokyo: Seiabō, 1956.
Omote Akira. "Utai-kō." *Bungaku* 25 (Sept. 1957):74–86.
Sanyūtei Itchō. "Enchō no shi." In *Dōkō shidan-kai,* ed., *Mandan Meiji shonen,* pp. 558–569. Tokyo: Shun'yōdō, 1926.
Sekijima Hisao. "Tokugawa makki no nōson jinushi no shōhi seikatsu." *Shakai keizai-shi gaku* 12(9) (Dec. 1942):69–108.
Sekine Mokuan. *Kōdan rakugo konjakutan.* Tokyo: Yūzankaku, 1925.
Sendai-shi Shi Hensan Iinkai. "Sendai han shoki no nō ni tsuite." *Sendai-shi shi: 5 beppen 3,* pp. 44–64. Sendai: Sendai Shiyakusho, 1951.
Shimizu Ikutarō. "Taishū goraku ni tsuite." *Shisō* (Aug. 1951):1–4.
Suzuki Bokushi Kenshōkai. *Bokushi.* Shiozawa-machi, Niigata-ken: Suzuki Bokushi Kenshōkai, 1961.
Takamura Kōun. *Kōun kaikodan.* Reprinted as *Takamura Kōun kaikodan.* Tokyo: Shin Jinbutsu Ōraisha, 1970.
Takano Tatsuyuki. *Nihon kayōshi.* Tokyo: Shunjūsha, 1926; rev. ed., 1930.
Takeuchi Makoto. "Tenmei no uchikowashi." *Edo sanbyaku-nen,* vol. 2, pp. 73–102. Tokyo: Kōdansha Gendai Shinsho, 1975.
Takeuchi Michitaka. *Kinsei geinō-shi no kenkyū.* Tokyo: Nansōsha, 1982.
Tanabe Wakao. *Haiyū.* Tokyo: Shunjusha, 1960.
Tōkyō-to. *Tōkyō-shi shikō.* 1913–present.
Tsurumi Shunsuke. *Taishū geijutsu.* Tokyo: Kawade Shobō, 1954.
Uzuki Hiroshi. "Tsū: sharebon no shudai to shuchō o megutte." *Nihon bungaku kaishaku to kanshō* 21(2) (Feb. 1956):25–28.
Wakatsuki Yasuji. *Kinsei shoki kokugeki no kenkyū.* Tokyo: Seijisha, 1944.
Wakita Osamu. "Jinai-machi no kōzō to tenkai." *Shirin* 41(1) (Jan. 1958):1–24.
Watanabe Ichirō. "Kinsei Echigo ni okeru chijimi-nuno san-ichiba no seiritsu to sono hen'yō." *Tōkyō Kyōiku Daigaku bungaku-bu kiyō* (Shigaku kenkyū, vol. 5).
Yamamoto Shōgetsu. *Meiji sesō hyaku-banashi.* Tokyo: Dai-ichi Shobō, 1922.
Yamazaki Gakudō. "Yōkyoku to haiku." *Haiku kōza,* vol. 7 (*Tokushu kenkyū hen*), pp. 227–238. Tokyo: Kaizōsha, 1932.
Yamazawa Hideo. "Manku awase." *Kokubungaku kaishaku to kanshō* 23(7) (July 1958):27–38.

Sources in English

Brandon, James R. *Kabuki: Five Classic Plays.* Cambridge, Mass.: Harvard University Press, 1975.
———, ed. *Chūshingura: Studies in Kabuki and the Puppet Theater.* Honolulu: University of Hawai'i Press, 1982.
Brandon, James R., and Tamako Niwa, trans. "Kanjinchō." In *Kabuki Plays,* pp. 19–48. New York: Samuel French, 1966.

de Bary, Wm. Theodore, trans. *Five Women Who Loved Love*. Rutland, Vt.: Tuttle, 1956.

Dunn, Charles J. *Everyday Life in Traditional Japan*. Rutland, Vt.: Tuttle, 1969.

Ernst, Earle, ed. *Three Japanese Plays from the Traditional Theatre*. London: Oxford University Press, 1959.

Fenway Court: 1992 (Competition and Collaboration: Hereditary Schools in Japanese Culture). Boston: Isabella Stewart Gardner Museum, 1993.

Gerstle, C. Andrew, Kiyoshi Inobe, and William Malm. *Theater as Music: The Bunraku Play "Mt. Imo and Mt. Se: An Exemplary Tale of Womanly Virtue."* Michigan Monograph Series in Japanese Studies, no. 4. Ann Arbor: Center for Japanese Studies, 1990.

Hall, John Carey, trans. *Japanese Feudal Law*. Yokohama: n.p., 1979; reprint.

Hoff, Frank. *Like a Boat in a Storm: A Century of Song in Japan*. Hiroshima: Bunka Hyōron, 1982.

Hsu, Francis L. K. *Iemoto: The Heart of Japan*. Cambridge, Mass.: Schenckman, 1975.

Jones, Stanleigh H., trans. *Sugawara and the Secrets of Calligraphy*. New York: Columbia University Press, 1985.

Keene, Donald, trans. *Chūshingura: The Treasury of Loyal Retainers*. New York: Columbia University Press, 1971.

————. "The Courier for Hell." In *Major Plays of Chikamatsu*, pp. 161–194. New York: Columbia University Press, 1961.

————. "The Love Suicides at Sonezaki." In *Major Plays of Chikamatsu*, pp. 39–56. New York: Columbia University Press, 1961.

Kinoshita Junji. *Twilight of a Crane*. Translated by Takeshi Kurahashi. Tokyo: Miraisha, 1952.

Kominz, Laurence. "Ya no Ne: The Genesis of a Kabuki Aragoto Classic." *Monumenta Nipponica* 38(4) (1983):387–407.

Leiter, Samuel L., ed. and trans. "Benten Kozō." In *The Art of Kabuki: Famous Plays in Performance*, pp. 2–58. Berkeley: University of California Press, 1977.

McCullough, Helen Craig, trans. *The Taiheiki: A Chronicle of Medieval Japan*. New York: Columbia University Press, 1959.

Markus, Andrew L. "The Carnival of Edo: *Misemono* Spectacles from Contemporary Accounts." *Harvard Journal of Asiatic Studies* 45(2) (1985): 499–541.

Morris, Ivan. *The Nobility of Failure: Tragic Heroes in the History of Japan*. London: Secker & Warburg, 1975.

Miyamoto Musashi. *A Book of Five Rings*. Translated by Victor Harris. Woodstock, N.Y.: Overlook Press, 1974.

Nakamura Matazo. *Kabuki Backstage, Onstage: An Actor's Life*. Translated by Mark Oshima. Tokyo: Kōdansha, 1990.

O'Neill, P. G. "Organization and Authority in the Traditional Arts." *Modern Asian Studies* 18(4) (1984):631–645.

Ortolani, Benito. "Iemoto." *Japan Quarterly* 16(3) (1969):297–307.

Read, Cathleen, and David Locke. "An Analysis of the Yamada-ryū Sōkyoku Iemoto System." *Hogaku* 1(1) (1983):20–52.

Rodd, Laurel Rasplica, with Mary Catherine Henkenius. *Kokinshū: A Collection of Poems, Ancient and Modern*. Tokyo: Tokyo University Press, 1984.

Scott, Adolphe Clarence, trans. *Genyadana: A Japanese Kabuki Play*. Tokyo: Hokuseidō, 1953.

Shaver, Ruth M. *Kabuki Costume*. Rutland, Vt.: Tuttle, 1966.

Tsubouchi Shōyō and Yamamoto Jirō. *History and Characteristics of Kabuki: The Japanese Classical Drama*. Yokohama: Yamagata, 1960.

Further Reading

The English-language literature on Edo-period society and culture is sizable and growing steadily. Here I have listed books that do not appear in the bibliography but may be useful as a starting point for readers who wish to know more about Edo-period culture, especially some of the subjects that Nishiyama treats in this volume.

Bellah, Robert N. *Tokugawa Religion: The Values of Pre-Industrial Japan*. Boston: Beacon Press, 1957.

Blasdell, Christopher Yohmei, and Yūkō Kamisangō. *The Shakuhachi: A Manual for Learners*. Tokyo: Ongaku no Tomosha, 1988.

Blyth, R. H., trans. and ed. *Senryū: Japanese Satirical Verse*. Tokyo: Hokuseido, 1949.

Chibett, David. *The History of Japanese Painting and Book Illustration*. Tokyo and New York: Kodansha International, 1977.

Dalby, Liza. *Kimono: Fashioning Culture*. New Haven: Yale University Press, 1993.

Dunn, Charles J., and Bunzo Torigoe, ed. and trans. *The Actor's Analects*. New York: Columbia University Press, 1969.

Ernst, Earle. *The Kabuki Theater*. Honolulu: University of Hawai'i Press, 1974; originally published in 1956.

Gerstle, Andrew, ed. *18th Century Japan: Culture and Society*. Sydney: Allen & Unwin, 1989.

Gluckman, Dale Carolyn, and Sharon Sadako Takeda. *When Art Became Fashion: Kosode in Edo-Period Japan*. New York: Weatherhill, 1992.

Gunji Masakatsu. *Buyo, the Classical Dance*. Translated by Don Kenny. New York: Walker-Weatherhill, 1970.

Hall, John, and Marius Jansen, eds. *Studies in the Institutional History of Early Modern Japan*. Princeton: Princeton University Press, 1968.

Hanley, Susan B., and Kozo Yamamura. *Economic and Demographic Change in Preindustrial Japan 1600–1868*. Princeton: Princeton University Press, 1977.

Itō Ihei. *A Brocade Pillow: Azaleas of Old Japan*. Translated by Kaname Katō, with an introduction and commentary by John L. Creech. New York: Weatherhill, 1984; originally published in Japan in 1692.

Keene, Donald. *The Japanese Discovery of Europe: Honda Toshiaki and Other Discoverers 1720–1798*. London: Routledge & Kegan Paul, 1952.

————. *World Within Walls: Japanese Literature of the Pre-Modern Era, 1600–1867.* New York: Holt, Rinehart & Winston, 1976.

Kelly, William W. *Deference and Defiance in Nineteenth Century Japan.* Princeton: Princeton University Press, 1985.

Konparu Kunio. *The Noh Theater: Principles and Perspectives.* Translated by Anne Corddry and Stephen Crane. New York: Weatherhill, 1983.

Kornicki, P. F. "*Nishiki no Ura:* An Instance of Censorship and the Structure of a *Sharebon.*" *Monumenta Nipponica* 32(2) (1977):153–188.

————. "The Publisher's Go-Between: *Kashihon'ya* in the Meiji Period." *Modern Asian Studies* 14(2) (1980):331–344.

Lane, Richard. *Masters of the Japanese Print: Their World and Their Work.* Garden City, N.Y.: Doubleday, 1962.

Leupp, Gary P. *Servants, Shophands, and Laborers in the Cities of Tokugawa Japan.* Princeton: Princeton University Press, 1992.

Leutner, Robert W. *Shikitei Sanba and the Comic Tradition in Edo Fiction.* Harvard-Yenching Institute Monograph 25. Cambridge, Mass.: Harvard University Press, 1985.

Lowe, John. *Japanese Crafts.* London: John Murray, 1983.

Markus, Andrew Lawrence. *The Willow in Autumn: Ryūtei Tanehiko, 1783–1842.* Cambridge, Mass.: Harvard University Press, 1993.

Morioka, Heinz, and Miyako Sasaki. *Rakugo, the Popular Narrative Art of Japan.* Cambridge, Mass.: Harvard University Press, 1990.

Nakane Chie and Ōishi Shinzaburō, eds. *Tokugawa Japan: The Social and Economic Antecedents of Modern Japan.* Translated by Conrad Totman. Tokyo: University of Tokyo Press, 1990.

Ooms, Herman. *Tokugawa Ideology: Early Constructs, 1570–1680.* Princeton: Princeton University Press, 1985.

Ouwehand, C. *Namazu-e and Their Themes: An Interpretive Approach to Some Aspects of Japanese Folk Religion.* Leiden: E. J. Brill, 1964.

Raz, Jacob. *Audience and Actors: A Study of Their Interaction in Japanese Traditional Theater.* Leiden: E. J. Brill, 1983.

Seigle, Cecilia Segawa. *Yoshiwara: The Glittering World of the Japanese Courtesan.* Honolulu: University of Hawai'i Press, 1993.

Shaver, Ruth M. *Kabuki Costume.* Rutland, Vt.: Tuttle, 1966.

Varley, Paul, and Kumakura Isao, eds. *Tea in Japan: Essays on the History of Chanoyu.* Honolulu: University of Hawai'i Press, 1989.

Waley, Paul. *Tokyo: City of Stories.* New York: Weatherhill, 1991.

Walthall, Anne. "Peripheries: Rural Culture in Tokugawa Japan." *Monumenta Nipponica* 39(4) (Winter 1984):371–392.

————. *Social Protest and Popular Culture in Eighteenth Century Japan.* Association of Asian Studies Monograph 43. Tucson: University of Arizona Press, 1986.

SOURCES OF CHAPTERS

Introduction: "Kinsei bunka e no teigen," *Nishiyama Matsunosuke chosakushū*, vol. 4, pp. 3–17. Tokyo: Yoshikawa Kōbunkan, 1983 (1983).

Chapter 1: "Ō-Edo no seiritsu," *Edogaku nyūmon*, pp. 16–37. Tokyo: Chikuma Shobō, 1981 (1975).

Chapter 2: "Edokko bunka," *Edogaku nyūmon*, pp. 38–53. Tokyo: Chikuma Shobō, 1981 (1976).

Chapter 3: " 'Iki' no bi ishiki to haikei," *Edogaku nyūmon*, pp. 200–219. Tokyo: Chikuma Shobō, 1981 (1979).

Chapter 4: "Ukiyo-e no haikei shakai," *Nishiyama Matsunosuke chosakushū*, vol. 5, pp. 395–408. Tokyo: Yoshikawa Kōbunkan, 1985 (1977).

Chapter 5: "Edo no shaji to shinkō," *Edogaku nyūmon*, pp. 222–235. Tokyo: Chikuma Shobō, 1981 (1978).

Chapter 6: "Edo bunka to chihō bunka," *Nishiyama Matsunosuke chosakushū*, vol. 4, pp. 143–188. Tokyo: Yoshikawa Kōbunkan, 1983 (1964).

Chapter 7: "Kinsei no tabi fūzoku," *Nishiyama Matsunosuke chosakushū*, vol. 5, pp. 461–492. Tokyo: Yoshikawa Kōbunkan, 1985 (1959).

Chapter 8: "Sesō to ryōri," *Nishiyama Matsunosuke chosakushū*, vol. 5, pp. 493–524. Tokyo: Yoshikawa Kōbunkan, 1985 (1958).

Chapter 9: "Nōgaku no shakaiteki haikei," *Nishiyama Matsunosuke chosakushū*, vol. 7, pp. 385–400. Tokyo: Yoshikawa Kōbunkan, 1987 (1958).

Chapter 10: "Edo jidai no kaisō to ongaku," *Nishiyama Matsunosuke chosakushū*, vol. 7, pp. 401–419. Tokyo: Yoshikawa Kōbunkan, 1987 (1967).

Chapter 11: "Kabuki no bi ishiki," *Nishiyama Matsunosuke chosakushū*, vol. 7, pp. 186–204. Tokyo: Yoshikawa Kōbunkan, 1987 (1978).

Chapter 12: "Taishū geinō ni okeru kinsei kara kindai e no suiten," *Nishiyama Matsunosuke chosakushū*, vol. 6, pp. 215–238. Tokyo: Yoshikawa Kōbunkan, 1984 (1960).

INDEX

About the author

NISHIYAMA MATSUNOSUKE is one of Japan's most influential historians of Tokugawa-period (1600–1868) culture. Born in 1912, and until recently professor of history at what is today Tsukuba University, Nishiyama has helped shape the thought of an entire generation of scholars and teachers. His prolific output, and especially the volume *Iemoto no kenkyū* (Iemoto Studies), has been instrumental in the recent reevaluation of Tokugawa-period culture. Largely through Nishiyama's efforts, the culture of this era is no longer considered "vulgar," but rather admired for its great variety and for the breadth of its basis of support.

About the translator

GERALD GROEMER teaches Japanese music and ethnomusicology at Yamanashi University in Kōfu, Japan. After earning a doctorate in piano performance from the Peabody Conservatory of Johns Hopkins University, he continued his studies of musicology at Tokyo University of Fine Arts and Music and became the first and so far only non-Japanese to be awarded a Ph.D. in musicology from a Japanese university. Among Groemer's other publications on Edo is *Bakumatsu no hayari-uta* (Popular Songs of the Late Edo Period), for which he received the 1995 Tanabe Prize, awarded by the Society for Research in Asian Music for the year's best book on music. He is the first Westerner to win that prestigious prize. Groemer has also published numerous scholarly articles on Edo-period performing arts in both Japanese and English. Besides researching the music and theater of the Tokugawa period, Groemer also continues to be an active pianist.